THE GETTING OF
GARLIC

John Newton is a freelance writer, journalist and novelist. He writes on food, eating, travel, farming and associated environmental issues. His most recent books are the prize-winning *The Oldest Foods on Earth* (2016), *Grazing: The ramblings and recipes of a man who gets paid to eat* (2010) and *A Savage History: Whaling in the Pacific and Southern Oceans* (2013). In 2005 he won the Gold Ladle for Best Food Journalist in the World Food Media Awards.

Dedication

To all the cooks and chefs, in professional and home kitchens,
who made Australian food what it is today.

THE GETTING OF
GARLIC

AUSTRALIAN FOOD FROM
BLAND TO BRILLIANT,
WITH RECIPES OLD AND NEW

JOHN NEWTON

NEWSOUTH

A NewSouth book

Published by
NewSouth Publishing
University of New South Wales Press Ltd
University of New South Wales
Sydney NSW 2052
AUSTRALIA
newsouthpublishing.com

ISBN   9781742235790 (paperback)
        9781742244365 (ebook)
        9781742248813 (ePDF)

A catalogue record for this
book is available from the
NATIONAL
LIBRARY
OF AUSTRALIA   National Library of Australia

Design Josephine Pajor-Markus
Cover design Peter Long
Front cover image Close-up of garlic bulb against black
background by Studio Omg / EyeEm. Getty Images

UNSW
SYDNEY

CONTENTS

INTRODUCTION
AN AROMATIC ABSENCE:
OR, WHY I WROTE THIS BOOK

I grew up in a world devoid of olive oil, garlic and
basil. A world where no one had ever heard of, let
alone smelled, fennel, parmesan or coriander.

English food writer and cook Nigel Slater (born 1958)

Garlic is banned from being included in
foods eaten by royal family members ...
The Queen is known to hate garlic and
has none of it in her food.

Express online <express.co.uk>, 26 June 2018

In 1991, after spending almost four years living in Spain,
I was sent by my editor at the *Sydney Morning Herald*
to cover the first Food of Orange District (F.O.O.D.)

dinner in the surprisingly orange civic centre in – Orange, New South Wales. That was when I realised a lot had changed in this country in my absence.

I remember being stranded in country towns for dinner before I went away. You had three choices: the RSL, the Greek cafe or the Chinese. The RSL stopped serving about six as I recall, the Greek was a long way from Athens, and the Chinese (usually my choice) would occasionally offer dubious delicacies like the deep-fried battered tomato that appeared on my plate one night in Singleton.

So, the most intriguing thing about the F.O.O.D. dinner in Orange wasn't that it was superb – the organisers had secured one of the greatest Australian chefs, Phillip Searle, to plan and cook it – or that Phillip had used, almost exclusively, food and wine from the district, but that 150 local Orange farmers and townspeople turned up, and lapped it up.

And was it an adventurous dinner. Not just adventurous (as some modern food is in the twenty-first century), but as delicious and satisfying to the palate as to the mind. Brook trout with a mousseline of its own milt (that's trout sperm) topped with fragrant and crispy leek slivers; Fricassee of wild mushrooms (slippery jacks, saffron milk caps, scotch bonnets) in puff pastry; Roast saddle of venison with spiced chestnuts; Goat's cheese salad with pickled walnuts; and Baked botrytis cream, caramelised apple and drunken black muscats topped by a flying-saucer-shaped glass biscuit. All accompanied by very good local wines. I still remember the earthy flavour of the Fricassee of wild mushrooms; many years after that dinner, I went foraging for them with Phillip in the Jenolan State Forest.

Later, he told me that never in his life had he seen so many plates (750 plates were served and filled in one-and-a-half hours) come back to a kitchen with not one scrap left on them. 'I was born further out west', he told me, 'and I know the country scene pretty well, and I was surprised'. He wasn't the only one. I was expecting some changes after that length of time away. But trout sperm?

My last book, *The Oldest Foods on Earth*, explored the way in which the animal and vegetable foods that were here when this country was invaded – first by the British and later by successive waves of migrants from across the planet – were almost entirely ignored by the invaders. I discussed the effects of that ignoring on the Indigenous people of the land, which were devastating and long lasting. Powerful stuff, food.

In this book, I look at what we Australians (and I'll explain my use of that term, see page 9) ate for the first 200 years of colonisation. And how the way we eat has changed since then, and what that means to us today. I explore the reasons Australians eat what they eat, and what that says about them. I am interested in what is cooked, who cooks it and where it is eaten: at home or outside the home at a restaurant, cafe or other form of public eating house. I will talk about the high tables (haute cuisine or, in Australian parlance, fine dining restaurants), where you will find what I have called mongrel cuisine (an all-in post-garlic construction); the low tables (those places most Australians who eat out, eat out at: the cafes and mid- to low-range restaurants); and the home tables.

The garlic conundrum

When I had finished researching *The Oldest Foods on Earth*, and began to wonder about Australia's non-Indigenous food history, I realised I had to start with the first Englishmen – not the first Europeans to visit, but those whose influence lingered longest – and what they brought with them.

In the journal of his first voyage around the world (1768–71) James Cook noted, in his account of what he called New Wales, that 'The Land naturally produces hardly anything fit for Man to eat …'. A curious claim, considering he was only here from April to August 1770, and barely spent time ashore.

Because of Cook's pronouncement, before the First Fleet set sail from Portsmouth on 13 May 1787 every care was taken to ensure they carried plenty of food with them: food fit for Englishmen (and although hardly mentioned, English women).

According to Barbara Cameron-Smith, in *Starting*

from Scratch (a note here – details for most books and articles mentioned in the text appear in the bibliography), they brought from England carrots, potatoes, lettuce, asparagus, onions, broccoli, beans, peas, watercress, wheat, barley, rye and oats. Also, apples, pears, plums, cherries and a selection of citrus including navel and Seville oranges and Tahitian limes. In Rio de Janeiro they picked up tamarind, coffee, cotton, lemon, orange and guava, as well as prickly pear plants complete with – and specifically for – cochineal grubs. The first but not the last example of a botanical blunder, prickly pear later ran rife and became an environmental problem. In Capetown, they added rice, maize (then known as Indian corn), apples, bamboo (the second mistake), pears, strawberries and quinces.

One plant appears to be conspicuously absent from this list. As it was from the British and Irish diet – and therefore from the Australian diet, remaining so for a good 180 years. Garlic. *Allium sativum*, otherwise known as the whiffy lily.

But on another list, compiled by Alan Frost in *The First Fleet: the real story*, garlic was included in the list of seeds brought from the old country: 'among the root garnishes horseradish, artichoke, garlic and shallots'). This intrigued me. My subsequent extensive research into the Australian diet and early Australian recipes showed that garlic was conspicuous by its absence. (A later entry in Frost's book lists garlic – among other food stuffs like rice, sago, tamarinds – as

'Surgeon's necessities': we can draw our own conclusions from this.)

That same research convinced me that garlic's passage from neglect to enthusiastic acceptance tells the story of the changing Australian food culture in a way that no other ingredient does. But what's with the British not only ignoring garlic but being loudly contemptuous of it?

That Victorian era authority on cooking and domestic subjects, Mrs Beeton, was not keen on garlic. And she was suspicious of the foreign roots of this vigorous bulb. In *Mrs Beeton's Household Management*, she wrote:

> The smell of this plant is generally considered
> offensive, and it is the most acrimonious in its
> taste of the whole of the alliaceous tribe ... On the
> continent, especially in Italy, it is much used, and the
> French consider it an essential in many made dishes.

And there is the clue – the French. The British have been at war with or involved in battles against France over 40 times between 1066 all the way to 1942 (when they opposed the Vichy government in France and sank eight French battleships). Antipathy towards the French found voice and material substance in antipathy towards French culinary culture, and a symbol of that antipathy in the garlic bulb. But it is not as simple as total rejection of French cuisine. Later in this book I'll examine the British upper-class obsession with French cuisine – which endured even while they were at war with the French – an obsession that was imported to Australia. That class divide between plain food in large quantities and upper-class worship of French haute cuisine has been present in Australia from the earliest days of European colonisation. While we're on the French, the French speaker will notice many grammatical errors in the French menus published here: I assure you that they are not mine, and not a sign of careless editing, but carefully transcribed from the original 'Franstralian'.

Overall, though, the evidence is clear. Those who colonised or invaded this country suffered from *Alliumphobia*, a fear of garlic. And so I have broken the history of non-Indigenous Australian food into two eras: BG (before garlic) and PG (post-garlic). That division introduces two themes that still reverberate in Australia today: racial intolerance and class division. A powerful plant indeed.

I have chosen garlic as a symbol of Australia's stubborn loyalty to the cuisine of its British/Anglo-Celtic founders, but this book will explore very much more as it traces the food that has been eaten by non-Indigenous Australians, in private and public, from 1788 to the present day.

I should warn the reader that in this book I'll be writing about theories of cuisine and culture. What is a cuisine? Does Australia have one? What is food culture? Does Australia have one? Why does it matter? Well, to quote from the great eighteenth century gastronome, Brillat-Savarin: 'The fate of nations depends on the way they eat'. Food and politics. Politics and food. Truer today than ever.

This a complex story, with many twists in the tale, and I am sure that I have missed large meaty chunks of it, but my hope is that it will add to the still-unfolding history of Australian food. In *The Getting of Garlic* I will chart Australian food from essentially conservative and British fare – not always as bad as it has been painted, but mostly plain and 'honest' – to the brilliant, polyglot, inventive and astonishingly varied cuisine we have now, the cuisine I call mongrel cuisine, the apogee of the post-garlic era. And I will also be introducing a new word to the language, *Essengeist*: 'way of eating'. All this will become clear as you move through the book.

Before we can arrive at an understanding of what it is, we must examine and reach some understanding of the circumstances that led us here. Only then can I attempt an answer to the question that underpins this book: if we do not have a food culture in the historical sense, what do we have? But first, I must answer the central question. How did we arrive at this state of being perhaps the only country, the only nation, without a discernible food culture or an identifiable cuisine when examined using the conventional cultural yardsticks? Is it just our youth? After all, the country known as Australia and inhabited by non-Indigenous populations has only been around for some 230 years.

It's important to state at the very outset that when I say 'we', and 'Australians', I will always mean non-Indigenous Australians. When I refer to the first non-Indigenous Australians, I will mostly use the terms British and/or Anglo-Celtic, defined by the *Australian National Dictionary* as 'of or belonging to the British Isles, including Eire'. Most often I have referred to British/Anglo-Celtic to lump together all the pre-1945 white population. Where I refer to other non-Indigenous Australians, I'll use European Australians, Chinese Australians, and so on. The matter of nationalities or origins is vexatious.

In examining the formative influences on today's Australian table, we must look at the two major waves of immigrants, and their descendants, who make up the non-Indigenous population of today – and the first wave begins with the officers, marines, soldiers and convicts of the First Fleet. They were followed by many others like themselves: between 1788 and 1868, about 162 000 convicts, all of whom would have been accompanied by officers and soldiers, were transported by the British government to various penal colonies in Australia. While not all convicts were villains, none came of their own volition. And it could equally be said that those accompanying them would not have chosen to relocate to this distant, unknown (to them) land. Surely, just as the Pilgrim Fathers – willing refugees from religious persecution in England – shaped American history, values and gastronomy, so too did non-Indigenous Australia's unwilling founders.

After 1793 came settlers, characterised by Eric Rolls in *A Million Wild Acres* as 'capable, adventurous, and extraordinarily adaptable, difficult, crude, vigorous, dishonest, selfish violent … They developed Australia'. Rolls points out that had they 'remained in Britain, they would have had no influence on their times' and that 'no other men could have done what they did'. (To which I would add, 'but women could' – as Rolls later comments, it was army officer, entrepreneur, politician, architect and pastoralist John Macarthur's wife Elizabeth who developed the family grazing business while he was exiled to England.) He goes on to write: 'No gentleman ever succeeds in doing much'. If you had to choose a word to describe the type of first-wave immigrant who populated Australia after 1788, it would not be 'gentleman'; more likely, it would be 'larrikin'.

Rolls' portrayal, which rings true to me, points towards the source of a 'get things done our own way' ethos that informs many Australian ventures (not all of them successful, cf. Bond, Skase …). We seem to have a built-in ability to improvise and make do: not so much the fair go as the give it a go. We haven't allowed a lack of traditions to hold us back; rather, we have invented our own, and they have propelled us forward. This characteristic has been noted in the wine industry, and I'll be exploring this 'nothing can stop us' tendency towards recklessness/brilliant innovation in our food culture – what I refer to as mongrel cuisine, a style you will encounter in detail at the other end of this book.

The next major wave of immigrants came after 1945. They arrived, as I wrote in *Wogfood*, 'with absolutely no intention of falling into whatever the natives of the new land ate …'. At the time I meant, by natives, the British/Anglo-Celtic population, but of course they, like all other arrivals, also ignored almost entirely what the original inhabitants ate.

One other group that I will touch on – as to cover them thoroughly would require at least one more book – are the Chinese. Here since (at least) 1817, then arriving in numbers during the mid-nineteenth century gold rush, their relations with non-Indigenous Australians, both personally and gastronomically, have been tricky.

OK, I was wrong

I have to admit to a shift in my opinion of the food eaten by British Australians. My attitude going into this book can be summed up by a quotation that Charmaine O'Brien took from a written opinion of mine and in turn quoted in her book *The Colonial Kitchen*: '… our 200 odd years of plodding along in the footsteps of the most boring cuisine on earth – Anglo Celtic – was a great tragedy for Australian history'.

A re-reading of these books in chapters 5 and 6, and a re-examination of the early history of the colony and – after 1901 – of the new country, has forced a turnaround. I have come to realise that I was harsh on our early food culture. My reappraisal has brought me down on the same side as Colin Bannerman in *A Friend in the Kitchen*, his review of Federation cookery: 'A search of more than 10000 recipes has produced examples of excellent eating and miserable eating'. While I doubt that I have examined 10000 recipes in this study, I have found myself getting hungry reading many, and wanting to cook them: a sure sign, for me, of approval.

And something O'Brien wrote made me think further.

> I wonder though that if what lurks behind our insistence on disowning our British food heritage is a much greater tension: the fact that our ancestors dispossessed Aboriginal people from their land and radically altered the place they had eaten well from for tens of thousands of years.

Having already written a book on that very topic, I also wonder whether culinary indignation may not have coloured my thinking on the substitute cuisine. As I write, we are living through another chapter in the culture wars, with both Australia Day and the statues of white heroes like Cook and Macquarie being called into question. Balance is required. Yes, we must acknowledge the sins of the past, but that doesn't mean damning all remnants of that past.

As I hope you will see as we follow this exploration of non-Indigenous Australian food from 1788, this nation of ours is a sum of its many contradictions, and its cooking, including its highest achievement – our mongrel cuisine – reveals and revels in those contradictions.

For at least thirty years, we've been asking what really is a misleadingly simple question: is there an Australian cuisine? By the time you get to the end of this book, you will ask yourself (as I write later), whether there is 'any point in continuing to slash through the thicket of difference and diversity in search of a single unifying idea that means Australia or Australian'. You will see that to do so is pointless and regressive. And that we should rejoice in the luscious and chaotic diversity of what our best cooks give us every day.

A quotation from Richard Beckett's *Convicted Tastes* more or less sums up my newfound tolerance: 'We may be a nation full of sheep, but we have never really been sheeplike in our attitude to food ...'. Not sheep, but larrikins and mongrels.

A note on Indigenous naming

The City of Sydney website states:

> There are about 29 clan groups of the Sydney metropolitan area referred to collectively as the Eora Nation. The 'Eora people' was the name given to the coastal Aboriginal peoples around Sydney. 'Eora' means 'here' or 'from this place'. The Gadigal are a clan of the Eora Nation.

The word 'Eora' was used by Indigenous inhabitants to describe to the British colonisers where they came from. I'll be using the word Eora in discussing the Indigenous inhabitants of Sydney at the time of colonisation.

1

TRADITIONS AND DEFINITIONS

We don't have a repertoire of dishes
that say what and who we are.

Barbara Santich, *Looking for Flavour*

Vegemite may be the best predictor of national
identity of any food in the world. That is, if you
eat Vegemite, you are almost certainly Australian.

Paul Rozin and Michael Segal, 'Vegemite as a Marker of
National Identity', *Gastronomica: the journal of food and culture*

[Food] culture gains its force through repetition,
reiteration, recapitulation, rigmarole, ritual,
rhythm, regulation, reproduction – recipes.

Michael Symons, *A History of Cooks and Cooking*

For some thirty years I have been writing books, newspaper and magazine articles, and academic papers on the subjects of Australian food and farming, cooks and cooking. I have worked as a restaurant critic for a number of publications and taught a short course on Writing About Food at the University of Technology Sydney. Recently, I wrote a doctoral thesis on Australian food culture – or the lack of it. All that time, I've been thinking about the food and the food culture of the country I live in.

I have lived through the elevation of chefs from being seen as fat old blokes (invariably blokes) in dirty white jackets who drank too much and tortured apprentices, to the moment – not that long ago – when they burst out of the kitchen, ripped off their clothes, shed blubber, grew pecs and attitude, and became the new rock stars, right down to having their own groupies.

More recently, I have looked on – even participated – as we as a nation have become food-obsessed and written and bought unprecedented numbers of cookbooks by an unprecedented number of chefs. Nielsen BookScan tracked 2.18 million units in the Food and Drink Category in 2016. It is currently the second largest non-fiction category – although this is down from 3.18 million units and the largest non-fiction category in 2011. Is our obsession with food subsiding? Or just our enthusiasm for cookbooks? The obsession continues on television, and has more recently been reflected in the vast audience for the show *MasterChef*: the new season launch in 2017 attracted an audience of 1.424 million. The show began in 2009, and its demise has been predicted ever since.

It began to dawn on me in the early 2000s, after some years of being immersed in food, that there was one important element missing from Australian menus, both domestic and professional. There are no dishes or recipes that could be identified as Australian – or more importantly, regional Australian. In his definitive book *Culture and Cuisine*, philosopher, journalist and author Jean-François Revel pointed out that (with one notable exception, as always) 'there are no *national cuisines* … The basic unit in gastronomy is the region, not the nation'.

On 17 October 1995, in my column 'Short Black' (in what was the *Good Living* – now *Good Food* – section of the *Sydney Morning Herald*), I noted that in her introduction to the 1983 *Australia the Beautiful Cookbook* fellow food journalist Cherry Ripe had asserted there were no regional dishes in Australia. While running this column, I would occasionally make use of the resource of tens of thousands of food-interested readers to do some research. In this instance, I asked my readers to write or ring in with any regional dishes that they knew of. After some weeks, and many submissions, I was only able to offer one.

Dishes that did not make the list included the Pavlova (like Barnaby Joyce, actually a New Zealander); the Anzac biscuit, which had neither place of origin nor creator; and Peach Melba, which honours an Australian but was named and invented by a French chef in London. And the Lamington, which, while most likely Australian, has a history so complicated that Professor Maurice French of the University of Southern Queensland has written a comprehensive 280-page analysis of it in *The Lamington Enigma: a survey of the evidence*. A reasonable summary of French's argument, for those unwilling to read the entire book, is that 'The lamington, like the Pavlova, was neither "invented" nor "created" in a particular place, at a specific time by a single person'. Interestingly, most of those 'dishes' nominated by my readers as Australian were sweet.

For the same reasons given above, I did not offer Cocky's joy, a flour dumpling swimming in golden syrup, or Damper, the flat bread baked over a campfire. Both examples of dishes developed in extreme circumstances and using limited ingredients, they are neither regional nor universally Australian. Nor did I nominate the roast leg of lamb, or steak and eggs, and especially not the inescapable 'spag bol' – again, none, with the exception of the last, is associated with any particular place or region. And even then, Spaghetti bolognaise is only vaguely related to the original Ragù bolognese, which in Bologna was traditionally served not with spaghetti, but rather with tagliatelle or fettuccine.

The only 'dish' I could offer my readers was Adelaide's Pie floater, a meat pie island in a pea soup sea, which was served – until quite recently – in three locations, all from pie carts, and all in Adelaide. The carts outside the casino and the one occasionally parked near Hindmarsh Square have disappeared in the years since my research. As I write this, the Norwood cart – which operates outside Norwood oval during home games of the local AFL team, the Redlegs – still exists. And on match days, there is a cart parked outside Adelaide Railway Station.

There are many places that serve pie 'n' peas, with the peas atop the pie. But only in Adelaide does the pie float in the mushy peas, preferably upside down. I offered two free copies of the *Australia the Beautiful Cookbook* to any reader who could supply more regional offerings (I came up with the Pie floater). It was the only contest I ran where the prizes went begging.

And it's relevant to the argument in this book, and in light of food historian Michael Symons' description of 'Australia's uniquely "pure" industrial cuisine', that even this one contribution to 'regional' Australian cuisine is an item of industrial food. The central thesis of Symons' most important book, *One Continuous Picnic*, is that because Australia was colonised at the beginning of the Industrial Revolution, we never had an agrarian, peasant society. From the outset our food production was industrial, our farming geared to mass production and export, and in more recent times much of our food produced in factories.

So, one important question to be answered is this: how is it that after 230 years we have no Australian or regional Australian food culture, nor even any evidence – through dishes – of its more tangible and visible sign, the recipe? The answer will require some definitions.

Defining terms

Food

Food can be defined as any substance that provides the nutrients necessary to maintain life and growth when ingested. Fine, as far as it goes, but it ignores the quagmire of cultural, religious, national, ethnic and habitual behaviour surrounding our choice of nutrient-giving substances and our ways of preparing and ingesting them – most importantly, by means of cooking.

Eighteenth century author and diarist James Boswell offers this definition of 'Man' as a 'Cooking Animal': 'The beasts have memory, judgement, and all the faculties of and passions of our mind, in a certain degree; but no beast is a cook'. Indeed, Richard Wrangham contends in his book *Catching Fire* that it was cooking with fire that made us human. Whether this is true or not, there is no doubt that what we eat and how we eat it demonstrates our humanity. We exhibit that by choosing food from a wide variety of sources, both in terms of produce and provedore; by the ways in which we choose to prepare our food; by choosing food and preparation techniques specific to the meal being cooked – breakfast is, usually, very different from dinner; by the occasion on which we are cooking – Eid, Christmas, Vesak; and by the group we choose to eat with.

More recently, ethics have been applied to our choices. We may choose to be vegetarians or vegans in order to support the rights of animals. Or we may still eat meat, but try to eat only meat that has lived well and died humanely, seeking out farmers like the American Joel Salatin whose animals, he assures us, have 'a good life and one bad day'. These issues are not new. The Indian religion Jainism, which advocates non-violence towards all living things, has been practised since at least the sixth century BCE. But these kinds of influences have been gathering force in relation to Western diets since the late twentieth century.

Food, then, is far from being a material substance that is merely ingested and excreted. It distinguishes and defines us to ourselves and to our fellows. It can be a primary cultural marker of our clan, tribe, religion, region, province, personal sensibilities and country. For instance, Italians divide themselves into *polentones*, those people whose carbohydrate of first choice is polenta, and *mangiamaccherones*, those who eat pasta – specifically referring to Neapolitans, from the city where the maccherone which we know as spaghetti was first eaten. The divide is also geographical, the *polentones* coming from the north of Italy and the *mangiamaccherones* from the south.

This culinary cultural specificity goes deeper than a choice of food type. It dictates the ingredients of dishes. Rosa Matto, an Australian-born Italian cookery teacher, told me a story that illustrates this point clearly. As a young woman, she went to live in Tuscany, to learn to speak and cook Italian. 'One day', she said, 'I was buying vegetables from a woman in the village, and practising my Italian. I told her that the night before, I had made a Ribollita [a vegetable soup specific to Tuscany]. "And what did the Signora use to make her Ribollita?", she asked me politely. I told her the ingredients I had used, and she sniffed and said: "Well, that may be all very well for those people over there" – and she waved towards a village no more than 20 kilometres away – "but we would never use a bay leaf in our Ribollita!"'.

Examples of foods specific to regions, ethnic groups and countries abound. A couple of examples. The Paella valenciana de l'horta of Valencia – as opposed to the tourist version of paella, greasy rice stuffed with frozen seafood, mostly served elsewhere in Spain – utilises the rice planted in the Ebro delta by the Moors some time between 711 and 1492. Now, officially, the Conselleria of Agriculture in Valencia allows only ten ingredients: olive oil, rice, chicken, rabbit, ferraura and garrofó beans (both specific to Valencia), tomato, water, salt and saffron. Dispensation is given for the addition of duck, snails and artichokes as regional variations. This was as a result of a recipe submitted in 2012 to the Conselleria by the restaurateur Rafael Vidal. His recipe was granted the status of *'paella valenciana tradicional con Denominación de Origen Arroz de Valencia'* – a Denomination of Origin.

Another example comes from Ethiopia. Injera bread is made from a grain called teff, grown only in the highlands of that country. Teff contains no gluten. Injera – which is made in the shape of a large pancake – is a soft, spongy bread. This bread and the grain from which it is made is specific to Ethiopia and Ethiopian culture, and over the centuries many meals have been created around its shape and texture. Until recently, practically every meal in Ethiopia consisted of Injera and 'Wat', stew, with the Injera used as both plate and eating implement for the meal. (Now even such a specific ingredient as teff has arrived in Australia, to fuel the ever-growing desire for gluten-free grains.)

Such foods and dishes epitomise and shape the culture, the customs, the habits and even the pastimes of a people. Paella, for example, is not just a dish but the centre of a ritual. On Sunday, a rural Valencian family visits their market garden – *horta* (*huerta* in Castilian Spanish) – which is tended to as a first priority. At lunchtime, a fire is lit (the wood must be either cuttings from an orange tree or vine shoots), over which a paella is prepared by the patriarch of the family. In a similar vein, Italian-Australian chef Stefano Manfredi has said that the only time a man entered the kitchen in northern Italy was to stir the polenta: 'That was', he said, 'for some reason, a male ritual'.

Culture/Food culture

So, food becomes culture in two ways. Firstly, when it is cooked: because once we have the basic products of our diet we transform them – by fire or other means of processing. Secondly, when it is eaten: because, although we can eat anything, we choose our food according to economic, nutritional or symbolic values. In these ways food becomes a key element of human identity and one of the most effective means of expressing and communicating ourselves to ourselves. Food has insinuated itself into the marrowbone of culture. Dishes and meals are central to family gatherings (the paella); and to religious ritual – the bread and wine of Transubstantiation at the centre of Holy Communion, the bitter root of Pesach and even, in their absence, the fasting of Ramadan.

Culture is a loaded word, with many layers of meaning.

For the purposes of this book, I will apply a narrower definition than that used by philosophers, ethicists and aestheticians. I am interested only in that which binds a people together, and so will offer one simple definition, from the *Macquarie Dictionary*, which states that culture is 'The sum total of ways of living built up by a group of human beings, which is transmitted from one generation to another'.

This is a useful definition, not the least because with the substitution (by me) of a single word, it can define food culture as 'The sum total of ways of *eating* built up by a group of human beings, which is transmitted from one generation to the next'.

We'll return to that idea of transmission.

The sum total of ways of eating of different groups of people using ingredients, recipes and ways of cooking to produce both their everyday and their festive food, and sharing what they cook with each other – that's food culture.

It can be seen in countless ways around the world: in Spain in the paella cooked in the *horta* (and only, as we have seen, in Valencia); in Italy in the countless *sagre* (originally feasts in honour of a patron saint) – celebrations of the food or the produce of a village or region; in Bali in the *pebantén*, the daily propitiatory offerings of fruits, rice, cakes and pigs to the gods. Even – or especially – in the archaic Christmas meal of roast turkey and Christmas pudding that some Australians stick to for cultural reasons.

A more precise definition of food culture can be found in Tim Lang and Michael Heasman's book *Food Wars*: 'a constellation of socially produced values, attitudes, relationships, tastes, cuisines and practices exhibited through food ...'.

This introduces the idea of the *social* production of food culture, and prompts a reflection on the ways in which these values, behaviours and choices are built up over time. Food culture – in this way of looking at it – extends from the table to behaviour, from the ways in which we sit to eat (on the ground, in chairs, reclining), to the ways we choose the implements with which we eat (chopsticks, knife and fork), to the ways in which we hold those implements. We are at once bound together by our food choices and by the ways in which we eat. Table manners are clear indicators of social class, and more. I was shown the correct use of chopsticks by a Chinese colleague while living in Singapore. She taught me that if I held them too low, I would identify as a lower class person; too high, and I would be accused of putting on airs.

Imagine food culture as a hand-woven oriental rug. The warp and the weft are the choice and ritual surrounding preparation and eating; the stuff that the rug is made of is the food — the produce of the land, sea and sky; and the pattern is the dishes created in domestic kitchens since the beginning of civilisation. It is an apt analogy. The rugs of the Middle East, like domestic cuisine and its dishes, are the creations of anonymous women working together. In each instance, the women creating recipes and the women creating rugs contribute their own idea to a 'general plan', which evolves into a legacy: that being, on the one hand, a collection of recipes which contribute to a cohesive local or regional cuisine, and on the other, a collection of rugs equally easily identifiable as emanating from a particular place.

Cuisine

The use of the word 'cuisine' illustrates to what extent the French have appropriated almost everything to do with eating, cooking and gastronomy – even the word *gastronomie* came into use first in France, in 1801, according to the *Larousse Gastronomique* dictionary of French cuisine.

Literally, the French word *cuisine* means kitchen, but it has been taken by the French – and since the seventeenth century, by English speakers – to denote both the kitchen and the manner or style of cooking undertaken there, as well as the task of the *cuisinier*, or cook. How does a cuisine arise? How is it 'created'?

There are two basic categories of cuisine – low and high. But there are many divisions and subdivisions including national, regional, peasant, bourgeois, global and modern.

One essential signifier of a food culture is a collection of named dishes that have exact or similar ingredients (see above, Ribollita, paella) eaten daily by all in a particular region, among an ethnic or religious group, or across a country and which originated in that country or region or with that group. Once that food culture has an established canon of named dishes, it is the foundation of most regional cuisines.

A cuisine, then, is what food culture becomes when it develops a canon of dishes accepted by, enjoyed by and understood by all members of a group. Put another way, a food culture is what a group chooses to eat, cuisines are the way they are cooked. But of course there is a hierarchy of cuisines, from the local and regional – very much dependent on local produce – to the highly formalised concoctions of haute cuisine which owe little to place, and much to skill.

A cuisine – of either type, low or high – is made by and requires a community. The people who regularly eat a cuisine know how it tastes, how it should taste, its ingredients, even variations on its ingredients, and how it should be cooked (remember Rosa Matto's Ribollita). It is their creation, their inheritance, they are proud of it and nurture it. It's the food of a community, often a very large community but, as anthropologist Sidney Mintz writes, 'a genuine cuisine has common social roots'.

When my wife De and I were living in Mallorca, we were invited by a group of Mallorquin friends to a 'bring a plate' celebration. De decided to prepare a local dish called tumbet, but, being Australian, she decided to 'improve it' or, as Gay Bilson would say, 'fiddle' with it. She added an ingredient that was not in the original and not very popular on the island. Chilli. After one of the locals tried it, and emerged from the experience coughing and spluttering, De asked him how it was. 'Very nice', he said, 'but it's not a tumbet'.

But there are exceptions, as there always are, to the concept of a 'canon-based' food culture. These include, firstly, many of those cuisines identified as modern;

and secondly, cuisines that the Italian food historian Rosario Scarpato identifies as 'global' – closely allied to 'modern'.

And thirdly, as I noted in a story for *Slow* magazine in 2000 on the food of gypsy (or Romany) culture, there is the cuisine that exists despite having no clearly defined recipes and ingredients. My Romany respondent Ina Bergin said:

> ... it is a concept. Food is a vehicle. We place great value on social gatherings. Food becomes the centre of repaying of debts of a social kind. All ceremonies have been based on giving hospitality, including, of course, good food.

Romany cuisine takes on the ingredients of whatever place they find themselves in. It is a cuisine of convenience, 'and very opportunistic', Bergin said, and it is also a dynamic cuisine. But there are no recipes. 'If people come and say you make the best whatever we have ever eaten, that becomes the recipe.' A cuisine evolved to work for a nomadic people.

Apart from those exceptions, the ancient food cultures of Europe and the Middle East supply a myriad of named dishes with exact or similar ingredients. In some cuisines, dishes have persisted for centuries in practically the same form. Claudia Roden, writing in her *A Book of Middle Eastern Food*, reports being 'thrilled to trace the origin of several of my family's recipes' to a thirteenth century compilation, probably of Syrian origin, the *Kitab al Wusla il al Habib* (*The Description of Good Dishes and Perfumes*).

With the advent of human culture came the divisions of high and low cuisines. Revel writes that 'Cuisine stems from two sources: a popular one and an erudite one, this latter necessarily being the appanage of the well-off classes of every era'. *Appanage*, a French word with no direct equivalent in English, means a benefit or right that belongs to your station in life.

Low cuisine

The first, 'popular', type of cuisine, Revel asserts, 'has the advantage of being linked to the soil' and thus being able to exploit the products of region and season 'in close accord with nature'. Low – or peasant – cuisine is not only linked to the soil, but from the outset has also been linked to language. A shared language was necessary for the sharing of recipes, especially in pre-literate times. The *recipe* is the carrier of the virus that spreads the cuisine. But without *language* these carriers would spread neither through time nor through place.

Before the advent of the hierarchical haute cuisines it was women who cooked, and women who devised and spread the recipes. While we will never know how a set of regional recipes was formulated, it is reasonable to assume that they would have been the work of many different women contributing their own idea to the general plan, over considerable spans of time – as was the case with other women's (traditional) creative work: pottery, woven rugs, quilting. So, a body of recipes – the foundation of any peasant cuisine – was created, over time, as the property of a language group. This process was repeated all across the world.

BW Higman writes in *How Food Made History* that the invention of cuisine was an 'element of human evolution' and 'an essential feature of a successful hunter-gatherer food culture', with the recipes, at first transmitted orally, providing 'continuity into the present'.

The cuisine community became larger with the invention of the printing press. Although there had been recipe and food books well before printing, they were written for two main reasons: to disseminate specialist information to the professional cooks serving in courts and the houses of the wealthy; and to link food and its preparation with ideas of health, spirituality (in the East) and even philosophy.

The first cookbook printed in Europe opened the floodgates. *De honesta voluptate et valetudine* (*On honourable pleasure and health*), by the Italian Bartolomeo Sacchi, better known as Sacchi, was printed in about 1475.

These books did more than transmit recipes far and wide to a newly literate audience. They began the process of 'fixing' – standardising and codifying – regional cuisines in a way that was far more rigid than in preliterate times. Indeed, had it been left to cooks, these recipes would have been far less rigid. Anyone who has worked with cooks, coaxing them to write down or at least quantify amounts of ingredients for their recipes, will be familiar with the difficulty. Cooks deal in handfuls and pinches and fair bits, long times and short times, fairly hot and warm. It was the cookbook that imposed precision on the domestic recipe. And it can also be said that cookbooks created the modern idea of cuisines of place – regional cuisines – beyond the boundaries of the place. Some by merely gathering recipes from a certain place and naming them as originating there – Tuscany, Sichuan, Catalonia – and putting them between covers; some by intent. Which brings us to a cuisine placed between high low and high, which should be discussed before we examine the more complex story of the development of haute cuisine.

Bourgeois cuisine

The arrival in the seventeenth and eighteenth centuries of the urban middle classes brought about the first 'fusion' cuisine, a marriage of high and low: bourgeois cuisine. This is haute cuisine roughed up, 'dumbed down', crossed with and elevating humble and traditional peasant cuisine, the domain of the female cook.

In France, perhaps the most influential book on this topic was *La Cuisinière Bourgeoise* (*The Female Bourgeoise Cook*) which, although written anonymously, was by the important chef and writer Menon. Published in 1746, it went through many reprints, the last being in 1880. Menon had previously written works for the nobility, but now, in the tenor of the times when cookbooks were reaching down from the heights of the professional cook and out to the home cook, he wanted to write for individuals of a lower station – and women. Women did not have any status above scullery maid in the kitchens of the nobility, but now here was a book written for the middle-class woman.

In Italy, beginning in the seventeenth century, perhaps as a result of stagnating economic conditions caused by the lack of progress there in agriculture and manufacturing, there was a retreat among the bourgeoisie to the regional cuisines and local culinary traditions that dominate Italy to this day. Rejecting the complicated dishes and heavy sauces of court cuisine – as was also the case in France – the Italian middle classes adapted and refined the stronger, simpler flavours of the lower classes. This was reflected in many of the cookbooks of the period, an important example being Antonio Latini's *Lo Scalco Alla Moderna* (*The Modern Steward*) of 1692, which examined the products and produce of the Italian south.

High cuisine

High cuisine is one of the perks of privilege, the privilege of kings, emperors, the nobility and the very rich.

Privilege began with inequality, and inequality with the slow and steady progress of agriculture over hunter-gatherer society. Fragments recovered from the village of Tell Abu Hureyra in what is today Syria show this was a process that could take a thousand years. Ancient Tell Abu Hureyra was occupied between 13 000 and 9000 years ago, and the site is significant because the inhabitants started out as hunter-gatherers and gradually moved to farming and the ownership of land.

At this point, you could ask: if the line from hunter-gatherer to agriculture and land ownership is linked, why then did the original inhabitants of Australia not go down that track? The answer is complex, and is to be found (at length) in Bill Gammage's book *The Biggest Estate on Earth: how Aborigines made Australia.* I'll try to explain briefly.

The first reason is linked to the fact that for Australia's original inhabitants, theology and ecology were fused. What is called in English 'the Dreaming' was the unifying principle of these people, and associated with it were two basic rules. Firstly, *obey the Law.* Secondly – and important in explaining why Aboriginal people did not take the path towards land ownership – *leave the world as you found it.* (Western agriculture does not leave the world as it has found it, as we are seeing in this country right now: the tragedy of the Murray–Darling Basin being one example.) Groups or tribes had stewardship of the land they lived in and used, but not ownership. They were caring for it for future generations.

The second reason is to do with their system of agriculture. To quote from Gammage: '... the skill with which Aboriginal people gathered food and resources is very well known. The key point is that they actually organized the landscape so as to make those resources predictable'.

Their system of agriculture allied with their theological beliefs meant that there was no need for them to own the land or to grow exponentially. They had found a stable system whereby they lived in balance with the land and its other non-human inhabitants, and adapted over millennia to the constantly changing environment.

By contrast, in the West, agriculture introduced to humanity the concept of ownership: of land and stock and, in feudal times, of entire countries. Those with the most land and the most stock and the most subjects needed to differentiate themselves from their inferiors, and part of that differentiation was the food they ate, the ability to eat from a more exotic menu than that allowed the common folk.

From their earliest times in Egypt and along the shores of the Mediterranean (more or less 3000 years BCE), royal courts employed men as cooks. They took over the women's recipes for daily cooking that were the signifiers of low or traditional cuisine, and transformed them into a court cuisine. Revel wrote that 'a truly great erudite [high] cuisine has arisen principally in places where a tasty and varied traditional cuisine already existed'. High cuisine, from the very outset, built upon its domestic foundation and then reached out, beyond the limitations of region and skill set, for ingredients and techniques from far and wide. Non-Indigenous Australia is the exception, in that its version of high cuisine – contemporary Australian cooking – arose despite there *not* being a pre-existing 'tasty and varied traditional cuisine'.

The invention and extensions of haute cuisine

French haute cuisine arose in the seventeenth century, around the court of Louis XIV (1638–1715) and among its aristocracy. But the real impetus for the rise and expansion – beyond the court and the aristocracy – of this style of cuisine was the advent of the restaurant, the first of which appeared in Paris in the 1760s.

Exactly who the first restaurateurs were is highly contested: Boulanger is championed by some, Mathurin Roze de Chantoiseau by others, including the author of *The Invention of the Restaurant*, Rebecca Spang. But what really matters is that restaurants increased in number and variety after the French Revolution and into the nineteenth century. The Revolution was about democracy and the rights of the individual. And the restaurant was one way in which the ordinary person could be served in a manner previously only available to a hereditary ruling class. Thus the French Revolution brought haute cuisine to the people.

Modern cuisine

And now we come to modern high cuisine – that form which Australia excels in. To exist and flourish, modern cuisine requires the following: an abundance of ingredients both local and exotic; sophisticated and critical consumers and commentators; and cooks and diners free from the restrictions of regional convention but with a more than passing acquaintance with the background to, and components of, the creations they are either preparing or eating. Sound like somewhere you know? This is a paraphrase of food historian Michael Freeman's description of one particular high cuisine in Sung Dynasty China. But it could well be a description of modern cuisine from the late twentieth century on. I will return to this very useful definition.

To extend the definition, modern cuisine could be called 'cooking with two foundations'. The first is what Brillat-Savarin calls 'gourmandism', which he defines as 'an impassioned, reasoned and habitual preference for everything which gratifies the organ of taste'. Modern cuisine from its very inception has been concerned more with taste than authenticity, with novelty rather than tradition.

European modern cuisine was born in the eighteenth century, hot on the heels of haute cuisine, where the new was sweeping through science, philosophy and art in the wake of the Enlightenment. As Revel writes, the French 'people of the period could not help but be amazed by the continuous renewal of their cuisine' and they 'constantly congratulated themselves on belonging to the century of modern cuisine'. This may sound familiar to Australians. This French new cuisine – like the new cuisine of the twentieth century – was a reaction against the sauce-dominated heaviness of haute cuisine. In one of the most important cookbooks of the time, *Le Cuisinier Moderne* (1736), author Vincent La Chapelle writes: 'The table of a great noble set out at present in the same manner as twenty years ago would not satisfy the guests'. Revel remarks: 'A mere twenty years!'.

This appropriation of the new and the search for culinary novelty was not confined to eighteenth century France. Wherever there was (and is) wealth, abundance and leisure, cuisine slipped its traditional and regional moorings and first and foremost – before hunger, before ritual traditional regional dishes – was about the sheer pleasure of eating and the delight of discovering the new.

The second foundation of modern cuisine is those traditional cuisines that are used as a base both to work *with* and to work *against*. A perfect example of this 'with and against' based cuisine was explained to me by José Antonio Campoviejo, in his restaurant El Corral del Indianu in the northern Spanish province of Asturias. Campoviejo cooks in the nueva cocina (new cooking) style. In 2000, when I ate there, I described his food as 'at once funny, exciting, disgusting and sensational ...'.

When I asked why he cooks the way he does, he told me: 'my mother is such a good cook, I couldn't possibly compete with her'.

In the twenty-first century, the modern has moved on radically from the stern instructions to chefs that La Chapelle gave in the preface of *Le Cuisinier Moderne*: 'Arts have universal rules', he told them, 'nonetheless, these rules do not suffice and perfection demands that one work untiringly to improve on a constant practice'. It was the boredom brought on by the constant repetition of classic dishes that moved restless chefs the world over to abandon that culture of constant practice of dishes from the canon of haute cuisine.

In his first book, *Los Secretos de El Bulli*, Ferran Adrià, the most influential chef of the Spanish modern movement, quotes Jacques Maximin. 'What is creativity?', Maximin once asked the young chefs in his kitchen – where Adrià was working. Answering his own question, he proposed: 'creativity is not to copy'. Adrià wrote that 'this response, so simple and forceful, completely changed my professional life'. Not for Adrià – or most modern chefs in the twenty-first century – the universal rules. There are no rules (at least for Adrià), other than do not copy. This cuisine exists in no place but the kitchen of the chef cooking it. This abandonment of the regional by the modern leads to the question of the existence or otherwise of national and international cuisines.

National, international and global cuisine

Is it possible to talk of Italian cuisine, Chinese cuisine – even (assuming it existed) Australian cuisine? I would argue no, recalling Revel's argument that there are no national cuisines, that the basic unit in gastronomy is the region, not the nation.

But here's the paradox. Once a regional dish leaves its place, it becomes a representative not of its region but of its country of origin. For example, when Spaghetti all'amatriciana, a dish from the town of Amatrice in northern Lazio, travels to a restaurant in New York or London or Sydney, it is served as an Italian dish. The same with Pork vindaloo – a dish devised in special circumstances in the Indian state of Goa becomes just another Indian dish. Such is also the case with Chinese and Spanish dishes.

These 'national cuisines', cuisines without borders, often suffer from two major, and related, disorders. Firstly, substitution of ingredients impossible to obtain – or deemed unsuitable ('they won't eat that') – in the host country. And secondly, chefs and restaurateurs becoming, over time, increasingly out of touch with the flavours they are attempting to recreate.

These uprooted cuisines are often taken, unquestioningly, for the national cuisines of their respective countries. Or the substitution of ingredients – if these end up becoming fixed – can lead to those dishes representing part of a transplanted regional cuisine (see the section on Barossadeutsch in chapter 7). Or they can take two steps sideways and become international or, latterly, global cuisines.

The exception here is France. When we talk of French cuisine – and by this we mean haute cuisine, that which was originally served in the palaces and houses of the aristocracy and the rich and, since the French Revolution, in restaurants dedicated to it – we are referring not just to food but to an all-encompassing aspect of French life. French cuisine is (some say was) a pillar of French culture, and is recognised as being part of the country's cultural heritage. And while it has its roots, as all great cuisines do, in popular cuisine, it no longer bears any resemblance to the regional cuisines of France, following centuries of refinement and creation by such culinary artists and philosophers as Carême, Escoffier and their modern equivalent, the late Paul Bocuse.

International cuisine is not new. Gastronomes have been gathering ingredients from far and wide for over 2000 years. *The Life of Luxury* was a gastronomic work written in the fourth century BCE by Archestratus of Gela, of whom Athenaeus (the author of *Deipnosophistae* – *The Dinner Party Philosophers* – another work of ancient Greek gastronomy, from the third century CE) wrote: 'This Archestratus, in his love for pleasures, travelled over every land and seas with precision, in a desire, as it seems to me, to review with care the things of the belly'. And don't we all know a few Archestratuses today, the journeys of their bellies accelerated by air travel.

But for the modern sense (of international cuisine), we must go back to Revel. While rejecting national cuisines, Revel does acknowledge international cuisine, by which he means 'an international culinary art ... a body of methods, of principles, amenable to variations within a given country depending on different local and financial possibilities'. He goes on to delineate two diametrically opposed branches of international cuisine.

The first is an often-debased version of true French haute cuisine, the basis of the multitude of so-called haute cuisines to be found in expensive restaurants around the world, especially the new world.

The second is one that all who travel for business are acquainted with: the anonymous cuisine of the hotel chain. To go from Holiday Inn to Holiday Inn around the globe (along with experiencing the same service, air conditioning and ice machine in the corridor) is to eat almost exactly the same Club sandwich, Chicken Kiev, Veal Marengo – recipes whose provenance is lost in the mists of jet trails. It is that which is best named 'global cuisine'. As we shall discuss later, the Australian version of haute cuisine – Modern or Contemporary Australian – is yet another of these 'rootless' cuisines, as described above by Revel. And we are well placed for it.

A cuisine without culture

In an article on *The Conversation* website, Julian Meyrick writes: 'we [Australians] are a net cultural importer, soaking up the art developed for other people and sensibilities'. Writing on the same theme in *Australia: a cultural history*, John Rickard states: 'My assumption has been that a provincial culture is by definition derivative'. How do these observations relate to our lack of cuisine?

In *Art, Culture and Cuisine*, Phyllis Pray Bober notes:

> how like the painting of Poussin is the sense of
> structure, of classical order, in the presentation of a
> formal French meal. A Chinese menu, on the other
> hand, unfolds melodically with an ebb and flow like
> landscape painting on a horizontal scroll ... Both
> consider the art of cookery and refinement of taste to
> be among the higher values in life.

This clearly conjectural hypothesis nonetheless points to the close connection between culture and cuisine (and is expanded on in Bober's book). By contrast, the (white) Australian art discussed and depicted in a survey of Australian works related to food, Gavin Wilson's *Cuisine & Country: a gastronomic venture in Australian art*, shows that we are indeed 'net cultural importers', in that our art is derived from and refers to that of Europe. One example from that book. Arthur Streeton's

Melon (c. 1926) is shown above Jean-Baptiste Siméon Chardin's *La Brioche* (1763), to illustrate that both are influenced by the mid-seventeenth century Dutch invention of the still life. So, too, the food depicted in Australian art – whether melons, steaks on a barbecue, oysters, bread or lemons – represents either imports from Europe or, in the case of the oysters, indigenous food of a type that was well recognised by non-Indigenous Australians.

It's not until the book begins to explore Indigenous art that uniquely Australian art and produce are found, as in the painting *Man with cooked emu* by William Bilinjara Maralngurru and the photograph by Kerry Trapnell entitled *Hunting and collecting food in the Aurukun 'supermarket'*, which depicts local Aboriginal people collecting what appear to be murnong (yam daises) and spearing fish in a river or billabong. As Bober writes: 'food serves as a template for examining numerous aspects of human experience'.

We can see this gap between culture and cuisine as both a positive and a negative in Australian cuisine: positive in that it allows us the freedom to create. Rickard expands on his idea of a derivative culture, writing that 'The paradox is that if one focuses on the derivative, one gains a new perception of what might ultimately be seen as "distinctive"'. And that's the first salvo fired in the culinary culture wars: Australian cooking is what it is because of, rather than in spite of, its freedom from the dead hand of tradition and culture. Because

Australian cooks stand so far apart from these traditions, they can draw on them or ignore them.

The proof of the magic pudding

As noted above, the recipe is an important signifier of a food culture, and the basic building block of a cuisine. Recipes can be defined as named dishes that have exact or similar ingredients and methods of preparation across a country or in a particular region or among an ethnic or religious group. Australia has none.

There has not been a single instance of invention or synthesis that has taken its place in a canon of dishes that could be pointed to or out as Australian, in the way that we can point to the pizza as Italian; the paella as Spanish; the rougail as Mauritian; pho as Vietnamese; or moussaka (even if it is a late construct) as Greek.

This has led to a state where the culinary signifier for Australians is an industrial product, originally made from a by-product of the brewing industry: Vegemite. And even that is derivative if you consider Marmite.

As we've seen, the structural definition of food culture is: a canon of easily recognisable dishes pointing to a national or regional cuisine. There is also a social definition of food culture: a self-conscious tradition of cooking and eating that implies the convergence of certain material factors – the availability and abundance of ingredients – with a set of attitudes about food and its place in life.

If we do have a self-conscious tradition of cooking and eating, it is not so much Australian as British, Irish, Scottish, Chinese, Lebanese, Greek and so on. There is not one single example of a widely used and accepted dish arising from a synthesis of the cuisines of more recent arrivals to Australia outside the transience of restaurant menus. Nothing has stuck; nor has anything broken out of the commercial kitchen into general domestic usage. Yet in other countries there is ample evidence of a culinary synthesis between two or more cultures forced into close proximity over a number of years. For example, the rougail and vindaye of Mauritius, the Kapitan chicken of Malaysia, the Rijsttafel of Indonesia, the Cotoletta alla milanese of Italy, the Kedgeree of India – all culinary souvenirs of the collision of cuisines.

By contrast, in Australia, outside the restless, ever-changing restaurant kitchens, there has been no forging of a 'collective bond' between the Anglo-Celtic dishes we have lived with for so long and the riot of imported cuisines. There is no Macaroni Melbourne, Souvlaki Sydney, Pad Thai Perth or Ballotine Brisbane with identifiable ingredients able to be reproduced and recognised anywhere.

By looking closely at the definitions of food culture and the delineation of cuisines, I think that we can safely say – with that one exception mentioned above

– we have neither cuisine nor food culture of our own. What we had, for many years, was a British/Anglo-Celtic food culture. But the best Australian cooking is anything but traditional.

Food cultural theory has moved on from regional and national cuisines to an attitude to food and cooking dictated by fashion and the media, more of a faddish approach to food than a deeply embedded culture, and a way of cooking informed less by tradition than by experimentation. This does seem to be the case, especially when we contemplate Australia.

If you've stayed with me so far, good on you. You've survived Food Culture 101. And it wasn't that hard: you might even have enjoyed it. If I could summarise the complex story above it would be this: a cuisine arises out of a food culture.

Recipes

*In line with this chapter, I've chosen three recipes that illustrate
'foods specific to regions, ethnic groups and countries'.*

....

PIE FLOATER

Serves 4 / Soak overnight

500 g blue boiler peas (not green split peas)
1 tsp bicarbonate of soda
2 litres chicken stock or water
4 pies of your choice
tomato sauce

1. Pick over the peas and remove any discoloured ones or
    foreign material.
2. Rinse the peas by putting them into a large non-reactive
    container, covering with water and swishing around with
    your hand.
3. Drain, then cover the peas with cold water again.
4. Add ½ tsp bicarb and mix well, making sure the peas are
    well covered with water to the top of the container.
5. Put the container in a cool place and leave overnight
    so that the peas can absorb as much of the water as
    possible.
6. Next day, when the peas have doubled in size, rinse
    them well and place in a thick-bottomed stock pot with
    chicken stock and the other ½ tsp bicarb. Do not add salt
    as the peas will not soften.

7. Bring the peas to the boil, watching carefully as they froth up. Stir regularly.

8. Reduce heat to a simmer and keep cooking, stirring occasionally.

9. Around 20–30 minutes into cooking, the skins will separate from the peas. Keep stirring the mixture so that it doesn't stick to the bottom of the pot. Cooking time depends on the seasonal quality of the peas, but around 1 to 1½ hours, depending on how mushy you want them.

10. When the peas are cooked, heat the pies.

11. Divide the mushy peas into 4 serves (there'll be some left over for next time) and spoon onto 4 shallow dishes.

12. Place the pies on the mushy peas – upside down if that's what floats your pie. Add tomato sauce to taste.

TIP Eat in front of the telly watching the Adelaide Crows or Port Adelaide.

PAELLA VALENCIANA DE L'HORTA

Serves 4 / Soak overnight

Paella is a dish named after the pan in which it is cooked, the paellera. In its purest form, it consists of rice and vegetables. Without the rice, it is very like another more ancient dish which did not contain rice, a dish called Adafina. But let Spanish food historian Clara María González de Amezúa tell us about it. 'Adafina is an ancient Sephardic (Spanish Jewish) dish: the origin of the name is Arabic and applied to both the food itself and the receptacle in which it is made, much like the modern-day paella.'

The Jews were in Spain as far back as the early Roman Empire. Some Judaic traditions have them there even earlier, from the destruction of the Kingdom of Judah in 587 BCE and the flight of the tribes of Benjamin and Judah to Sefarad, the Jewish name for Spain.

But Adafina was a meat and vegetable dish, and contained no rice, because there was no rice in Spain when the Jews arrived. The Arabs brought the rice.

The Arabs arrived in 711 CE. From there they travelled, explored, invented, and brought back from distant lands new plants and methods of cooking. From India and the Far East they imported rice, and planted it in the deltas along the Levante, the region of Mediterranean coastal Spain that runs roughly from Castellón to Alicante, whose centre is Valencia. And it is from Valencia that we get paella. And rice also made its way to Italy, so we can thank the Arabs for risotto as well.

For those of you who relish the authentic (Barbara Kafka's 'spectrum around an idea that changes even while we're trying to appreciate it'), here is the most authentic recipe I could find, adjusted for local (Australian) conditions. Once you understand the spirit of the dish, your own additions will only improve it.

One essential for your kitchen if you want to cook paella regularly is an enamelled 40 cm paellera, otherwise use a heavy frying pan.

100 g lima beans (fresh and newly shelled are best)
100 g cannellini or flageolet beans (ditto)
100 ml olive oil
salt
400 g organic chicken, cut into pieces
350 g rabbit, cut into pieces
125 g green beans, cut into pieces
100 g tomatoes, skinned, de-seeded and finely chopped
16 cleaned snails in their shells
2 strands saffron
1 tbsp pimentón (Spanish paprika, that labelled La Vera is best)
1.75 litres chicken stock
sprig of rosemary
350 g bomba rice (the finest Spanish rice, use Calasparra if you
    can't get it)

1. Unless you are using fresh beans, soak the lima and cannellini beans overnight in cold water, then drain and rinse.
2. Heat the oil in a 40 cm paellera with a little salt. When it is hot, add the chicken and rabbit and fry over a low heat until golden brown.

3. Add the green beans and fry for 5 minutes, then add the tomatoes and fry for 3 minutes.
4. Meanwhile, boil the snails in a separate pan for 5 minutes, then drain.
5. Crush the saffron, then dissolve it in a little boiling water.
6. Add the pimentón, then quickly add the stock and bring to the boil. The quantity of stock is difficult to specify and may need a little practice.
7. Add the lima and cannellini beans.
8. When the stock begins to boil again, add the snails, rosemary, saffron and a pinch of salt and simmer for 30 minutes.
9. Sprinkle in the rice and boil over a high heat for 5 minutes, then gradually turn down the heat and simmer for about 10 minutes until the rice is cooked and the liquid has evaporated.
10. Do not stir. If you have cooked the paella properly, you will end up with a brown, toasty, caramelised circle of rice in the centre of the bottom of the paellera. This is called the socarrat, and is given to the most honoured guest.

MARCELLYS

···

BOEUF À LA MODE

Serves 4

This recipe is from a curious book I found in my late father's kitchen. Published in England and in English in 1930. Its title, French Cooking for Everywoman, and author, Marcellys. Or, rather, translator, because on the inside title page it tells us it is translated from LES RECETTES DE GdMÈRE *(Grandmother's recipes). It is the closest I could get to an original recipe of the cuisine bourgeoise as it would have been originally published in the nineteenth century.*

Two points of interest. Firstly, in the notes to the recipes, presumably written by Marcellys (about whom I could find nothing), it tells its British readers: 'In many cases garlic is used. Few people know how much a small quantity improves the flavour of food to which it is added, but it may be omitted from any of the following recipes if the flavour is not liked'. By people, I am sure he/she means British people. Secondly, this recipe solves a problem I encountered. There are two dishes with almost the same name: Boeuf à la mode is beef stewed in red wine with carrots, and Boeuf mode is a similar dish but set in aspic (and famously written about by Marcel Proust in Swann's Way*). This recipe unites the two.*

But in the same manner as warning the British about garlic, I will add that you can omit the calf's foot, and replace it with gelatine, if you intend to serve it cold.

This can either be served hot with boiled potatoes or cold in aspic, with potato salad.

To serve hot

1. Take a piece of either rump or sirloin. Cut some bacon into little cubes, and with the aid of a knife, insert these into the meat. Some butchers will do this. Place in a saucepan, containing a large tablespoon of hot dripping or lard. Place over a good fire for about 15 minutes, and turn frequently so that it becomes brown all over.
2. Then remove the meat, and in its place, put 4 onions, 1 lb [500 g] carrots cut into thin slices, also 2 whole shallots [eschalots], 2 cloves of garlic, also whole. When the onions start to brown, put the meat back in with some bones and a calf's foot cut into 6 or 8 pieces.
3. Pour a liqueur glass full of brandy over the top, and light it with a match. Pour 2 wineglasses of dry white wine in, season well, and cover the saucepan. Let it simmer gently for 4 hours. Turn the meat occasionally, and when cooked, place on a dish, remove the fat from the sauce, to which more water can be added, if desired, and serve very hot.

To serve cold

1. Place the meat in a mould, either whole or cut into slices. If it is cut, it should be put together again, so that it appears to be whole.
2. Arrange the slices of carrot, and pieces of calf's foot, round the meat, and cover it with the sauce. Leave it in a very cool place or on ice for at least 12 hours, then remove any fat from the top of the jelly, and turn out the mould, having eased it with a knife.

TIP This makes an excellent dish in summer, and is served at many hotels and restaurants with potato salad or a French bean salad.

2

A BAD START.
THE FIRST FLEET.

Many cottagers and farm labourers ... moved to
the cities working in the new factories. There
under the slavery of long hours and pittance wages
their diet declined to bread, jam, sugar and tea.

Colin Spencer, *British Food*

If we're going to look at the history of Australian food, we have to go back, way back to the diet of the first non-Indigenous arrivals before they left the 'old country'.

What do we know of their diet? What attitudes to food did they bring with them? We know that the majority of those to arrive in the First Fleet did not come of their own free will: they were convicts. Most of the soldiers and administrators were volunteers.

And both groups, for the great part, were British, Irish or Anglo-Celtic. They totalled, according to Robert Hughes in *The Fatal Shore*, 1030, including 548 male and 188 female convicts. I cite Hughes because estimates of these numbers vary widely, and his represent an approximate average.

Their arrival in 1788 was significant. They had witnessed and been affected by the beginnings of both the Industrial and Agricultural Revolutions, social upheavals that had their roots in the United Kingdom. This meant that many of these new arrivals had been forced from the countryside – from involvement in the growing of food and the raising of livestock – into the cities and overcrowded, unhealthy, urban environments. Being on the whole among the poorest of the poor, many turned to crime – and after being convicted were transported.

During the entire eighteenth century, Britain was embroiled in wars with India, France and America, among many others – more than 22 wars and conflicts – and these were a major cause of the scarcity and high price of food. And then there were the land enclosures.

These had begun in the sixteenth century due to a favourable overall increase in trade, but most especially in the trade of wool and textiles – profits being so high that landowners did everything they could to find more land to graze wool sheep. This included turning over arable land previously used for food, enclosing waste land used by the poor to grow food, and raising rents to force tenants out. But that earlier era of enclosures was a drop in the ocean compared with what was taken from the ordinary people in the eighteenth and nineteenth centuries.

Most of the Enclosure Acts – over 4000 of them – were passed between 1750 and 1860. The result was that two to three million acres (eight to 12 million hectares) of open fields, commons and wastelands were enclosed – handed over to large and wealthy landowners – in the last half of the eighteenth century. Those who didn't move to the cities or migrate and who were left in the countryside often had their small allotments for growing crops and raising domestic livestock appropriated. Once the smallholdings and commons were absorbed, there was nowhere for the small farmers, labourers and cottagers to grow their own vegetables, gather fuel for their fires, or to keep their pigs or a few cattle. Every peasant had at least one pig, and often more, because they cost nothing to keep: they would live off scraps and leftovers. The loss of their pigs was disastrous for the rural poor.

What drove the later set of enclosures was the pursuit of agricultural efficiency. Just as the Watt steam engine, first introduced in 1763, fired up the Industrial Revolution, Jethro Tull's horse-drawn seed drill, which went into use in 1701, helped promote a revolution in agriculture. Because it was especially useful to large landowners, it was one driver of the changes in agricultural practices that resulted in small farms being gobbled up by big landowners. Colin Spencer quotes eighteenth century commentator Arthur Young, who laid out the prevailing view: 'No small farm could effect such great things as have been done in Norfolk. Great farms are the soul of Norfolk culture; split them into tenures of a hundred pounds a year and you will find nothing but beggars and weeds in the whole country'.

JC Drummond and Anne Wilbraham wrote in *The Englishman's Food*: 'The ruling classes, the nobility and the new rich had now absorbed most of the fertile land of England'.

Many of those displaced villagers and farm labourers were forced to move to the cities and take jobs in the factories springing up in the industrial towns. They were torn from their source of food and, living in cramped city conditions, often had no means of cooking nor indeed money to buy food to cook. As they were, for the most part, illiterate, and had been plucked from their village culture, deprived of their crops and livestock, they had no way of preserving the recipes they and their families had used for generations.

This had far-reaching consequences for the British. In *British Food*, Colin Spencer points out that in all the discussion about the merits – more efficient and productive farming – and demerits – the desolation of the villages – no historian had previously discussed what this had meant for English cooking culture.

Every cuisine has its roots within the peasant traditions … In such cooking there is a reliance on cereals, wild plants and game; many of these ideas are then filched by more affluent parts of society … and this flow constantly replenishes a national cuisine. It is this profound enrichment from below that our national cuisine was now to lose.

And which Australia never had. But these events – enclosures and the Industrial and Agricultural Revolutions – would also stunt the growth of Australia's food culture by sending here as convicts these impoverished unfortunates whose own had been destroyed.

Transported Londoners – many of our first settlers – were drawn, in the main, from places like Stepney, Poplar, Clerkenwell, Seven Dials between Soho and Covent Garden, and Spitalfields. These were the poorest parts of London in the eighteenth and nineteenth centuries, and here lived the petty thieves and minor criminals, driven to crime by grinding poverty, from whose ranks Australian convicts were drawn. At least four per cent of men tried in London were born in Ireland. And they also lived in these, the poorest parts of London.

For those at the bottom of the economic scale in Britain's industrial cities, life was a struggle, and even for those who could afford it – those in employment – food was scant and expensive. Here, from *London Life in the Eighteenth Century* by M Dorothy George, is a calculation of the content and cost of a week's worth of food and drink for an unmarried clerk in London in 1767, a year of scarcity and hence high prices. The details of this calculation are a mystery lost in time (note: 'd' is a penny, 's' a shilling).

Breakfast
Bread & cheese & small beef   £0 0 2[d]

Dinner
Chuck beef or scrag of mutton or sheep's
trotters or pig's ear soused; cabbage or
potatoes or parsnips, bread, and small
beer with half a pint of porter   £0 0 7[d]

Supper
Bread and cheese with radishes or
cucumbers or onions   £0 0 3[d]

Small beer and a half a pint of porter   £0 0 1½[d]

Per week   £0 7[s] 10½[d]

An additional repast on Sunday   £0 0 4[d]

Total for the week   £0 8[s] 2½[d]

Even such miserable food and drink left little money over for lodgings – for which this labourer paid half a crown a week – and for washing and clothes. And this was someone well above the starvation line, whose annual wage was around £135.

Not all the inhabitants of London were supping on 'scrag of mutton or sheep's trotters or pig's ear soused', as this contemporary verse affirms.

> While the epicure alderman's cramming his belly
> And feasting on pheasants, on ven'son and jelly;
> While turtles and turbots his tables bespread,
> A poor family dines on a morsel of bread.

At the big end of town, the roast beef of old England or mutton surrounded by many other dishes of the fabled Georgian table was more the norm.

But it was, for the most part, the undernourished, underprivileged and uneducated citizens of the overcrowded industrial cities who found themselves on the convict ships on a voyage to the other side of the planet.

At sea

British naval food has acquired a perhaps undeserved bad reputation; yet as bad as it was or wasn't, it would have represented plenty beyond imagination to the convicts on board the First Fleet. Although the convict class was voiceless, Sydney Living Museum's resident gastronomer Jacqui Newling tells us that if we assume they were served what naval tradition called 'salt rations', each male prisoner would have received *two-thirds* of the following, on a daily basis.

Salted pork 4 lb (250 g per day); or beef 7 lb
(450 g per day)
Flour or bread 7 lb (450 g per day)
Pease (dried peas) 3 pints (1 cup per day)
Rice ½ lb (30 g per day)
Butter (ghee) 6 oz (25 g per day)
In addition, there was sometimes rice, dried fish,
and soup.

Why two-thirds? Because they were not doing any physical work. And women convicts were given half of the two-thirds, just because they were women. This was supplemented en route by fresh meat, fruit and vegetables taken on board at various supply stops. Watkin Tench – a British marine officer who sailed on the *Charlotte*, and who wrote two contemporary narratives of the experience as well as an account of the 'settlement' of Port Jackson – tells us that in Tenerife they bought pumpkins, onions, chickens, figs and mulberries; although, as he wrote, 'fresh meat … is neither plentiful or good'. They also stopped for fresh provisions at Rio de Janeiro, and at the Cape of Good Hope, where they took on board the live animals which formed the foundation of the colony's herds: one bull, one bull calf and seven cows, all black (one cow died at sea). Along the way they also picked up goats, geese, pigs and poultry.

Only one marine and 22 (some accounts give 24) convicts died on the long voyage. That was counted as a good result. In *Sickness and Death on Male and Female Convict Voyages to Australia*, researchers Hamish Maxwell-Stewart and Rebecca Kippen point out that, surprisingly: '… death rates on the First Fleet … were remarkably low given the scale of the operation … the monthly death rate of under seven convicts per 1000 embarked was benign by late-eighteenth century standards'.

A reason for this could have been that Arthur Phillip (who was in charge of the fleet), had insisted that all convicts sentenced to make the gruelling four-month journey be fed well once they had boarded the transport ships, in good time before the fleet set sail.

The same researchers tell us that the death rate on the Second Fleet was much higher, 49 per thousand per month. And that they arrived, according to the Reverend Richard Johnson, Sydney's first chaplain: 'wretched, naked, filthy, dirty, lousy, and many of them utterly unable to stand, to creep, or even to stir hand or foot'.

Those 'wretched, naked, filthy' arrivals were convicts. According to the website 'Food at sea in the age of fighting sail', officers aboard Royal Navy ships enjoyed considerable variety both of foodstuffs and cooking technique: 'The officers' cooks made bread, cakes' and had 'plenty of varied meats'.

While we can't be sure that their choice of food-stuffs was as wide and luxurious as those reported on that website (items listed for the officers' mess included anchovies, bacon and ham, chutneys and pickles, pickled oysters, capers, horseradish and olives, mustard and curry powder), we can conclude, as the writers did, that, 'At sea as on land, the Georgian age was not so bad a historical place for the better sort of Briton to eat'. But it was not predominantly the better sort who landed in 1788.

Recipes

SKATE WINGS AND WARRIGAL GREENS

Serves 2

In his journal on the voyage with James Cook, botanist Joseph Banks records this meal:

> 1770 May 6. We dind to day upon the stingray and his tripe: the fish itself was not quite so good as a scate nor was it much inferior, the tripe every body thought excellent. We had with it a dish of the leaves of tetragonia cornuta boild, which eat as well as spinage or very near it.

This is the first record of a British meal of Australian native produce if not on Australian soil, at least in Australian waters.

The Tetragonia cornuta, *which Cook and Banks elsewhere called New Zealand spinach (it grows on both sides of the ditch), is today known as warrigal greens.*

Stingray in today's parlance is skate, and the parts usually eaten are the wings. As for 'his tripe', it's hard to know what was meant by that, and I've concluded (after consultation) that it probably means skate offal, which we need not trouble ourselves with; although, as Banks pronounced it 'excellent' perhaps some intrepid reader might like to try it. This is my modern intepretation of the dish.

2 skate wings
50 g plain flour, seasoned with salt and freshly ground black
    pepper
25 g butter
1 tbsp olive oil
175 g butter
3 tbsp caperberries, rinsed
3 tbsp capers, rinsed
4 tbsp lemon juice
500 g warrigal greens
2 tbsp roughly chopped flatleaf parsley, to serve

1. Dredge the skate wings in the seasoned flour.
2. Fry the seasoned skate in butter and olive oil until done.
3. Throw in caperberries and capers before removing from
    the heat.
4. Plate each skate wing with capers and caperberries.
    Squeeze over the lemon juice.

5. Drop the warrigal greens into boiling water for no more than 1 minute, then drain.
6. Squeeze out excess water from the warrigal greens. Serve with the skate and chopped parsley.

....

LOBSCOUSE

Serves 6

We can't be certain that this signature dish of the great port of Liverpool, and a staple for sailors during the eighteenth and nineteenth centuries, was served on the First Fleet. That it was served at that time on Royal Naval vessels, there is no doubt. So here is a traditional recipe, adapted somewhat to the modern day.

1 kg lamb shoulder, cut into 5 cm chunks
500 g beef chuck, cut into 5 cm chunks
1 tbsp lard
beef stock to cover the meat (about 1 litre)
2 onions, sliced into crescents
6 or so cups of coarsely chopped root vegetables in any
    proportion, including leeks, parsnips, and white and yellow
    turnips
4 potatoes, peeled and cut like the vegetables
1 tsp dried thyme
½ tsp dried marjoram
3 bay leaves
salt and pepper
chopped parsley, to serve

1. Brown the meat in the lard, then dump everything else except the parsley into the pot, bring it to the boil, cover and cook over medium–low to low heat for between 2 and 3 hours.
2. Serve with the parsley.

3

PUTTING DOWN ROOTS

With respect to the resources of the settlement,
there can be little doubt, that at this moment it is
able to support itself in the article of grain; and
the wild stock of cattle to the westward of the
Nepean will soon render it independent ...
in the article of animal food.

David Collins, *An Account of the English Colony
in New South Wales*, 1798

While science fiction writer Robert Heinlein may well
have taken the name for his novel *Stranger in a Strange
Land* from the Old Testament (Exodus 2:22), the idea
of a Martian-raised human landing on earth could just
as easily have come from a reading of the arrival of the
First Fleet on the east coast of Australia in 1788.

Put yourself in the place of one of the Indigenous population witnessing over 1000 men, women and children disembarking from the 11 ships of that fleet, eventually pouring into the forest of eucalypt, red gum and angophora at the edge of Sydney Harbour. You have seen nothing larger than a canoe in your life.

If you wore anything, it would be a possum-skin cape in winter. And here, looming over you these huge – canoes? – with things like tree trunks stuck in them, hung with white bark. In her book *The Colony*, non-Indigenous Australian historian Grace Karskens reports that 'the ship made them think of *boorowan*, an island, or a great bird with billowed wings'. Pouring from these unfamiliar vessels were over 700 of what you did not know at the time were convicts, victims of a system of justice unthinkable in your culture; and more than 400 marines, officers and soldiers – warriors.

The Aboriginal people would have seen that some had red tops, white legs and strange headdresses like black or white half-moons on their heads. They carried black sticks and had short shining spears by their sides. The others, the majority, who were being shouted at by the red-and-white men carrying sticks and spears, were shuffling around, looking dazed. And their skins – what you could see outside their strange covering, not as colourful as that of the red-and-white men – as pale as ghosts or pink like lilly pilly fruit. Some with hair the colour of oysters.

Hello. And thanks for all the fish.

Fast forward to 1988. What was called the Bicentenary year, the year when white Australia celebrated 200 years since the arrival of the First Fleet. It was and remains a contentious issue, especially the proclamation of Australia Day on 26 January, the day when the ships sailed into Port Jackson.

I was on the harbour's edge, along with thousands of other Sydneysiders, watching the parade of tall ships, commemorating this arrival. I was looking north across the harbour straight at Bradley's Head. It struck me then that the only terrestrial features surviving from that time were the sandstone rocks around the edge of the harbour, the rocks that the city is built upon. Turning to the west, there in all its concrete and glass glory, its jamming traffic and roaring trains, was the city that had been built on the site of what had once been the home of the Eora.

Although it is impossible to know – and would have been impossible to know at the time – just how many Indigenous people were in the Sydney region when the First Fleet landed and began building, Phillip estimated 1500. If that was the case, suddenly there were an extra 1000 mouths to feed, which put a strain on resources, especially on the fish population in the harbour. And that strain began to tell immediately.

Jacob Nagle was an American seaman who had sailed on the First Fleet vessel *Sirius*. He was a member of the crew who rowed Phillip, with some officers and seamen, from Botany Bay to Port Jackson, but when they went ashore he stayed aboard the boat. Throwing a line over the side as he waited, he caught 'a large black bream'. Coming back to the boat, Phillip saw the fish and said to Nagle, 'Recollect that you are the first white man that ever caught a fish in Sydney Cove where the town is to be built'. But not the last.

By July 1788, just six months into the life of the colony, the locals had had enough of the colonists scooping up the fish. Phillip recorded that 'they [the Eora] highly resent the encroachments made upon their fishing places'. They showed this resentment in a very straightforward way. About 20 of them came down to the shore with spears and 'violently seized the greatest part of the fish which was in the seine'. The officer in charge of the fishing party 'very prudently suffered them to take away what they chose, and they parted on good terms'. Phillip went on to say that 'this is the only instance in which these people have attempted any act of unprovoked violence, and to this they probably were driven by necessity'.

But Phillip's attempt to redress this incursion into the Eora food supply showed just how little the Europeans understood the traditional division of labour. He ordered that a proportion of the fish caught by the non-Indigenous fishers be given to the locals. Newling points out in her book *Eat Your History* that 'this had a hidden cost to the Aboriginal women', for whom harbour fishing was their principal and ordained role. As Newling learnt in a personal exchange with an Indigenous man, 'early in a girl's life, a portion of the little finger of her left hand was removed and cast into the harbour as an offering to the fish ... [which] gave the fisherwomen the right to harvest fish from these waters for food'. The well-meant donation of fish diminished the status of the Eora fisherwomen.

Fresh-caught fish were an important part of the diets of both the British and Indigenous populations at the time, but far more important for the locals because 'the others' brought large quantities of their own food.

An account by Karskens sums up the vast gulf between those who were here before 1788, and those who arrived on 26 January. It is a story of costume and, more importantly for this book, gastronomy – to quote the wisdom of Brillat-Savarin again: 'The pleasures of the table belong to all times and all ages, to every country in every day ...'.

Bennelong and Barangaroo, both members of the Cameraigal clan, are two of the best-known Aboriginal people from the time of Arthur Phillip. Bennelong, at first cautious of fraternising with the invaders, befriended Phillip, and gradually persuaded his partner, Barangaroo, to join him. Soon, as Karskens writes, they began to visit Government House to eat with Phillip, accompanied by two children they had adopted. And although Bennelong would often wear a red jacket with silver epaulettes given to him as a gift, 'Baranga-roo remained defiantly naked'.

That is an image that struck me the first time I read it, and continues to do so. Firstly, it indicates what a proud and powerful woman Barangaroo was. And sec-ondly, the image of this woman – then some 40 years old – at the Governor's table, eating the beef and bread offered but, apparently, never touching the wine (unlike Bennelong who became too fond of it), naked among all those over-dressed Georgian gentlemen. What was the reaction of those Georgian gentlemen?

In another account of Barangaroo's encounter with the British, at a picnic also attended by Phillip and Bennelong, Tench describes her as having a petticoat put on her by an Indigenous man, Araboo – which she discarded 'with hesitation' after being ridiculed by Bennelong and the British. She then 'stood armed cap-a-pee [from the French *cap-à-pie*, head to foot] in her nakedness'. Tench goes on to say that 'in short she behaved so well, and assumed the quality of gentleness and timidity to such advantage that … amidst a roam-ing horde of savages in the desert wastes of New South Wales might be found as much feminine innocence, softness and modesty … as the most finished system could bestow'.

That description by Tench – 'a wandering horde of savages' – is how the officers of the First Fleet viewed the Indigenous inhabitants of the land they were col-onising. To turn the table, and to contemplate dining with them – with Bennelong and his cohorts – would have been unthinkable.

First culinary encounters

In eighteenth century England, most food was cooked in a pot hanging over an open fire. And that was adopted in the colony. Much of the colonists' food was boiled, both meats and puddings (sweet and savoury). This would hold for every meal, from the governor's table down to the convicts, except that convicts and lower ranks would have eaten a one-pot meal that could have consisted of rice or peas or maize cooked with vegetables (if there were any), and most likely salt meat.

Each day, according to Newling, the convicts were given '450 g bread, 450 g meat, a cup of maize, a couple of tablespoons of salt, $^1/_4$ cup of sugar, and 15 g tea, which, when compared to a 2 g tea bag today, would make almost 2 litres of tea!'.

The English do love their tea, and one of the most popular native plants used by the new arrivals was sweet sarsaparilla (*Smilax glyciphylla*): a tea was made from the leaves, which Watkin Tench believed saved many from scurvy. But it must have been more than its health properties that made it so popular. Convicts gathering the plant away from the camp were beaten and in one case killed by locals. It would be fair to say that at this stage the new arrivals had no idea how

much their presence was angering the Aboriginal population, who had realised these strange beings were not
going to leave: they were in danger when they left the
confines of the camp.

More than sarsaparilla tea supplemented the diets
of convicts and their keepers. They gathered red berries (perhaps native cherries, *Exocarpos cupressiformis*),
and much else, as told in the diary of midshipman
Daniel Southwell.

> Balm is here in plenty and sevral vegetable have
> been lately found that are of some kind tho not
> so good as at home. Here is Spinach, parsley, a
> sort of B'[road] Beans several wholesome unknown
> vegetables ... a Sort of green Berries ... and a
> species of sorrel &c ...

They hunted and ate kangaroo, duck, cockatoos
and the magpie goose. Two of the ships' surgeons,
Arthur Bowes Smyth and John Worgan, recorded their
hunting experiences. Worgan wrote of kangaroo that
he had 'several times tasted the flesh of this animal',
but that he could not say of it (as others had) that 'it
equals venison'. He reported a 'delightful excursion' in
a boat upharbour, at the end of which the party ate 'a
cold kangaroo pie, a bottle of wine etc'. After another
such trip Worgan wrote that a bird had been shot that
'answers the description given by Dr Goldsmith of the
emu ... its flesh proved very good eating'.

Roo even made it to the table for the first major feast in Sydney, on 4 June 1788, the birthday of King George III. After the handing-out of a pint of porter to each marine guard, and half a pint of spirits for every convict, the officers and gentlemen went to dinner. And what a dinner.

Mutton, roasted kangaroo, fish, fowl, salad pies and preserves. And to drink: Port, Lisbon, Tenerife and Madeira.

Two traits of British society were exhibited even at this early stage. Firstly, the class divide, which would increase as time went on (and as land was grabbed by the wealthy). Secondly, the adherence (with a few exceptions, such as the roasted kangaroo) to British fare. The key phrase in midshipman Southwell's diary entry is 'tho not so good as at home'. Newling admits in her essay 'Dining with Strangeness: European food-ways on the Eora frontier' that although some early settlers did seek to find out about Indigenous food, and that there was 'much experimentation and con-sumption of local produce', this was only practised '… until introduced foods were successfully produced and in good supply in the colony'. Britannia ruled the dining table, and continued to do so for some time, in both what was eaten, and the way it was cooked.

Away from home, on expedition or excursion, food — meat, or fish and small birds caught on the way — would have been grilled over an open fire, an early ver-sion of the barbie. Indeed, advantage was taken of the weather and picnics became very popular among the 'better class of people'. By the early nineteenth century, the picnic in the bush had become an accepted pastime. Patrick White writes of one in *Voss*. Voss and Laura Trevelyan are seen 'approaching the spot where the most solemn rites of the picnic were in the course of being celebrated', where 'little boys were holding chops over the coals on sticks specially sharpened by the coachmen, so that an incense of green bark mingled with the odour of sacrificial fat'. Rural idylls aside, there was building to be carried out.

First farmers

In *The Farming of Australia*, Robin Bromby calls the beginnings of early Australian agriculture 'the conquering of the island continent'. And conquer it the new arrivals did – so successfully that, by 1801, John Oxley (later an explorer, but in that year a visitor to the new colony) could write of settler farms in New Town Bay in Tasmania that 'White cottages in the midst of tolerable good gardens afforded a pleasing contrast to the wilderness of their surrounding scenery'.

This will be only a brief look at the establishment of European agriculture, for several reasons – among them the fact that this topic has been covered extensively in other books, including Bromby's. And because this is a book about the food of the country, which arose, initially, from that agriculture. Where the agriculture directly affects the food and food culture, I will examine it more closely.

As is generally well known, the first attempts at growing food crops in the penal colony were not successful. A combination of poor soil, lack of skilled agricultural workers and that bane of farmers in Australia to this day, usually labelled drought – but which is really the normal state in a dry continent – frustrated all efforts to farm large amounts of food. Although 'cottage' gardens – one grown at Government House and tended to by men Phillip had brought from England (three convicts in the First Fleet were described as 'gardeners'), and others cultivated by convicts – also contributed to their diet.

In May of 1790 the colony faced starvation, which would have been widespread but for the supplementary use of native foods. In November, Phillip wrote: 'I do not think that all the showers of the last four months put together would make twenty-four hours' rain'. He reported that his crop of potatoes 'turned out very badly when I dug them up two months ago'.

Realising he would have to look elsewhere for good farming land, in 1788 he had surveyed Broken Bay and the Parramatta and Hawkesbury Rivers, and settled on Rose Hill, now Parramatta, as the site to establish a government farm. This was only the first of many government farms, a version of early agricultural socialism planned by the representative of the British Crown. The public farm established in November 1788 at Rose Hill was followed, much later, by similar efforts in Bathurst and Wellington. All the produce from those farms was the property of the Crown's representative, Governor Phillip, and distributed as rations. Any additional food grown by convicts, officers, soldiers or (later) settlers was their own. In 1791, Elizabeth Macarthur noted in a letter that while the government farm had had little success with grain, 'the grape thrives remarkably well' and melons 'were raised with little or no trouble'. Food in the colony was still scarce – and expensive – and its supply was dependent on imports from convict ships.

After the Rose Hill farm had been established, Phillip allowed convicts whose sentences had expired to occupy and farm land there. The first to do so, and therefore Australia's first non-Indigenous farmer, was James Ruse, whose 30 acres (12 hectares) was called Experiment Farm. By May of 1790, when Ruse had reaped his first crop (the year before he didn't yield sufficient grain to produce flour, but produced enough seeds for next year's crop), the food situation had improved somewhat, and by the end of the year 200 acres (80 hectares) had been planted at Rose Hill.

By the time Phillip left New South Wales in 1792, he had established 68 emancipated convicts on farms west, north and north-west of Sydney. Even so, few of them had knowledge of farming. Governor Philip Gidley King (who took over in 1800 from John Hunter, Phillip's successor as governor) remarked, perhaps unkindly, that it was impossible to make farmers out of London pickpockets; he neglected to say that they were not all pickpockets, many had stolen to feed their families. And the only crime of many others was to be poor.

In addition to the poor soils, the lack of rain and skilled workers, there were other problems, including crops sown with the same poor seed year after year, and different varieties of seeds mixed together – which meant that crops ripened at different times, which meant wastage. Added to that were the problems with livestock: the Bengal cattle were bad milkers, many of the horses were ill-bred, and the wool of the sheep was coarse.

But some livestock were thriving. Ironically, those left to their own devices, which had escaped in the early days of the settlement and wandered into bushland 65 kilometres up the Nepean River from Parramatta. In 1795, they were accidentally found by two convicts. The original runaway herd of four (some reports say five) cows, one bull and one bull calf had, by 1800, grown to 300. The area where they were found, named by Governor Hunter 'Cowpastures', is modern-day Camden (today there is a Cowpasture Road at Wetherill Park, 20 minutes north of Camden). Although wild, they were claimed as a government herd.

Hunger eased, markets opened

One of the inevitable by-products of food short-ages was theft. With government farms and no open market, and with rations cut in 1790 when the *Sirius* was wrecked off Norfolk Island on its way to the Cape of Good Hope to import more food supplies, theft from private gardens and the Governor's garden increased. In April 1790, a seaman was given 500 lashes for steal-ing from Phillip's garden. He wasn't the only one. In August, the convict Hugh Lowe was sentenced to be hanged for stealing a sheep.

The 1790 King's Birthday found the colonists hungry and in no mood to celebrate. And then relief of sorts sailed through the Heads on 3 June. The *Lady Juliana*, one of the convict transports of the Second Fleet (the fleet carried over 500 passengers), arrived ahead of the other vessels, with a cargo of very sick and dying convicts – as well as provisions, which were sold in a sort of a barter market. It was the first time pri-vately owned goods had been openly sold in Sydney.

Why didn't Phillip confiscate the cargo and stop the market? Perhaps he saw that the time for such mar-kets had come.

Notwithstanding the arrival of provisions, Lieu-tenant Governor David Collins wrote in 1791 that 'the governor thought it expedient to make a reduc-tion of flour, rice and salt provisions', with flour, rice and pork being reduced for everyone over the age of ten from 4 pounds to 3 pounds of each, and the beef ration reduced from 6½ to 4½ pounds. He added that 'the flour was the best article; the rice was found to be full of weevils, the pork was ill-flavoured, rusty and smoked and the beef was lean being cured with spices, truly unpalatable'.

The continued arrival of the ships of the Third Fleet from July through to October 1791 helped to further ease the food shortage, and early in the new year Phillip moved to free up private food supplies. In January of 1792, he advised the colonists that free men and convicts were at liberty to dispose of the food they had grown, and any excess would be purchased by the public commissary at a fair price.

Major Francis Grose, who arrived that year to take up a position as Phillip's acting lieutenant, recorded some of these signs of material progress. He was delighted at the gardens that surrounded his house. In a letter home, he wrote: 'Vegetables are here in great abundance, and I live in as good as house as I wish for'.

The King's Birthday of 1792 proved a far more prosperous one than that of two years earlier. Patients at the hospital were served fresh meat and vegetables; guests at private dinner parties no longer had to bring their own bread, as shortages had forced them to do for some time. And the royal toast was drunk for pleasure rather than to drown feelings of despair.

It was the arrival of merchantmen – such as the *Atlantic* in June of 1792, and others of the East India company some months later – that transformed the Sydney and Parramatta jetties into what were the first produce markets, although regulations governing them didn't come into play until 1806.

Regulations or not, it seems that the Sydney and Parramatta markets were lively affairs, with one account likening them to a village fair. Hawkers shouted out their wares, 'piping hot, smoking hot' mutton pies and Banbury cakes (for which a recipe is given on page 92). For sale were ducks, geese, suckling pigs, fowls, and maize and wheat, melons and cabbages. And 'a number of respectable persons, especially of the fair sex, lounge about the market ...' according to one contemporary account. It would be fair to say that the word 'respectable' was used at least ironically.

Collins listed the prices for that first market, both in Sydney and Parramatta; the differences between the two indicate the cost of transport. I'll record just a few items from the list (where 'd' is a penny, 's' a shilling).

Sydney
Flour from 6d to 1s a pound
Eggs 3d each
Fresh pork 1s a pound
Salt pork 8d–9d per pound
Potatoes 3d a pound
Cabbages 1d each

Parramatta

Flour 1s a pound

Eggs 3s a dozen

Fresh pork 1s 1d – 1s 3d per pound

Salt pork 10d–1s per pound

Potatoes 3d–4d per pound

Cabbages 10s per hundred

To put that in perspective, in 1790, pay in the New South Wales Corps was as follows: for a captain, 7s 6d a day; a lieutenant, 3s 6d; a sergeant, 1s; a private, 6d. It is easy to understand how crime and corruption flourished.

And flourish they did when Phillip left in December 1792 and handed over to Major Francis Grose.

One of Grose's first acts in 1793 was to allocate parcels of land – 100 acres (40 hectares) to officers, 30 acres (12 hectares) to emancipated convicts – the idea being to increase food production, the unintended consequence being to entrench inequality. At the same time, he allowed convicts employed on government farms to work on private landholdings on their own time. Another unintended (or, I would imagine, even unnoticed) consequence was the beginning of the alienation of the Indigenous population from their land and their food sources, which had long-term and disastrous consequences. Once the fences went up, they were locked out.

Although only an acting governor, Grose (and Paterson after him) was the officer in charge of the New South Wales Corps (aka The Rum Corps). Soon the unofficial rule was, 'what's good for the Rum Corps is good for the colony'.

How did the name of the corps arise? Because it was illegal to distil liquor in the colony, it had to be imported. The officers of the New South Wales Corps were the only ones with access to imported goods, so it wasn't long before they were selling these goods at anything from 100 to 1000 per cent profit. And the most profitable item sold was rum, which arrived at 8 shillings a gallon and was retailed at anything up to £8.

Back then were laid the foundations of the Sydney we know today: freewheeling, free marketeering, property-obsessed and with an ever-present whiff of corruption.

Writing in her *Companion Guide to Sydney*, Ruth Park makes an interesting connection with the name of this rambunctious metropolis:

> Sydney is a corruption of 'St Denis', St Denis being the saint who converted the Gauls to Christianity. But the name Denis is another corruption of the Athenian name, Dionysius. Thus we may say that Sydney's patron is Dionysius, which, in view of the blithe and irrepressible character of the city, as it has developed, is gratifyingly suitable.

In the same year that Grose began to allocate land grants, the first free settlers arrived aboard the *Bellona*, five men, two women and six children. These immigrants were the first free settlers to receive land grants. The granted land was at Liberty Plains, now Strathfield and Homebush, and they joined emancipated convicts in taking up freeholdings (or selections). After building themselves huts to live in, with slabs of bark for walls, and roofs held up by saplings, they began to farm, with mixed success. They were no more skilled than the emancipated convicts.

The land they farmed often suffered from overcropping, and having run out of land at Parramatta, many, including Ruse (who sold his Rose Hill farm), turned to the Hawkesbury River, where some cultivated the low-lying lands and were inundated when the river rose. Floods were not the only problem.

A protracted drought lasting until 1799 – the worst since the First Fleet arrived – played havoc with the crops, Bromby reporting that 'the wheat proved little better than chaff and the maize was shrivelled to the ground'. Then came fire, and then the rains, which flooded the river. One farmer drowned. But in spite of Governor Macquarie's attempts to persuade them, they would not leave, in spite of almost annual floods. Many had their land seized by creditors.

By 1820, the colony was beginning to move into a new stage. The officer class had lost dominance, and free settlers were in much greater numbers. In 1822, the Agricultural Society (later the Royal Agricultural Society) stated in its prospectus:

> It becomes us therefore to provide for ourselves;
> to make the most of the land we have cleared; to
> improve our fleeces; to look out for new exports;
> to improve the present; to distil our own grain;
> and to grow our own tobacco.

From the outset, they demonstrated a determination to continue with the methods of agriculture that would prove disastrous for the land. And spread them across the entire continent.

Although Sydney was still the centre of the colonists' world, they began to expand outwards: south to the Shoalhaven River and the Illawarra, north to the Hunter Valley, and west to Bathurst. Agriculture was on the march. The frontier wars began.

Although it is difficult to choose a date when self-sufficiency was realised, it was in 1823 that the British government took the approach that it would be limiting its direct expenditure to the transportation of convicts and food and supplies, and handing responsibility over to the colonial administration.

The foundations of a metropolis

Although Phillip had an elaborate plan for a new town, which he originally called Albion, the plans and the name were abandoned. Government House was built where the Museum of Sydney now stands – at the front of which can be seen the footings below ground level under glass, and an installation called *Edge of the Trees*, by Fiona Foley and Janet Laurence, which symbolises the juncture of the old Eora world and the new European one. Phillip also built a row of brick houses for officers in what is now Bridge Street. This was, according to Karskens, for the elite, 'the town'. The rest, to the west, were 'clear of the town' or even (my interpretation) 'beyond the pale'. It is interesting to note how long that east–west divide lasted: the east for the silvertails, the west for the 'westies'.

The west, at that time, was The Rocks, so named by convicts who built their homes there. Firstly of wattle and daub, later of more durable materials, with gardens. Immigrants settled there, including the Chinese, and the city's first Chinatown was in lower George Street where – although I can find no evidence – there must have been Chinese eating houses, such as were to be found around Dixon Street from the late nineteenth century on.

The Rocks was not only where the newly arrived convicts and later immigrants went to live, it was the place where visiting seamen came to carouse and often to stay. Over time there arrived pubs and shops, bread ovens, boarding houses and bawdy houses, and it became not just a working class area, but the outsider's Sydney, a place of revelry, debauchery and gambling, the early Sydney equivalent of a much later Kings Cross.

Here, as historian SH Roberts wrote in the *Sydney Mail* in 1938, 'were the grog-houses where the convicts, the sailors and the lower classes of the free community gathered for their dram drinking, swallowing execrable Bengal rum neat from wine glasses and smoking foul-smelling Brazil twist in dudeens or clay pipes' in places like the Sheer Hulk and the Black Dog.

But now it is time to move out of the developing and Dionysian capital on the harbour, and follow the spread of the colony across the continent.

Recipes

JACQUI NEWLING

....

SWEET BREAKFAST HOMINY

Serves 4

From Jacqui Newling, Eat Your History: stories and recipes from Australian kitchens, *Sydney Living Museums/NewSouth Publishing, Sydney, 2015.*

In her book Eat Your History *Jacqui Newling points out that 'maize', or 'Indian corn', proved to be the grain best suited to Sydney's soils and climate, although the bread made from it was not so popular. Children visiting the Hyde Park Barracks on living history tours make this dish which, according to Newling, receives mixed reviews, depending upon how much brown sugar is added. In twenty-first century Australia, cornmeal, with the Italian name polenta, is a fashionable food.*

170 g (1 cup) coarse polenta
250 ml (1 cup) milk (optional)
1 heaped tbsp brown sugar
1 heaped tbsp currants (optional)
1 tbsp butter (optional)

1. Put the polenta in a large saucepan with ¼ tsp salt and 500 ml (2 cups) water. Cook over a low heat, stirring for about 10 minutes or until the polenta has thickened and starts to come away from the sides of the pan as you stir. Be careful – the mixture will bubble and pop as steam tries to come through the polenta as it thickens.
2. Add the milk, if using, or 250 ml (1 cup) water, and stir for a few seconds to loosen up the mixture.
3. Add the sugar and currants, if using, and stir for a few minutes until the sugar dissolves and the currants have softened. Taste, adding more salt or sugar to your liking.
4. If using the butter, stir it through until it has melted. Serve hot.

– Banbury cakes –

Banbury cakes were sold at the original Sydney Markets in 1792 along with 'piping hot, smoking hot' mutton pies. The 1615 recipe from Gervase Markham's The English Huswife, Containing the Inward and Outward Virtues Which Ought to Be in a Complete Woman *I reproduce for your interest. Below it a more practical recipe from renowned baker Dan Lepard, first published in* The Guardian, *inspired by Markham. My thanks to Dan Lepard for permission to publish his recipe.*

GERVASE MARKHAM

BANBURY CAKES

To make a very good Banbury cake take four pounds of currants and wash and pick them very clean, and dry them in a cloth: then take three eggs and put away one yolk, and beat them and strain them with good barm [yeast], putting thereto cloves, mace, cinnamon and nutmegs; then take a pint of cream and as much morning's milk and set it on the fire until the cold be taken away; then take flour and put in a good store cold butter and sugar and then put in your eggs, barm and meal and work them all together an hour or more; then save a part of the paste and the rest break in pieces and work in your currants; which done mould your cake of what quantity you please; and then with that paste which hath not any currants cover it very thin both underneath and aloft. And so bake it according to bigness.

DAN LEPARD

....

JACOBEAN BANBURY CAKES

Makes 8

Based on the Gervase Markham recipe, miniaturised and topped with sugar, very much like a slender, elegant black bun.

75 ml Guinness, at room temperature

2 tsp fast-action yeast

1 medium egg, separated

100 g unsalted butter

300 g strong white flour

100 g wholemeal flour

75 g dark brown sugar

1 tsp salt

75 ml each double cream and milk

⅛ tsp each ground cloves, mace and cinnamon

500 g currants

demerara sugar

1. Beat the Guinness, yeast and egg yolk in a bowl and leave for 30 minutes. In another bowl, rub 75 g butter through the flours, 25 g sugar and salt. Warm the cream, milk and 1/2 tsp of each spice in a pan, then pour this and the yeast mixture into the flour. Mix to a soft dough, knead lightly, cover and leave for an hour.

2. Mash 250 g of the dough in a food processor with 25 g butter, 50 g sugar, spices and a third of the currants. Stir in the remaining currants. Roll half the

remaining dough very thin (0.25 cm, ideally), cut into 8 equal pieces, place a golfball-sized scoop of the currant mixture in the centre and stretch the dough around it. Dampen the edges and seal. Repeat with the remaining dough. Gently roll each cake seam-side down into a 1.5 cm thick oval, place on trays lined with nonstick paper, brush with beaten egg white, sprinkle with sugar, slash the tops and bake at 220°C (200°C fan-assisted)/ gas mark 7 for 15 minutes.

4

AGRICULTURE, CLASS
AND COMMODITY

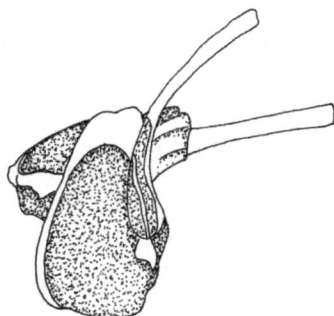

The most important economic resource [of the
new colony] was land. Accordingly, the governor's
primary socioeconomic function was to distribute
what were called 'Crown lands'.

Philip McMichael, *Settlers and the Agrarian Question*

How did we get to the point where an industrial product, originally made from a by-product of the brewing
industry, can be called, as it was in an article in *Gastronomica*, 'the best predictor of national identity of any
food in the world. That is, if you eat Vegemite, you are
almost certainly Australian'?

I'm going to argue – and I'm not the only one – that
this process began with the second lot of land grabs

on the Australian continent. The first of course being when the officers of the First Fleet raised the Union Jack and claimed not only sovereignty over New South Wales – then comprising the whole eastern half of Australia – but also ownership of the remaining 1.5 million square miles. Done on the pretext that there were no other peoples living there, and later to be called the principle of *terra nullius* – empty land.

The second land grab began with Phillip handing out what was Crown land, first to freed convicts, then to ex-marines. As we saw in the previous chapter, after 1793 Acting Governor Grose began dispersing 100-acre lots to officers. It wasn't long before land grants were being extended to whoever was deemed by the governor of the day to be worthy. Those grants from 1793 were significant.

They were the first drafts of an Antipodean version of the English class system. That is, the rise of landed property with all its imported prestige, privileges and rights. And more importantly for our food culture, the foundation of a system of farming and food production that had more to do with export markets than putting food on the domestic table.

At first, the colony's priority – and resources of time and labour – had been given to providing food and raw materials for the survival of the colonists. The emphasis of the early governors, especially Phillip, was therefore on the establishment of smallholding farms. Before 1821, in spite of the larger grants to officers and other influential gentlemen, three-quarters of all land grants were less than 100 acres.

After 1821, and with the spread of settlement, large blocks of land were held by those individuals who became known as squatters under temporary grazing rights, and some very large grants were given. For example, in 1824 a million acres of prime land was granted to the Australian Agricultural Company (which today is still going strong and still largely British-owned).

As the settlement grew, the emphasis began to shift from agriculture to pastoralism. A pastoralist is defined by the *Australian National Dictionary* as 'the owner of a substantial stock-raising establishment or a number of such establishments'.

From those first land grants in 1793, our agriculture morphed from the mixed farming originally envisaged by Phillip and others to monoculture, broadacre farms and the production of commodities intended in the main for the imperial market.

Phillip's vision of a land of smallhold farms went against the tenor of the times. The colony was established at the outset of the Industrial – and Agricultural – Revolutions. Both these mitigated against the small farm. The development of broadacre farming, the giant squatter holdings, saw the industrialisation of our food supply – or, more correctly, food industry.

After 1825, responding to a larger rural population, emphasis was shifted to encouraging a mix of large grazing properties and small agricultural holdings. The official desire to continue encouraging small farming was reinforced, and a limit of 9600 acres was set on land grants.

At the same time, a system originally called 'tickets of occupancy' was initiated. This gave security to those who had occupied land illegally by taking possession of those areas around towns that had not yet been surveyed and settled, a practice later known as squatting.

Who were the squatters? The *Macquarie Dictionary* defines a squatter as 'one who has settled on Crown land to run stock, especially sheep, initially without government permission, but later with a lease or licence'. In other words, a land thief, at first regarded as a quasi-criminal, who rose to the ranks of what became known as the 'squattocracy' amid the hurly burly and devious dealing in land that marked Australia during most of the nineteenth century. When the Melbourne Club – then as now an enclave of class and privilege – was founded, Bromby tells us, 'the majority of its members were squatters ...'. They were thieves twice over. First the land was stolen from the Indigenous population. Then the squatters stole the land from the Crown.

As various administrations bent to their wills, these squatters became more powerful. It was widely believed that any move against them would be dangerous for the economy, which began to slide into depression in the 1840s. By now, there was consensus that pastoral capitalism would be the backbone of the colonial economy.

Big food

So it proved, and this is where Australian culinary habits begin to be set in the soil. The number of livestock grew exponentially – even faster than the human population, which doubled between 1860 and 1890. By 1890, with a population of 3.2 million humans, stock numbers had grown to 10 million cattle and 100 million sheep. While many of the sheep were grown for their wool, the 10 million cattle were clearly more than were required for Australian tables.

This was seen not as a problem, but as an opportunity: an opportunity in search of technology to solve the problem of how to get all that beef – and lamb – to export markets. As early as 1830, individual producers had been using an ancient preservation technology, sending salted meat to markets including England and Mauritius.

The next step was canning, the invention of which began in France and was developed in England in 1810. By 1869, manufacturers in Queensland were exporting over a million kilograms of canned meat each year to Great Britain. Then came freezing, which ran into problems. Shipments sent to England in 1873 and 1877 were unsuccessful. But by the early twentieth century, Australia was able to export chilled beef, and by 1937–38 the export trade had grown to 28 000 tonnes.

And it was not just meat being sent offshore. Richard Twopeny, writing in the 1880s, observed that '... the finest qualities of flour are all shipped to England instead of being used here'.

Food was something you grew not to eat, but to export. This was pretty much the prevailing attitude right up to the mid-1990s, when I recall hearing an industry leader addressing a 'mob' of beef farmers. 'What youse blokes have to understand', he told them, 'is that you're in the food industry'. As fine an example as any of the attitude of a broadacre cattle farmer who raises his stock, herds them onto the trucks to the abattoirs, closes the farm gate, and that's the last he hears of them. Thankfully, this attitude has changed dramatically in more recent years.

There is the core of the difference for Australian food culture. In his book *One Continuous Picnic*, Symons writes that 'There has never been the creative interplay between society and the soil ... almost no food has ever been grown by the person who eats it, almost no food preserved in the home ... Our history is without peasants'. But that is only one of a number of causes which will be examined.

This land, as first settled, before refrigeration, before any means of taming the weather, was for the great part a harsh and unforgiving place for the colonists to live. And it was populated by Indigenous people who appeared to the ill-advised colonists (the majority, but no means all) to be from another planet or, at the very least, another time – the stone age. As the colonists spread further across the country, these people fought back ferociously against the theft of their lands.

Under such conditions, the development of a food culture was the very last thing on their mind. Food was primarily fuel.

The subsequent development of a vast grazing industry, pioneered by John Macarthur, locked the gate against culinary development. 'Grazing's success', wrote Symons, 'turned us into a nation of meat eaters', and in the main, primitive ones at that – eating slabs of meat thrown onto the fire.

That, and the rations of 'Ten Ten Two & a Quarter' (10 lb of flour, 10 lb of meat, 2 lb sugar, ¼ lb tea and salt). These were paid to an itinerant workforce who, according to Symons, glorified 'the drifting, shiftless way of life [of workers on the large grazing properties]' and 'prevented the food supply from ever really developing beyond the high dependence of the convict stage', putting paid to anything but the 'characteristic and monotonous' diet of fried meat, damper and tea at our early stage of development. This diet, replaced by a big slab of meat and potatoes, continued almost into current times.

A meal in Australia was (and in some cases still is)

generally not measured by the excellence of the produce or the skill of the cooking but by its size on the serving dish. A steak was a 'good feed' if it hung over the edges of the plate. About twenty years ago, while doing research for the pilot of a television show on Australian food, I visited the highway cafe voted best in the country by truck drivers. Why, I asked, did it get the prize? Because we serve really big helpings I was told. Having eaten there, I can vouch for that.

In such a culinary absence, skill and 'daintiness' on the table was provided by women cooking cakes. The woman who cooked a 'tea' of mutton and potatoes for the shearers practised her skills on the cakes, jellies, jams and trifles served around the edges of the main meal. And the preponderance of dessert and cake recipes in Australian cookbooks attests to this. Chapter headings in the first edition of the Country Women's Association's *Coronation Cookery Book* (1937) included Tea Cakes, Tea Loaves, Pikelets, Buns, Cakes, Small Cakes, Home Made Sweets – the book was predominantly recipes for sweet things. In later chapters, I'll examine the Country Women's Association recipe books more closely.

From the outset, by the design of those who ran the colony – or at least by the design of those who 'grabbed' the land – our food was produced industrially, as commodity. But the food culture here in the nineteenth century, what I call our British or Anglo-Celtic food culture, remained in place virtually unchanged until after the Second World War – when things changed dramatically. There was, however, one curious exception to that dictatorship.

Rosbif and roast beef

For all but the wealthiest Australians in the nineteenth century, the juxtaposition of an imported Anglo-Celtic food culture with the harshness of the environment and copious quantities of poorly cooked second-rate meat (the best was exported) on the table, resulted in a diet of abundance and poor quality. Slabs of meat, washed down with tea, followed by cake, would be a short definition of the average meal.

This is not to say that there were no good cooks, both professional and domestic, in Australia; but the overall standard of food, as confirmed by visitors and locals, was generally poor.

Curiously, and following the tradition of the British upper classes, public eating – celebratory banquets for example – were predominantly French in content and form. Where did this English awe of French culinary arts begin?

According to Colin Spencer, around 1660, with the publication of *The Accomplisht Cook* by Robert May: a book that showed its influences by listing nine recipes for snails. The year 1660 saw the return of Charles II to the throne. Spencer writes: 'For though the King had to pretend to pursue Protestant policy, all knew that he and his family had strong Papist sympathies and a love of France and French cooking'. As did May, who had spent five years in France and cooked for Royalist nobility. This association of the nobility and the upper classes with French cooking continued through to the eighteenth century. Even while Britain was engaging in battles against Louis XIV in the early eighteenth century, and although France was at the time a 'highly emotive subject', Spencer wrote, '… French chefs and the food they produced were popular with the aristocracy who thought that French recipes were superior to the English'. In her 1747 book *The Art of Cookery Made Plain and Easy*, Hannah Glasse wrote: 'So much is the blind Folly of this Age, that they would rather be imposed on by a French booby, than give encouragement to a good English cook'.

This reverence towards French cuisine arrived in Australia with the officer and governing classes, undimmed by distance, undeterred by unavailable produce, unfazed by the challenges of climate, and took root immediately. It is perhaps understandable that this marker would be adopted in a new society carving out a class structure based largely on that which they had left in Britain. There were early hotels and restaurants serving French food – including the first licensed hotel in New South Wales, the Freemason's Arms in Parramatta, built in 1800 – but the mainstays of nineteenth century French culinary dominance were the extravagant public banquets held in Sydney. The Mitchell Library, in the State Library of New South Wales, holds menus from these events in its ephemera collection.

On 26 January 1888, the Centennial Dinner was held at the Exhibition Building (demolished in 1954) in Sydney's Prince Alfred Park, to celebrate the first one hundred years of European occupation. It is an archetypical Victorian blowout. Almost the entire menu is in French:

Potage.

Tortue.

Poissons.

Saumon à la Royale.

Filet de Sole, Crême des Anchoies. Schnapper à la Maréchal.

Entrées.

Les Pâtes à la Reine.

Salmi des Perdrix.

Chaud Froid de Volaille.

Releves.

Dinde Rôti à la Perigord. Dinde Boulli,

Sauce aux Champignons.

Jambon de Yorc. Langues de Bœuf.

Selle d'Agneau. Haut de Bœuf.

Bœuf en Preserve.

Gibier.

Faisans, Sauce au Pain.

Pâte de Foie Gras en Aspic.

Salade à la Russe.

Mayonnaise des Crevettes.

Entremets.
Gelée à l'Australienne.
Gelée des Oranges. Gelée au Ponche.
Charlotte aux Fraises.
Pouding à la Princesse. Pouding aux Amandes.
Crême à la Vanille. Crême au Fleur des Oranges.
Crême au Chocolat.
Nougat au Crême.
Fanchettes.
Bouchées des Dames. Tartelettes au Crême.
Pouding Glacé à la Nesselrode.
Eau Glacé aux Oranges.
Dessert.
Café
Wines
Sherry, Hock, Chablis, Australian Wine.
Champagnes: Ruinart, Irroy, Pommery and Greno.
Clarets: Mouton de Rothschild, Latour.
Port.
Liqueurs: Curacao, Maraschino, Old Brandy.

The meal displays only a vague connection with the new land. There are many such menus for many such meals in the library's collection. But what is of particular interest in this context is the number of dishes styled 'à l'Australienne'. A little earlier, at a Mayoral Banquet in June 1884, there is on the menu a Jelly à l'Australienne. And then in 1889 at a dinner at New South Wales Parliament House, Glace à l'Australienne. These curious early descriptions of things as 'à l'Australienne' persisted. What did they mean? Did they have to do with the news filtering through to local chefs of the codification of the 186 French and 103 foreign sauces of the French cuisine, published by Marie-Antonin Carême in his *L'Art de la Cuisine Française au Dix-Neuvième Siècle* in 1833? These included à la Russe, à l'Italienne and à la Polonaise. But these had at least a tenuous link with their names. Not so the dishes labelled 'à l'Australienne'.

Very few of the dishes at these French feasts were made using Australian native produce. For example, at a banquet for the Earl of Carnarvon in the Parliamentary Refreshment Room in Sydney on 19 December 1887, in addition to the Filets de pigeon à la Parisienne (the pigeon, hopefully, would have been local, and not 'hung' for the trip from 'home'), we find Murray cod à la Normande. The early European inhabitants were very fond of Murray cod, and had even sent a live specimen back to England. Huîtres natives Australienne or Huîtres au naturel were served at a banquet for Henry Parkes' eightieth birthday on 28 May 1894, then again on 7 September 1897 at a banquet to celebrate the Federal Convention, and again on 4 October 1913 at a Banquet for Rear Admiral Sir George Patey we find Huîtres native Australiennes.

When I asked food historian Colin Bannerman about any possible meaning for 'à l'Australienne' he suggested that it could have to do with the early stirrings of Republican sentiment leading up to Federation. In his own database he found a recipe for Peach à l'Australienne in *Australian Home Cookery* by Emily Futter, published in 1924. This was an elaborate confection using a mould lined with Florence paste, royal icing coloured with carmine, and employing complex techniques which, Bannerman said, were totally out of context with the rest of the book, suggesting a restaurant, hotel or banquet dish.

Whatever the naming of these dishes meant, apart from an expression of pride in a century of occupation, and apart from the designation of oysters as native – they could hardly have been imported – they did not represent any move towards the development of a cuisine or food culture. Indeed, it is somewhat ironic – or an indication of alienation – that when we do refer to the country and its food for the first time, it's in French!

Recipes

JANE LAWSON

....

STEAK WITH VEGEMITE BUTTER
Serves 4

From Jane Lawson, Grub: favourite food memories, *Murdoch Books, Sydney, 2007.*

Jane Lawson's book of Oz culinary nostalgia, Grub *(out of print), contains this simple and nifty way to combine two elements of our culinary heritage. Explaining this recipe (which I love), Jane says:*

> While I don't personally do the 'Vegemite on toast' thing (yeah, crazily un-Australian but I don't really dig it), I am not averse to people chucking a little in a stew, soup, meat pie filling etc. for a little added oomph if it needs it. I rarely use it myself these days – but when I was learning to cook, my grandmother suggested it as a way to increase flavour – I assume it was because when times were tough during/ post World War II that you couldn't access many decent ingredients. Or she was just a crap cook?

80 g butter
3 tsp Vegemite
1 garlic clove, crushed
1 tsp finely chopped thyme
4 x 200 g fillet (or scotch fillet/sirloin/hanger steaks)
olive oil for brushing

1. Combine the butter with the Vegemite, garlic and thyme and season with freshly cracked black pepper. Pat into a log and wrap in plastic wrap. Twist the ends of the wrap in opposite directions to form a smooth sausage, or pat into a rectangular shape.
2. Refrigerate until ready to use, but bring to room temperature 5–10 minutes before serving to soften slightly.
3. Heat a barbecue grill plate to high. Brush the steaks with a little olive oil, then season with salt and freshly cracked black pepper.
4. Grill the steaks for 3–4 minutes a side or until cooked to your liking. Remove from the heat, cover loosely with foil and allow to rest for 5 minutes.
5. Slice the Vegemite butter and place several discs on top of each steak.
6. Serve with potatoes and a green salad or a mixture of lightly cooked green vegetables such as snow peas, asparagus and perhaps some baby carrots.

SCHNAPPER À LA MARÉCHALE

This dish, which appeared on Sydney's Centennial Dinner menu in 1888, has been known since the eighteenth century at least. It may be associated with the Maréchale de Luxembourg (1707– 87). According to food historian William Pokhlyobkin, the dish had to be so tender that 'even a marshal (a synonym for an elder, satiated and toothless man) could eat it'. Although a specific recipe is very difficult to find, a good cook could prepare it by following the instructions below.

To make the fumet
5 litres water
4 cups fruity white wine
1 cup grated carrot
1 cup grated white onion
thyme
500 g mushrooms
500 g ripe tomatoes

Bring to the boil, simmer for 30 minutes. Cook the day before and cool.

To cook the fish
Any firm white fish can be prepared à la Maréchale. Poach the fish in the fumet, then take the fish from the liquid. To make the sauce, reduce the liquid and then mix it with meat glaze and butter. Serve the fish with the sauce.

5

COOKING BY THE BOOKS

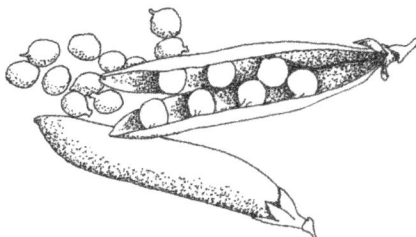

On the whole, our forebears seemed determined
to ignore the riches around them and to implant
a familiar but unsuitable cookery. In much the
same way, town and city dwellers bought their
vegetables from John Chinaman, but made no
attempt to learn his ways with them.

Colin Bannerman, *A Friend in the Kitchen*

The first cookbook published in this country was *The English and Australian Cookery Book*. Written in Tasmania and published in London in 1864, its frontispiece proclaimed it to be *For the Many, as Well as for the 'Upper Ten Thousand'*. It was written by 'An Australian Aristologist' – aristology being defined as the art or science of cooking and dining. The book encompasses the preparation, combination and presentation of dishes and the manner in which these dishes are integrated into a meal. The Aristologist was later revealed to be one Edward Abbott, a pastoralist and parliamentarian whose family had arrived in Australia in 1790: in other words, one of the 'Upper Ten Thousand'.

In many ways, this curious book set the tone for various Australian cookbooks to come, although, in the fashion of the time (and especially in the manner of Mrs Beeton), it was as much an instruction book for its dedicatees – 'His Fair Countrywomen of the "Beautiful Land"' – as a compilation of recipes. The recipes were mainly British, with a smattering of 'continental' – 'gazpacho', 'sour-krout', Turkish pilau – and a nod in the direction of his homeland: roast 'emeu', roast wombat, and a selection of kangaroo recipes, including the famous Slippery Bob, kangaroo brain fritters. Bannerman remarks that 'his recipes for kangaroo suggest it was widely accepted both as a survival food and as meat for the well-served table'. But such local delicacies are overshadowed by imports like Devonshire squab pie, Jugged hare, Irish stew, Banbury cakes and, from the Raj, Mulligatawny soup. To give Abbott his due, he does offer a comprehensive list of Australian game and fish, somewhat marred by the inclusion of unavailable produce like salmon, turbot and ortolan.

Of special interest to this book is that, unlike most of the other cookbooks I've researched (and especially the entirely garlic-free *The Art of Living in Australia*, dicussed below, which appeared almost 30 years later), Abbott uses and lists garlic.

Unlike his close contemporary Mrs Beeton (first published in 1861), whose sniffy and xenophobic dismissal ('The smell of this plant is generally considered offensive …') we have come across before, Abbott, in his list of what he calls 'Condiments', more a potpourri of ingredients, quotes the seventeenth century essayist Sir William Temple on 'Health and Long Life':

Garlic has, of all our plants, the greatest strength, affords most nourishment, and supplies most spirits to those who eat little flesh, as the poorer people seldom do in the hotter, and especially the more eastern climates … no other food of herbs or plants yielding strength enough for such labour.

It's surprising then, that after such extravagant praise, garlic should appear in only a handful of the 1000 recipes in Abbott's book: a garlic gravy, Roast goose à la françoise and in his savoury, French and plain sausages. Perhaps this is not so surprising when you read a little further into Sir William's praise of garlic; he claims that it is 'a specific remedy of the gout' from which he suffers, but also that 'I could never long bear the constraint of a diet I found not very agreeable myself, and at least fancied offensive to the company I conversed with'.

In Abbott's book there is also a wonderful story, reading like a modern Extreme Food Adventure ('I ate dog in China!'), of Abbott and a group of friends in Bordeaux. They were 'anxious to taste "a gigot a l'ail" (roast leg of mutton with garlic)'. Their 'anxiety to taste' is reminiscent of a group in an exotic location daring themselves to eat a bizarre local specialty. We see them sitting eagerly around the table awaiting this thrilling dish.

> When the roast was placed on the table at the second course, it appeared to us all to be a gigot aux haricots [a leg of mutton and kidney beans]; but the meat was delicious, and the beans certainly superior to and bearing a different flavour from any haricots we had ever tasted before.

Abbott and his friends quizzed the landlord and asked why he had substituted beans for garlic.

'The dish you have eaten', the landlord replied, 'and which your guests seemed to have liked was a gigot a l'ail, and what you have mistaken for beans is garlic'.

Incredulous, they asked how this was possible. 'Again we tasted the garlic; its rankness was gone.' They politely asked the landlord how he had achieved this miracle.

'The process is very simple,' the landlord told them. 'The garlic is thrown into five boiling waters, with a little salt, and boiled five minutes in each. It is then drained and put into the dripping pan under the roasting mutton'. Very simple.

The second of the early didactic cookbooks, *The Art of Living in Australia*, was published in 1893, and written by Philip Edward Muskett, who at different times was a surgeon and senior resident medical officer at Sydney Hospital. He was a health reformer, and in private practice about one-third of his patients were children, which prompted him to write two books on health care for children. Muskett had very clear ideas about what Australians should and should not be eating, and was most concerned about what he saw as maladaptation to the climate.

> The Australian people [have] never yet realised their semi-tropical environment. It would naturally be supposed that [this would have] exercised an irresistible effect on their mode of living. But, on the contrary, the type of the Australian dwelling-house, the clothing of the Australian people and, what is more significant than anything else, their food habits, prove incontestably that that they have never recognised the semi-tropical nature of their climate.

Most of his dietary advice is, to a modern eye, sensible: more fish less meat, more salads and more vegetables, wine instead of beer. A good part of the book is dedicated to the planting of vineyards and the best grapes for the country. His criticism of the meat-heavy diet did not stop at content but included cooking. 'The abuse of flesh food in a climate like Australia's would be serious enough under any circumstances, but it is intensified and aggravated by the direct unoriginality of dealing with meat.' He wrote indignantly that there was no attempt to break through the conventional chain of joints, roasted or boiled, and the inevitable grill or fry: '... In how many houses does the breakfast consist of anything but the ubiquitous chops, steaks or sausages? Indeed, one might almost term them the "the faith, hope and charity" of domestic life'. That just about summed up my Anglo-Celtic father's invariable breakfast.

Muskett advocated the planting of asparagus, globe artichokes, Jerusalem artichokes, eggplant and many other vegetables that would have been strangers to Australians of the time. He added at the end of the book a number of recipes and Mrs Beeton-like 'kitchen information' from a Mrs H Wicken, a lecturer on Cookery at the Technical College, Sydney. That the dietary advice offered by Muskett was ignored for the next sixty years was testament to the power of culture over cuisine. Regardless of the unsuitability of the climate, Australians persisted with – many still do – the ritual of Christmas dinner, turkey and pudding, in December, one of the hottest months of the year. In his book *Food Is Culture*, Massimo Montanari writes, 'food takes shape as a decisive element of human identity and as one of the most effective means of expressing and communicating identity'. And Australians, for over 160 years, identified as British/Anglo-Celtic. Indeed, Muskett himself recognises the dominance of culture in deciding diet:

> It must be remembered that Australia has been peopled chiefly by the Anglo-Saxon race. In such a stock the traditional tendencies are almost ineradicable, and hence it is that the descendants of the new comers believe as their forefathers did before them. It's in the blood. For there can be no doubt but that the Anglo-Saxon thinks that there is only one way of living in every part of the world – no matter whether the climate be tropical, semi-tropical or frigid. Those in the old country live in a certain manner, and all the rest of the globe have every right to follow their example.

Curiously, given Dr Muskett's assertion – printed on the title page of his book – that 'Australia is practically Southern Europe' and his enthusiasm for a Mediterranean diet for Australia, as mentioned above, there is not one clove of garlic in any of Mrs Wicken's recipes.

One of the most interesting asides in Muskett's book is this question – asked, let's not forget, in the early 1890s: 'Is it not strange that so far ingenuity, universal approval, or general consensus of opinion, call it what you will, has not up until the present given us an

Australian national dish?'. He hopes that when it does it will be a macédoine of vegetables, a vegetable curry or some well-concocted salad. Some 130 years later, we're still waiting.

Brazilian stew and
other curiosities

More typical in many ways of those cookbooks to follow, including freedom from garlic, was Mrs Lance Rawson's *The Antipodean Cookery Book and Kitchen Companion*, first published in 1895 and still being reprinted in 1907. 'Once more', she wrote, 'I come before my sister housewives with a cheap and useful work on cookery, expressly written for those living in the far bush as well as those within the reach of the amenities of civilized existence'.

Where Rawson differed from her contemporaries was that while the majority of her recipes were straight up and down British, she not only embraced native ingredients but wrote that 'I would advise every housewife in the Bush to experiment and try everything; the blacks or her own common sense will soon tell her what is edible and what is not'. Her relationship with Aboriginal people was complex and nuanced. Demonstrating an understanding of the dispossession of land occurring in Queensland at the time, she wrote sympathetically of: 'The lessons white men should learn from the blacks before the work of extermination which is so rapidly going on has swept all the blacks who possess this wonderful bush lore off the face of the earth'.

Her recipe for cooked parrots calls for one dozen parrots, a recipe that today would land you in considerable trouble with the law. She adds 'the hindquarters of a wallaby, kangaroo tail and any wild fowl or small birds' to her recipe for beef stock. We have had to wait until the twenty-first century to see Mrs Rawson's wise words being enacted and be thankful that her prediction didn't come true.

One section that endeared itself to me was her 'Hints for the Literary Worker', the last of which was, 'The literary worker is seldom a large eater, therefore he requires what he does eat to be of the best and most strengthening'.

The Goulburn Cookery Book was also first published in 1895, with no revision of the text for thirty years. It was the work of Jean Rutledge (Mrs William Forster Rutledge), and written, as she said herself, for 'women in the bush who often have to teach inexperienced maids and would be glad of accurate recipes that anyone of fair intelligence could carry out'. My edition, the thirty-third, was printed in 1928. What is interesting is the similarity of the *Goulburn* and another, later, cookbook published in 1909, *The Schauer Australian Cookery Book* (discussed in further detail in the following pages): for example, Steak Gerard and the mysterious 'Brazilian stew' appear in both. In the *Goulburn* there is no mention of unnamed sauces involved in the stew as is the case in the *Schauer*, but there is vinegar, which is presumably what makes the dish Brazilian wherever it crops up. (I've done some research on Brazilian food, and nowhere can I find vinegar as an ingredient in 'stews'.)

'Barrier goose' in the *Goulburn* is a leg or shoulder of mutton, disguised to relieve the monotony of mutton, mutton, mutton, for which there are 23 recipes in the *Goulburn*. Why so much mutton? It was, by this stage, the by-product of the wool industry. Growing sheep for meat was no longer profitable. The result was, it was cheap, and not of very good quality. GC Mundy, described as a 'soldier and an observer', wrote in 1852 in his book *Our Antipodes*: 'for meat is nothing in price when mutton is merely the soil on which wool is grown'.

Mrs Rutledge presents her oyster-stuffed steak as Carpetbag steak à la Colchester, more than likely because Colchester is an English town famous for its oysters. In the section entitled 'What to Do With Cold Meat', three 'foreign' sounding dishes are discovered. Firstly, Bobotjes, a baked pudding of minced mutton and bread served with 'a good brown gravy'. Although this is originally a South African dish, in his book *Thirty Five Receipts From 'The Larder Invaded'*, the American William Woys Weaver tells us it was 'considered indispensible at hunt breakfasts in England'.

Secondly, a recipe for Cannelon of meat contains no pasta, but is a boiled pudding of minced mutton.

Another 'foreign' sounding dish, but much changed from the original, is Kromeskies. In Mrs Rutledge's version they are chopped cold meat rissoles; in *Larousse Gastronomique* they are salpicons: chopped meat, fish or vegetables bound by a thick sauce, cut into rectangles and wrapped in thin pancakes or caul. Kromeskies is another dish ubiquitous in these years.

Where did all the Brazilian stew and Kromeskies go?

My copy of *The Commonsense Cookery Book* (issued by The New South Wales Cookery Teachers' Association for use in cookery classes) is undated, but judging by one of its advertisements for Dr Waugh's Baking Powder, featuring a light horseman (headline: 'Call to Waugh'), more than likely published between 1914 and 1916. It is inscribed by hand 'Mary Kalnin, Wolmar' (Wolmar, I'd guess, is the name of the family's country property), and also contains several laid-in cut-out and typed recipes. One for Cheese biscuits; another for 'strong-lite' layer cake; Maize meal layer cake; Caramel layer cake marshmallow sauce; Economy Christmas pudding; Christmas cake; Almond paste; Substitute almond paste; Christmas pudding; Wine sauce; Mock cream; Lemon spread; and finally, Cream of potato soup and Scotch broth – that is, 75 per cent sweet dishes.

The contents of the book itself are remarkable for containing not one recipe that would identify its origin as other than Britain. The only vaguely 'foreign' dish is a curry in the Cold Meat Cookery section, made from chopped meat, apple, onion, sultanas and a tablespoon of curry powder – in other words, a proper 'British' curry.

There is a charming and intimate 'review' for the following book in the *Sydney Mail*, 1923:

> Miss Emily Futter has compiled an 'Australian Home Cookery Book'. It is dedicated to her cousin, Dame Alice Chisholm, and to her niece, Kitty Owen and has an autographed preface by Dame Nellie Melba. The authoress herself is a competent cook: therefore those who buy her effort will have the satisfaction of knowing that every recipe has been tried and tested by her before being included.

Dame Nellie tells potential readers that 'I feel sure that this book will receive the hearty reception it merits'. Kromeskies appear again, this time identified as Russian. A recipe for 'kangaroo steamed' calls for the cook to 'Cut the kangaroo into small, neat pieces ...', indicating that the writer of the recipe had never done so. The book is thorough but naïve, with a recipe for Italian sauce specifying sherry but no garlic, there or anywhere else, and the usual surfeit of sweets, cakes, bread and biscuits – 80 pages of recipes.

Amy Schauer was born in Sydney, and taught cooking at Brisbane Central Technical College from 1895 to 1936. *The Schauer Australian Cookery Book* (my copy without front and back pages circa 1946) was first published in 1909. It does contain one concession to place. After the recipe for Ox tail soup, there is an instruction that 'Kangaroo tail soup can be made in the same way'. As for other than Anglo food, the only concessions to 'exotica' are things like Brazilian stew, with instructions to 'Mix 1 dessertspoon each sauce and vinegar, salt and pepper together' with no instructions as to what 'each sauce' is; Madras steak, whose Indian flavour comes from '1 large teaspoon curry powder'; and Wakefield or French steak, a recipe very close to Steak Diane. Garlic does not make a single appearance. Bannerman traces the Lamington back to the first edition of the *Schauer*, when it appeared as a cake. It was not until 1916 that a Western Australian book (unnamed) printed a recipe for the small squares of today. The *Schauer* I have, from some thirty-five years later, offers Lamingtons as small squares. (The origin and lore of the Lamington will be discussed in chapter 7.) There are recipes for Steamed kangaroo or wallaby in both the *Schauer* and the *Goulburn*; the *Schauer* gives a Roast wonga pigeon but makes no other concession to place apart from the Lamingtons.

The book from which the epigraph for this section was taken, *A Friend in the Kitchen*, concentrates on Federation cookbooks, which Bannerman dates from the Centenary – 1888 – to 1914 (not the accepted architectural dates of 1901–14), contending that: 'the wave of nationalistic sentiment stirred up by those celebrations [the Centenary] must have been one of the driving forces behind the federation of the colonies ... I have taken it as ending formally in 1914 when Australia first went to war as a nation'.

In discussing the general problem of finding out what was being eaten in these times, Bannerman cites various primary and secondary sources – newspapers, great grandma's scrap books, oral history and old cookery books. He breaks these down further into gatherers, teachers and personal collections, as well as contributors: those containing a collection of recipes, like the Country Women's Association books compiled since 1937 using members' recipes. The teachers' books contain, he writes, 'a wider range of everyday dishes and even a few advanced ones'. And as such, provide an insight into what was being prepared in the home at the time.

Australian meals imagined

If, as I am contending, and others have observed, there are no specifically Australian recipes, nor apart from one exception discussed later, examples of regional cuisine, how then can an 'Australian' meal be created? Below we can see some attempts, from visitors, writers and contemporary chefs.

Firstly, the observations of Arnold Haskell, a writer, journalist and ballet critic, who wrote the book (not the song) *Waltzing Matilda: a background to Australia* on a second visit to Australia in 1938. In it he notes that 'Apart from certain regional dishes there is an amazing uniformity about the menus all over the Commonwealth'.

In his book he runs through 'a typical tea' as served at 6.30 pm in a small country hotel (lunch is much the same). This comprises 'Vegetable soup (not tinned); fried fish usually schnapper [as snapper was then called]; choice of roast beef, mutton, lamb, pork or turkey; salad of young lettuce, tomatoes, spring onions; boiled or baked potatoes; fruit salad with lashings of cream or apple pie with good apples and medium pastry; very poor cheese'. In a footnote on the schnapper he refers to Louisa Ann (Mrs Charles) Meredith writing a century previously that the snapper was:

> very nice though not esteemed a proper dish for a dinner party why I am at a loss to guess; but I never saw any native fish at a Sydney dinner-table – the preserved or cured cod and salmon from England being served instead, at a considerable expense and, to my taste, it is not comparable with the cheap fresh fish.

Haskell's summary of his experience of the food he encountered on this visit is that: 'Undoubtedly the gastronomic mission of Australia seems to be to preserve the good old-fashioned English cooking, the grills and roasts that it is becoming impossible to find in England'.

This process of 'mummification' of a food culture by émigrés is common. Often, dishes long disappeared from the 'old country' – be it England, Italy or Germany – are still cooked as they were when the emigrant left many years before.

In 1925, the *Melbourne Punch* published an all-Australian Christmas menu, 'from cocktails to coffee', devised by an anonymous writer who claimed to have 'dined in most parts of the civilised world' (based on that, I'd take a stab at it being George Meudell – see chapter 9). While the author has gone out of his way to use only Australian produce, the menu is French/English in conception and execution with, once again, no sign of any recognisably Australian dish, although the blackfish is native:

Salted almonds. Olives.
Oysters on the shell.
Beche de Mer soup.
Fresh water Blackfish Maître d'Hotel.
Fillet of beef. Pique. Sauce Béarnaise.
Roast Teal. Port Wine Sauce. Orange Salad.
Ice pudding.
Devilled Prawns.
Dessert.
Coffee.
'Sautern' or Chablis. Burgundy.
Champagne. Cognac.

Much later, in 1968, writing in *Epicurean* magazine, bon vivant and writer Oscar Mendelsohn used two English Gallup Polls, one from 1947 and one from 1962, 'to ascertain the perfect meal at any cost', to introduce his own idea of 'the perfect Australian meal.' Once again, we find a meal devoid of any Australian-ness betraying its roots in the old country, minus the earlier slavish Francophilia. It included Avocado oysters, Poached fillets of flathead, Caper sauce, Roast turkey, Walnut stuffing, Fig sauce (in season) or Brown gravy sauce, ending with Girgarre blue cheese. It would appear that since the time of Haskell some cheese had found a name and was, we must assume, no longer 'very poor'.

A curious entry into this section is the Celebration Dinner devised by Colin Bannerman and members of the Canberra Food and Wine Club in 1980. 'At the end of a dinner of French regional dishes', he writes in *A Friend in the Kitchen*, 'we lingered over coffee and an excellent sauternes, talking of future dinners. Why not do a traditional Australian dinner? Back came the question "what could one eat at a traditional Australian dinner that wouldn't be boring?"'.

Bannerman devised the menu using *The Schauer Australian Cookery Book*, then the oldest book that he owned. 'With a singular exception, [the dishes] were English.' This is what they ate, when the dinner was presented to the club in 1982:

Angels on horseback
Sydney Soup
Chicken and tongue croquettes
Braised fillet of beef with vegetables
Jam Roly Poly

The Angels on horseback my mother served in the 1970s (bacon wrapped around prunes and baked in the oven) were different from those from the *Schauer* (bacon wrapped around oysters, skewered, placed on a hot plate and served on toast).

In 2010, the *Independent* newspaper wrote, under the heading of 'Minor British Institutions: Devils on horseback':

> The origins of the name are mysterious, and perhaps
> derived from the dish's diabolical shades of black
> and red. Or as a play on angels on horseback, which
> is oysters wrapped in bacon, or anges à cheval, a
> French dish. Add stilton to the stuffing or use dates
> in place of prunes as variations on the theme. Last
> popular as a party food in the Seventies and early
> Eighties, these little devils are surely well overdue
> a comeback.

From the above constructions, it is plain to see that from 1925 all the way to 1982 the dishes form- ing an 'Australian' meal were, firstly, British in origin, then French, with occasional items of local produce (Girgarre cheese, blackfish). It's very hard to discern an Australian identity from these meals.

Moving closer to the present day, for Australia Day 2012, on Tuesday 24 January, the front page of the *Sydney Morning Herald Good Living* supplement asked: 'What's the Ultimate Australia Day Dish?' A cover photograph of a lamb pie provides one of the answers. The dishes, submitted by a collection of Australian chefs, display a multiplicity of roots, both new and old.

For instance, pastry chef Jean-Michel Raynaud, who 'arrived in Australia in 1988 at the height of the bicentennial fever', chooses to present Pavlova, a recipe of, at the very least, Australian and New Zealand provenance (the origin of this disputed dessert will be discussed in chapter 7); chef Lauren Murdoch proffered a Lamb pie with sautéed mushrooms; provedore Brigitte Hafner, Barbecued marron with Thai green mango salad; chef Cheong Liew, Prawn and king salmon dim sims with salmon roe; chef Daniel Puskas, Sand crab with macadamia nut milk and chamomile; chef and writer Karen Martini, Salad of calamari, jamòn, curly endive and goat's cheese; and baker Tim Cooper, another purportedly Australian but actually French dessert, Peach Melba, devised in singer Dame Nellie Melba's honour by the French chef Auguste Escoffier in 1893. And from chef Ian Curley, Kangaroo Wellington.

The hallmark of the list is the ethnic diversity of

the dishes, none of which would be familiar generally to Australians (other than someone who was familiar with a chef's menu that had featured one or more of these dishes).

In spite of realising (as Muskett and later Bannerman stated) that much of the British household domestic larder was unsuitable for Australian conditions – and apart from the occasional adaptation (Christmas pudding ice cream) and the massive influx of non-British residents bringing their own food cultures – it is clear that, in the 230 odd years that Europeans have lived here, there has been no emergence of any dishes that speak with a broad or even mild Australian accent.

Recipes

CHARMAINE O'BRIEN (ADAPTED FROM MARGARET PEARSON)

....

MULLIGATAWNY SOUP

Serves 6

The recipe on the following pages is not from Edward Muskett's book, but is an adaptation by food historian Charmaine O'Brien of a recipe by Australian Margaret Pearson, from Pearson's Cookery Recipes for the People, *1888.*

The name 'mulligatawny' comes from the Tamil millagai/milagu *and* thanni *meaning pepper-water, also known as* rasam. *According to* A Historical Dictionary of Indian

Food *this is not a soup but a liquid dish that is taken before a meal as an appetite stimulant, throughout a meal as a digestive, and poured over rice at the end of the meal – also as a digestive. Soup is the European construct it has been slotted into.*

Later versions were British modifications that included meat, though the local Madras recipe on which it was based did not. Larousse Gastronomique says that it's a soup of Indian origin, adopted by the British and 'particularly popular in Australia' where, according to Larousse, smoked bacon and tomatoes are added – neither of which are in the (Australian) recipe below. I'm including it because it is delicious, but also because it is indicative of the kind of culinary fusion that has not happened in Australia. O'Brien says:

> The original recipe [from Pearson] is based on a rich meat based brown stock for this soup, however I more often prepare it with good chicken stock. This recipe calls for 'currie' powder but Pearson does not give a recipe for such, presumably because she thought the cook would either know how to compound one or would use a commercial preparation. I highly recommend you avoid the latter option and make your own from the recipe I have given below – it will ensure this soup is a delight.

75 g butter or 3 tbsp vegetable oil
2 onions, sliced
1 chicken, skinned removed and cut into 12 pieces
1.5 litres stock

2 tbsp currie powder*
2–3 tbsp cream
juice 1 lemon
½ bunch parsley, finely chopped
To serve
plain boiled rice
lemon wedges

1. Melt the butter, or heat the oil, in a pot large enough to hold all the ingredients and the stock.
2. Add the sliced onion and allow to cook until browned, stirring as needed to ensure these do not stick and burn.
3. Remove from the butter/oil and drain on kitchen paper.
4. Coat the chicken pieces with a mixture of plain flour and a little salt. Add the chicken pieces to the hot butter/oil in which you cooked the onion and brown these (you may need to do this in batches; also, the chicken does not need to be cooked through as you are just putting a little colour on the pieces and developing flavour).
5. When all the pieces have been browned, return them to the pan and add the stock and the cooked onions along with the currie powder. Simmer until the chicken is cooked through (about 1 hour). Remove the chicken pieces from the stock and set aside.
6. Strain the liquid and then return it to the pan (you are straining out the onions). Mix the cream and lemon juice into the soup liquid and heat for 1 minute (do not boil).

7. Check for salt and add more if required. Add the chicken pieces and leave on the heat for another few minutes. Just before serving stir the parsley through the soup.

8. To serve, place 2 chicken pieces in a bowl and then ladle the liquid over these. Place the cooked rice in a bowl on the table along with extra lemon wedges. The way to eat this soup is to squeeze the lemon over it and then eat the chicken pieces (remember to provide a side plate or bowl for the bones) first, after which a few spoonsful of rice are added to the soup left in the plate.

Currie powder from Dr Kitchener

Dr Kitchener was in fact William Kitchiner MD (1775–1827) an optician, inventor of telescopes, amateur musician and exceptional cook. His name was a household word during the nineteenth century. He was also the creator of Wow-Wow sauce. A Victorian food celebrity.

3 tsp coriander seeds
1 tsp whole black pepper
1 tsp black mustard seeds
5 allspice berries
5 green cardamoms
1 tsp cumin seeds
1 tsp powdered ginger*
1 tsp turmeric powder

Grind all the spices except the ginger and turmeric powder to a fine powder in a mortar and pestle or an electric grinder. Mix in the turmeric and ginger powder. If not using immediately, store in an airtight jar.

*I do mean dried powdered ginger, not fresh.

JEAN RUTLEDGE

....

BRAZILIAN STEW

The intriguing Brazilian stew, from the 1928 edition of The Goulburn Cookery Book *(first published in 1895) by Jean Rutledge. I would use red wine vinegar. I've converted to metric.*

1.2 kg shin or stewing beef
1 carrot
½ turnip
3 small onions
bunch of herbs
1 stalk celery
1 tsp salt
½ tsp pepper
2 tbsp vinegar

1. Scrape the vegetables [skin them] and cut them into slices or cubes; put all together [including the beef but not mentioned in the recipe] in a saucepan, packing them closely together.
2. Add seasoning and herbs.
3. Cover the saucepan with a piece of calico and put the

lid on; this is to prevent the steam escaping [you can use foil].

4. Cook slowly on the side of the stove [low heat] for at least 3¼ hours from the time it commences to simmer. No water is required for this dish, but if properly made, there will be plenty of gravy from the meat.

6

WOMEN: CO-OPERATING, SWEETENING AND COMPETING

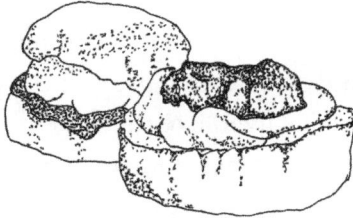

She has few pleasures to think of as she sits here
alone by the fire, on guard against a snake. All
days are much the same to her, but on Sunday
afternoon she dresses herself, tidies the children,
smartens-up baby, and goes for a lonely walk along
the bush track...she does this every Sunday.

Henry Lawson, 'The Drover's Wife', from
The Drover's Wife edited by Frank Moorhouse

Life was grim for women in the colony. The gender
ratio was, at first, seven to one against them (from 1788
to 1868 a total of 157000 prisoners were sent from
Britain to Australia; only 25000 were women). It was
a tough, masculine world. Later, as free settlers began
to arrive, they still found themselves isolated, living

in leaky, slab-timbered, thatch-roofed huts with dirt floors and tar-paper walls. Many settlers couldn't afford farm hands, and were not assigned convict labour, so the women did much of the physical labour around the farm, as well as bear and care for children, often far from medical help. Feminism wasn't even a dirty word in the world invoked in Henry Lawson's haunting and complex story *The Drover's Wife*. With her four children and her husband away droving '... She is used to being left alone. She once lived like this for eighteen months'.

In 1922, such women joined together to form an association to help one another, to improve conditions for rural women everywhere and, later, to form a lobby group for their rights. This was the Country Women's Association, the CWA. Today, that body advocates for the environment and education, as well as for health and social security issues.

Along the way, as cooks do, especially when they are isolated, members swapped recipes. In 1937, at the instigation of one remarkable woman member, Sara Moore-Sims, the New South Wales branch of the CWA published their first recipe book, *The Coronation Cookery Book* which, in various forms, names and editions, has not been out of print since.

Because of this activity, and their annual tea and scones cafe at the Royal Easter Show in Sydney and other agricultural shows, members feel the need to reiterate that there is a lot more to the CWA than scones and recipes. I assure them that I know this, but as this is a book about Australian food, and their contribution is invaluable, that is my focus.

I've spent hours poring over their archives, first at their Potts Point building and most recently at the New South Wales branch's new headquarters, CWA State Office in Mascot. And it was in Mascot that I learnt something fascinating about that first edition of the *Coronation Cookery Book*.

'Some enjoy a little garlic'

The title page lists two names as compilers. They are Jessie Sawyer, OBE, State President of CWA of New South Wales and Sara Moore-Sims, President Mallowa Branch CWA, Gwydir Group. Of these, Sara Moore-Sims was the driving force behind the first edition, having spent twelve years collecting recipes for it, and lobbying for its publication, as she told friend and fellow member Mrs Dulcie Hunter Jnr before she died. Which she did, right after, as Dulcie Hunter tells us, having 'completed everything for a second edition'.

It occurred to me when I read this, that most of the recipes in that first edition of the *Coronation Cookery Book*, collected in the late 1920s and early 1930s from CWA members from all stations in life, have survived into the twenty-first century. At the time of writing, that first edition has been reprinted, in various forms, with changes and additions, 16 times, the latest in

2018. Here is the table of contents of the first edition, which gives an idea of the scope and thoroughness of the book.

Aspic
Beverages, Cool Drinks, Tea and Coffee
Biscuits, Scones, Tea-cakes, Tea-loaves, Pikelets etc.
Bread, Buns
Cakes, Small Cakes, Sponges, Meringue and Eclairs
Cool Kitchen with illustrations
Diet for Diabetics
Diet and Sample Diet
Emu Egg Recipes
English Cooking Terms and Meanings
Etiquette and Useful Information, Serving of Wines
Fish and Oysters
French Cooking Terms and Meanings
Fritters, Pancakes, Doughnuts, Waffles
Home-made Sweets
Hors d'oeuvres
Household Hints (Medical and General)
Infant Feeding
Invalid Cookery
Ice Puddings, Ice cream, Water Ices, Fruit Salad
Icings, Fillings, Filling Butters
Kitchen Remedies
Meats, Mutton Dishes, etc. Suitable for Entrées
Omelettes, Egg Dishes, Chaudfroids
Pastry, Pies and Tarts

Pickles, Sauces, Chutney, Spiced Fruit
Poultry and Game
Preserves, Jams, Jellies, Conserves, Crystallised
    Fruits
Puddings, Hot and Cold
Right Accompaniment, Correct Sauces for Various
    Dishes
Salads and Salad Dressings
Sandwiches, Sandwich Fillings, Club Sandwiches
Savouries, Canapes, Caviars
Savoury Dishes, Cheese and Cheese-made Dishes
Sauces, Sweet and Savoury
Soufflés, Hot and Cold
Soups
Table of Proportions
Tomato and Fruit Cocktails
Vegetables
Waiting at Table
Weights and Measures
Woolly Down, and Mattress

Reading through many of the recipes in this book made me hungry. Roast duckling with mushroom stuffing, Jellied chicken, Quince dumplings, for example. The famous Australian goose – 'take two or three flaps of mutton' – is there (perhaps not so appealing), and wine is used in cooking, in Lapin à la Saint Avertin. But not in the Australian goose, which advises 'a spoonful of sherry if available'. Apart from recipes, the book offers much practical advice, for example on choosing game.

> To test if game is young, hold the bird by the lower beak, and when young it will snap off. The legs will look smooth and the quill feathers soft. The breast of the bird will be hard and firm and well covered with flesh when it is in good condition ...

And a paragraph on how to choose poultry, which would still hold today, if only we had the choice of birds for roasting or boiling.

> When young the feet will be pliable and the tip of the breast bone will be soft. Choose fowls with dark legs for roasting and white legs for boiling ... An old fowl left covered with water in which 2 tablespoons of vinegar is added overnight will be tender when boiled and will not take so long to cook ...

This tells us, perhaps, that the women reading this book were not accomplished cooks, because of either their status (used to having servants) or their youth.

The recipes also betray class differences. Posh recipes such as Jugged hare, Salmi of pigeon and Chicken Maryland (attribution 'Chef at Cavalry Club') live democratically alongside such dubious combinations as Fillet of beef with fried pineapple and economical dishes like Rolled mutton flap.

Baked ox heart, Tripe and onions, and Brains and potato pie in batter remind us that we have not always been averse to offal. And Lamb cutlets and spaghetti displays a touch of the cosmopolitan. 'Curries', Mrs Moore-Sims tells us, 'are becoming very popular' – and in them, she adds daringly, 'some enjoy a little garlic'. Interestingly, some of the recipes contain almond milk and coconut milk.

And I did find one other mention of garlic. A recipe for Roast leg, Spanish style, of either lamb or mutton, with instructions to 'pierce the meat with a skewer and insert small bits of garlic (using not more than a clove of garlic to a leg of 4lb [1.8kgs]'. Curiously, this recipe, and the same amount of garlic, lasted until the 2009 version, *The Country Women's Association Cookbook: seventy years in the kitchen*, which changed it to metric.

The fascinating Chicken Maryland, which my parents ate at the 1950s equivalent of fine dining restaurants, almost lasted the distance, with changes. The 1937 version is garnished with grilled halves of banana, grilled bacon and croquettes of maize flour or fresh corn cobs. In 2009, the bananas had disappeared. But where did Chicken Maryland originate?

Well, apparently, and curiously enough, Maryland in the USA where in *Harvest of American Cooking*, a 1956 collection of stories and recipes by Mary Margaret McBride:

[it] was probably born in the kitchen of the 1600s,
when the hot corn bread came from the oven at the
exact moment that the floured, salted, peppered
and fried golden-brown chicken was ready. And so
the two were put together and another southern
classic was created. The corn bread must be made
with white cornmeal, sliced in half and the fried
chicken placed on top, the boat of rich cream gravy
alongside.

The bananas appeared in the UK of the 1960s,
where it became Fried chicken, often in breadcrumbs,
served with sweet corn fritters and fried bananas.
And how did the anonymous contributor to the 1937
Coronation Cookery Book get the recipe? The first mention of a Chicken Maryland (Poulet au Maryland) with
grilled bacon, potato croquettes and fried bananas is to
be found in, of all places, *Ma Cuisine*, Auguste Escoffier's
last cookbook, first published in 1934.

Escoffier spent much time in London cooking at
the Savoy and Carlton Hotels. And the recipe in the
Coronation Cookery Book was the result either of a British
chef trained by Escoffier coming to Australia or, more
likely, a wealthy member of the CWA bringing it back
from a visit to one of Escoffier's hotel restaurants.

Two further sidelights to the Chicken Maryland
story (which could probably fill a book on its own).

In F. Scott Fitzgerald's tragic novel *Tender is the Night*,
the female protagonist, Nicole Diver (certainly not a

heroine), is discovered lying on the beach, trying to hold her life together and claiming that: 'everything is all right – if I can finish translating this damn recipe for chicken à la Maryland into French'. And finally, Chicken à la Maryland was featured in the very last luncheon served on the *Titanic*, on 14 April 1912. Was it served with bananas? The menu – the one surviving copy of which last sold in 2015 for US$88 000 – doesn't say.

A dish that definitely did not come via Escoffier or the first-class dining room of the *Titanic* was A drover's dream, a down-to-earth casserole of shoulder chops, onions and turnips. This economical and deeply Celtic-Australian dish – under the name of Irish stew included in my father's very limited culinary repertoire – lasted all the way to 2009, before being dumped from the radical 2011 edition, *The Country Women's Association Cookbook 2: more treasured recipes*.

Of the 15 editions of the original *Coronation Cookery Book* printed between 1937 and 2011, the last three were the most different in format and content (there was a compilation in 2012, *Jam Drops and Marble Cake: 60 years of CWA award-winning recipes* – as the name suggests, it was all cakes and desserts). But let us have a brief look at a few of these editions along the way to get an idea of Australia's changing food.

In 1958, for the first time, there was a chapter on Chinese Cookery: ten dishes, which included that Australian-Chinese restaurant perennial, the Prawn cutlet, and a recipe for Savoury duck, which allowed one clove of garlic per duck. From the restaurant- and nightclub-frequenting set of wealthier country women, we find two other 1950s favourites: Prawn cocktail ('Serve very cold in cocktail glass'); and Steak Diane, another dish that arrived in the pages of the *Coronation Cookery Book* via a circuitous route.

When I wrote the 'Short Black' column in the *Good Living* section of the *Sydney Morning Herald*, I conducted a quest to find the origin of Steak Diane. Various correspondents wrote to insist that it had been invented by Tony Clerici of Chiswick Gardens restaurant in Sydney, or by the head waiter at Prince's nightclub; another that he had learnt it as a waiter in New York in the 1950s. Many more chimed in, but the definitive answer, I decided, came from the grande dame of Australian food, Margaret Fulton, whose 1982 book *Superb Restaurant Dishes* offers a recipe from The Ivy in London, where, she claimed, it was invented. In Sydney, the late Beppi Polese used to prepare it tableside when he was working at Romano's nightclub. If you decide to cook a Diane (from the recipe at the end of this chapter), here's a tip from Beppi:

> They [the other waiters at Romano's] used to reduce the sauce too much, and get a too strong flavour of Worcestershire. I didn't cook the meat in the brandy, I'd take the meat out, then do the brandy, add more butter and reduce the sauce and pan juices. When

the sauce was nearly right, I'd put back the meat for a few minutes, and add some chopped up parsley.

Two comments on this. Firstly, looking at the list of claimants, and where the dish was served, it is obvious that the women of the CWA were not all struggling farmers' wives. And secondly, it is touching that the recipe in the *Coronation Cookery Book* specifies the much cheaper cut of round steak, when all other recipes for Steak Diane specify fillet. I recommend you go with that – and definitely the brandy, which is optional in the CWA version.

In 2009, the book was spruced up by a new publisher (Murdoch Books) with nostalgic black-and-white shots of early CWA members, and published as *The Country Women's Association Cookbook: seventy years in the kitchen*. 'Choosing Poultry' went from a long paragraph to just three lines, and articles on boning turkey and fowl were added, either because it was fashionable or no longer done by the (supermarket) butcher. There was a chapter on International Cookery, which included ten Chinese recipes. Some old stalwarts remained: Beef and grilled pineapple, and Baked stuffed lamb flaps being just two.

The 2011 edition, *The Country Women's Association Cookbook 2: more treasured recipes*, as I have said, has undergone the most radical changes. Gone are Chicken Maryland and A drover's dream, added is a chapter on Microwave Dishes. And garlic sprouted everywhere: in

Moroccan eggplant, and in Greek style roast chicken a massive three bulbs! Although in the Spanish style leg of lamb, one clove is still spread over 1.8 kilograms. There is a Spanish tortilla and a Potato moussaka. Multiculinarity had arrived, although it is pleasing to note that Lamingtons made it to 2011 (and to 2018, see page 151).

It's worthwhile stopping here to examine the *Coronation* phenomenon. I'm sure that Sara Moore-Sims would have been astonished that the book she began had lasted, in one form or another, for eighty years, and contained recipes she could never have envisaged while retaining many of those she had gathered from members in the 1920s and 1930s.

So what are these books about?

Thinking in broad terms, the recipes gathered were not primarily about food. They were about isolated women bonding. For women, at that time, the recipes were what they had to show for their existence – apart from their children – and they would have been difficult to place in the covers of a book. For all that these women were, more often than not, equal partners on the family farm, they were seen as subsidiary: farmers' wives. The exchange of recipes, as women had done for hundreds of years, was a demonstration of creativity and meaning. The success of the books would have given collective confidence to the CWA women.

But from 2009 on, the heritage passed into the hands of other publishers and editors. To a great extent, the decisions on what recipes stayed and were dropped and what was added was no longer solely in the hands of the CWA. Decisions were made by urban women who worked in publishing and not on the land. Decisions were made based on what was cool rather than on camaraderie.

Consequently, I believe that the reprints, from 2009, are more for urban middle class women – offering nostalgia on a plate. The dropping of A drover's dream reflects this (although why did Baked stuffed lamb flaps stay? Go figure). To substantiate my theory, let me offer this.

In 2013, I had lunch with the members of a CWA branch not far from Sydney. As we ate the lunch they had cooked, I quizzed them on the food they ate, on why and how it had changed. And listened.

The meal they cooked was determinedly rooted in the 1960s and 1970s – delicious but dated. By no means were the dishes chosen for nostalgic reasons: this was the food they ate. I've reproduced the menu on page 150.

At one stage I asked them for their favourite cookbooks. They offered Margaret Fulton, Maggie Beer, Tess Mallos, the 1970 *Australian Women's Weekly Cookbook* (edited by Ellen Sinclair), *The Commonsense Cookery Book* (first published 1914, but still in print) and Donna

Hay. Not one of them mentioned any of the *Coronation* books. Here is the lunch menu:

Before lunch:

Cheese twists and water crackers (both packet) with dips:
corn relish and cream cheese; sun-dried tomato and olive;
sun-dried tomatoes, cream cheese and mixed dried herbs.

Lunch:

Pumpkin soup
Beef burgundy and rabbit stew
(both cooked in crock pots)
Boiled potatoes
Carrots and beans

Dessert:

Impossible pudding
Apple turnovers
Cream
Blue Ribbon ice cream

One final note. While researching in the imposing new CWA State Office in Mascot, I ate lunch at a little sandwich bar in the same building. Mascot (for those of you who don't know) was, until relatively recently, as well as the home of Sydney's airports, a working class suburb of modest houses and factories. No more. This coffee shop epitomised the new Mascot. My lunch there was a toasted sourdough sandwich of poached chicken, aioli, rocket and basil. Beyond a drover's wildest dreams.

A curious feature of Australian cooking has been the emphasis, right from the start, on scones, cakes and sweeties. Many theories for this abound. I will add one of my own.

Postscript: While editing this book, yet another CWA book turned up: *Everything I Know About Cooking I Learned From the Country Women's Association of NSW*, 'a selection of 120 tried and true recipes, in a giftable format, from the Country Women's Association archive'. The recipes have been selected from the 2011 edition, *The Country Women's Association Cookbook 2*, and there does seem to be a mixture of the old and the new. Japanese golden mushroom soup, and Bruschetta, then Jumbuck stew, as well as exhibition tips – including the correct size for Lamingtons (no higher than 3.7 centimetres, although some allow 4.5 centimetres). For a publisher (Murdoch again) it's the list that keeps on giving.

Sweet and dainty

Bannerman's explanation as to why most early Australian cookbooks – and here he is talking about Federation (1888–1914 by his reckoning) – were so dessert-heavy is that the experienced cook didn't need recipes to 'boil, roast, grill or stew a piece of meat, to boil vegetables or to make a white or melted butter sauce'.

But they did need guidance for the 'unforgiving' puddings and cakes.

Such a surfeit of desserts did not occur in French or Italian cookbooks because there were recipes for dishes other than boiled, roast, grilled and so on meat. But here desserts predominated because (as Bannerman states later) the cook's reputation depended on her cakes, pies and biscuits. These products were her chance to show her skill: skill little needed at the front of the meal, where to satisfy the men of the household she had only to cook a large hunk of roast or fried protein, perhaps with a couple of veg. The cakes and scones, as the women of early Australia saw it, were necessary to maintain some civilisation in the midst of the overriding masculinity of the time and place. And then there was Barbara Santich's assertion in *Looking for Flavour* that: 'It's hardly surprising that this area of culinary endeavour has been neglected. Cakes and biscuits and afternoon tea are seen as frivolous accessories. They belong to the domain of women – women produced them, women consumed them'.

And women were not held in high regard in early Australian society. The little woman makes a nice cake, can knock up a beautiful batch of scones. The dessert top-heaviness of early Australian cookbooks is illustrated by this analysis of the numbers of recipes in the first edition of the CWA's *Coronation Cookery Book*:

Sweet dishes

Biscuits:	43
Cakes, small cakes, sponges, meringues, éclairs:	111
Icings, fillings, for cakes etc.:	50
Scones and tea cakes:	30
Pikelets etc.:	9
Puddings hot and cold (sweet only), including jellies:	104
Pies and tarts:	27
Home made sweets (toffees etc.):	29
Soufflés (sweet):	29
Total sweet dishes:	<u>432</u>

Savoury dishes

Vegetables:	21
Fish and oysters:	31
Poultry:	48
Rabbit:	6
Salads:	32
Meat (beef):	45
Mutton (includes lamb):	37
Veal:	10
Pork:	19
Bacon and ham:	5
Sweetbreads, brains, meat patties (including kidneys and tripe)	11
Curries:	9
Total savoury dishes:	<u>274</u>

Symons writes of the importance of 'daintiness', which embodied feminine qualities 'such as lightness, prettiness and gentility', seeing it as 'part of a long campaign [by commercial interests] to twist the traditional, caring concerns of women into petty materialistic preoccupations'. Rather, I would suggest that the 'daintiness' was part of that attempt to impose some civilisation on the rough-hewn, mutton-fuelled, predominantly masculine Australian culture. In 1833, to take a random year, the Australian Bureau of Statistics tells us there were 44 643 males and 16 151 females in New South Wales.

Taking up the theme of daintiness from Symons, Santich, citing the results of a 1953 American survey on 'the real test of a woman's ability to cook', stated that 'women believed their culinary prowess in the eyes of other women was demonstrated through baking'. But Santich also posited that 'another possible and more persuasive reason for all these cakes and biscuits [was] they represented female creativity'. In Australia, this prowess would have often been for an audience of one: the female cook herself. Patrick White's novel *The Twyborn Affair* sets up just such a set of circumstances.

Although the events in this part of the book took place between the two world wars, the Australia it depicts was still a tough country, founded by tough men with women only at the periphery.

To a great extent, this masculinist character has carried down into the present day. In writing of the construction of the Australian national character 'underwriting 1980s nationalism', in *Making it National*, Graeme Turner describes the Australian male character as 'prescriptive, unitary, masculinist and excluding'. Turner goes on to assert that this is not a version that reflects Australian identity in the 'postcolonial nation state'. Perhaps not. But our parliaments, board rooms and universities still mainly comprise men. For example, the Australian Institute of Company Directors' quarterly gender diversity report in 2017 found there were 25.4 per cent female directors across the ASX 200 by the end of August. In 2018 that percentage had climbed to 47. But at the time of writing there are still only five female ministers in Malcolm Turnbull's cabinet. Australia is still a land of blokey blokes.

In *The Twyborn Affair*, White played with this by creating Eddie Twyborn, who is also Eudoxia and Eadith Trist – three gender-ambiguous male/female protagonists, more transsexual than transgender. Eddie Twyborn steps off the train at Fossickers Flat on the way to Bogong, a sheep station in the Monaro region in southern New South Wales, where he is to take up the position of jackaroo. Don Prowse, the manager of Bogong, who picks him up 'in a car of sorts', lets him know the lay of the land. Prowse points out a nearby town: '"This is the way to Woolambi", he tells his passenger, "where the good times are – six pubs, four stores, the picture-show. Get a screw too, if you're interested in that … there's a root or two closer to home if you get to know. I always say there's roots for the lookin' anywhere'".

The housekeeper/cook Peggy Tyrell is more comfortable in this hyper-masculine world than is the gender-ambivalent Twyborn. But she, like many such women in such a world, must carve out – and bake out – her territory. His first breakfast, 'chops and veg followed by wedges of sponge cake and dobs of enormous floury scones', more or less sets the tone: mutton for bulk, and cake and scones to allow the cook to show her prowess – and to add a little refinement (daintiness) to the meal. As they begin a later meal, dinner this time, White writes: 'Everyone, it seemed, even the newcomer, was involved in a primitive ritual, no grace, but plenty of tomato sauce'. They ate 'black mutton' and slug-infested cabbage: 'Eddie had sighted another slug'. And yet again, Mrs Tyrell 'tossed several charred chops and a mountain of fried up cabbage and potato on the plate'. In the face of this mountain of mutton and to save (feminine) face as a cook, Mrs Tyrell continues 'sifting flour for a batch of scones'.

As the country grew, the prowess of women's baking reached another level and took on another dimension: competition.

Cake vs cake

In the introduction to this book, I admitted to a reappraisal of my initial harsh judgment of Australian cooking. Of course, there must have been good cooks here before the Second World War. Not chefs at first, no fine dining, but good, plain home cooks. And the evidence of the truth of this is to be found in the archives of the Royal Agricultural Society (RAS), the body that holds the Royal Easter Show every year and which has, since 1869, in conjunction with 'the Show' as it is called in Sydney, hosted, judged and awarded prizes to thousands of those (almost exclusively women) who had never heard that Australia was a land of bad food: they were too busy cooking. And competing. In an article published in the culinary magazine *Petit Propos Culinaire*, '"The Cleverness of the Whole Number": social invention in the golden age of Antipodean baking, 1890–1940', Symons writes:

> About one hundred years ago, Australian and
> New Zealand women took control of their new
> industrially-provisioned kitchens in an unrivalled
> burst of domestic creativity. They developed
> Lamingtons, Anzac biscuits, Afghans, the Pavlova
> and many other still cherished cakes and biscuits.

Although his research covered Australia and New Zealand, both nations were closely aligned in this kind of cooking, with continuing spats over who first developed the Pavlova or the Lamington.

In Australia, the country women began by swapping recipes. Then the CWA published the first compilation of these recipes. The next step was to compete against one another. They enjoyed cooking, but they needed something to engage with. The men ran the farm or business, and had their sport. The women needed to find an area where they could excel. There were two basic arenas for this competition. First was the agricultural show – in New South Wales, this was Sydney's Royal Easter Show's Perishable Foods Competition, which began in 1910 (other states had their competitions, but New South Wales was first). And then the CWA competition held in conjunction with the *Land* newspaper, the first one in 1949. Now here's my theory.

Yes, it was women supplying the creativity in the kitchen with their cakes and scones, and perhaps Bannerman is right in claiming there was no need for recipes for the simple meat dishes first cooked in Australia.

But the cakes and scones, the pickles, chutneys, jams and preserves were much easier to transport and to judge, being either sculptural (cakes) or contained (pickles and so on in jars). The difficulties in judging Best Roast Leg of Lamb or Best Australian Goose would have been insurmountable.

Even then, the logistics of the show imposed restrictions and favoured some recipes over others. As Symons points out:

since entries must be displayed for many hours
or even days, decorated cakes (keeping fruitcakes
with elaborate hard icing) have long been well
represented. Conversely, cream puffs, if they
appear, are specified as 'unfilled'. The favourite of
both nations, the Pavlova, being a large meringue
topped with whipped cream and fruit, hardly ever
appears.

I maintain it was this intense and continued competition over many years that resulted in a cake- and sweet-dominated collection of recipes, from Lamingtons to Jazz cake.

In 2010, I researched in the archives of the RAS for a story in *Slow*, the magazine of the international Slow Food Movement. There are kept the leather-bound catalogues of RAS competitions recording the entries in and judging of everything from wood chopping contests to prize cattle and sheep, dogs and cats, lucerne, sorghum, cucurbits (squashes) – if it's agricultural, there's a competition for it. These dusty old catalogues record every name, and in spidery handwriting in the margins, in ink browned by time, are recorded the winners of first, second and third prizes – if indeed a prize was awarded. Hopes and heartache are here engraved.

It wasn't until 1888 that any form of food was included in competition, and then only preserved food – one category being 'preserved fish of all kind', another, 'preserved vegetables'. Only 14 entries were recorded, but no winners.

The competition called Perishable Foods didn't appear in the catalogues until 1910, in the Agriculture section. In that year, added to the candied and dried fruit, pickles and calf's foot jelly, was a section for Pastry. Sadly, there was only one entry, from a Mrs George Bagnell. Even more sadly, she did not win the prize of £3 3s donated by Dr Waugh's Baking Powder for her 'collection of pastry (14 lb) and biscuits (28 lb)'. All that work, and Mrs Bagnell didn't take home the prize because her entry was 'not according to schedule'.

Such strict rules apply to this day. The schedule for chutney in 2005 stipulated that it must be delivered 'in matching 500 g jars, round or square with straight sides. No brand names on the lids'.

By 1920, the category now called Cookery had moved back into Agriculture, and men were banished: 'Only female exhibitors are allowed to compete in this class' is the stern admonition on the title page. Why did the women feel they had to put their stockinged feet down firmly against male cooks? Men had everything else. They had their cookery.

The kitchen was their territory. Men had everything else in those early days (in many ways they still do), but the kitchen, cooking and baking was where women found creativity, competition and meaning. The menfolk could 'bugger off'.

We don't know for sure why there was no food competition between 1928 and 1938. We can only speculate. These dates coincided with the Depression years in Australia, which hit farmers hard. All we know is that on 11 November 1938 an item in the *Sydney Morning Herald* announced the 'Reintroduction of women's industries including cooking in next year's Show'. Then there was another gap, between 1940 and 1945, when there was little thought given to the icing, let alone the cake.

But that 1939 competition was packed with entries in 42 classes, and we must record in this brief period of respite between Depression and war that the Rainbow cake with white icing was won by Miss EM Leech of Randwick. That we know Miss Leech is from Randwick is due to the fact that, for the first time, the addresses of the ladies who entered Cooking were recorded.

And still they cook. Every year, hundreds of women from Sydney and rural New South Wales arrive at the Showground with their pickles and jams, their iced cakes and scones, their Lamingtons and rich fruit cakes.

Mrs Glad Shute is from Earlwood in Sydney and has been a competitor for twenty-six years. 'In 1975, I won first prize for my first entry of patty cakes. Flushed with success, I went back the next year. There was only one year I didn't win anything.'

In 1998, the year that the Show moved to its current location at Homebush (near the site of the 2000

Olympics), Glad Shute also became a judge. 'Judging is very stressful', she said, when I interviewed her for the *Slow* story, 'all the contestants are sitting there watching – and although you don't know who owns any cake, you've got to be careful'. Standards are high.

> Take the Orange cake section. It must be baked in a loaf tin. The cake has to have a nice crust around the edges, and have a nice bottom. When you cut the cake in half it'll be in the centre where it's under- or over-cooked. There must be no holes, nice texture which cuts well without crumbs everywhere. And it must smell and taste like an orange cake. It must be nicely presented, not with icing dribbling down the sides. Some you can see at a glance, but when it gets down the to the last four, it gets hard.

Glad Shute is from a large family, and learnt to cook from her mother. 'I started to make cakes on a fuel stove. I've made every wedding cake in the family for years – that's four sons and now five grandchildren married.' And they loved their food. 'With my kids', she said, 'if I stood in the same place too long, they'd eat me'.

And we must record that today, men are welcome. In 2008, Neil Willis of Normanhurst beat a strong field to take first prize for his American fruit cake. Willis, an engineer for a construction company, had been entering for over thirty years. 'Beating the women is a joy', he said, 'because they bake on a daily basis and I don't – it upsets them greatly when I walk in and win'. I don't blame them for feeling that way.

Australian food not so good? Well, yes, maybe in the restaurants and hotels of the cities, where poorly trained chefs battled to find the kinds of ingredients being eaten in Paris and London. But in the kitchens of the suburbs and the farms, as attested to by the honour rolls in the RAS catalogues, thousands of anonymous but talented (mostly) women baked and preserved their way to glory.

(Disclosure: For some years I have judged in the Preserves section of the RAS Arts and Crafts Show.)

Recipes

COUNTRY WOMEN'S ASSOCIATION (CHEF AT CAVALRY CLUB)

CHICKEN MARYLAND

Serves 4

Both this recipe for Chicken Maryland and the next one for Quince dumplings are from the 1937 edition of the Coronation Cookery Book, *compiled for the Country Women's Association of New South Wales by Jessie Sawyer and Sara Moore-Sims.*

The Cavalry Club was an English gentlemen's club at 127 Piccadilly in Mayfair, which in 1975 merged with the Guards Club. This recipe would have been contributed by a wealthy member of the CWA, perhaps a member of the squattocracy. I'm reproducing it as it was published, as a narrative recipe. As I could not find the devilled sauce anywhere in the Coronation Cookery Book, *I'm supplying a recipe for the horseradish sauce from the book, to which I've added metric conversions.*

Have 1 medium-sized chicken (very tender) cut into 5 pieces, 2 wings, 2 legs and the breast. Lay in a very well buttered casserole dish. Season with salt and a little pepper. Put lid on and cook in a hot oven. When cooked, sprinkle some fresh bread crumbs on and brown nicely under the grill. Place the pieces of chicken on a dish and keep hot. Before being served, garnish round with grilled halves bananas, grilled bacon and small fried croquettes made with maize flour or fresh cob corn. Two sauces may be served – a devilled sauce or a hot cream horseradish sauce – the former being generally preferred.

Horseradish sauce

Scrape a stick of horseradish very finely, and mix it in a basin with 1 tsp of flour, a little salt and cayenne. Add a gill [240 g] of cream and then, very slowly, stirring all the time, 2 tbsp of vinegar [although I suggest white wine].

COUNTRY WOMEN'S ASSOCIATION

··

QUINCE DUMPLINGS

Makes 4

I've added the metric measurements.
4 medium-sized quinces
½ pound [230 g] short or suet pastry
sugar or honey

1. Peel the quinces, core but not quite through, fill the hollow with sugar, make the pastry, divide into 4 equal parts, roll each piece out a little, mould evenly round the quinces.
2. Sprinkle a pudding cloth lightly with flour, tie each dumpling separately in the cloth, drop into plenty of boiling water, cook about 2 hours, lift out, remove cloth, serve with sugar or honey.

COUNTRY WOMEN'S ASSOCIATION

··

STEAK DIANE

From the 1958 edition of the CWA's Coronation Cookery Book. As already mentioned, I would suggest eye fillet steak – and definitely use the brandy.

allow ½ lb [230 g] topside or round steak, from which all fat and gristle has been removed, per person
1 clove of garlic
1 tbsp of butter

1 dessertspoon lemon juice
1 tsp of Worcestershire sauce per 4 servings
flour
pepper and salt

1. With a meat mallet, pound the steaks carefully until they are $\frac{1}{3}$ inch (8–9 mm) thick. Rub with garlic and lightly flour them.
2. Cook in a thick-bottomed frypan in butter, quickly browning on each side.
3. Add the lemon juice and sauce and cook slowly on each side for 2 minutes. Serve immediately with the juice from the pan as sauce. If desired a little brandy or wine may be added to the sauce.

BERNICE KING

PLAIN SCONES

From the 1996 Land *Cookery Competition, run by the CWA and sponsored by the* Land *newspaper. Bernice King is from Goonellabah, NSW.*

1. Place ¾ cup cream, 3 rounded tbsp sifted icing sugar and 1 cup milk in basin and beat with beaters for 1 minute.
2. Stir in 3 cups sifted self-raising flour and combine well.
3. Press out on a flat surface and cut to whatever shape required. Bake in a hot oven for 20 minutes.

7

BUT WHAT ABOUT...?

Our chosen 'national' sweet dishes are loved
everywhere ... Pavlova, lamingtons and Anzac
biscuits are embraced by Australians in the
heart and on the plate.

Sarah Jane Shepherd Black, 'Tried and Tested'

When explaining to friends or colleagues my belief
that we have no food culture in the traditional sense,
I'm often met with derision, protestations, sometimes
anger, and then attempts to disprove that premise: 'But
what about ...?'. Once, when I was chairing a panel at
the Sydney Writers' Festival and attempting to debate
the matter, I got the response, 'Who cares?'. Well, I do.
Not because of any nationalistic pride (which appears
to be what denying it offends), but because it is a curiosity, an anomaly, and I think a very important key to
understanding why we eat what we eat.

Before beginning an exploration of what we have evolved in its place, I'm going to analyse the list of dishes and the one (and a bit) cuisine(s) offered as a real exception, in an attempt to counter my core premise. It's a bit of a detour, but I believe a necessary one: because exceptions tend to underline general rules.

The exceptional Barossadeutsch

And the one exception to the general rule that there are (or were) no regional food cultures is the food of the Barossadeutsch, that group of immigrants who arrived in South Australia having sailed from the port of Cuxhaven, downstream from Hamburg, in July 1841. They were Lutherans, and were escaping what they saw as their persecution following the unification of the Lutheran and Reformed churches, a process instigated by Kaiser Frederick William III in 1798. When the journey began, they were 270, but 50 died on the voyage. They came from the provinces of Posen, Brandenburg and Silesia in Prussia, and although many did not know each other, they were led by a pastor, Gotthard Daniel Fritzsche, who had 'ministered to their several parishes in Prussia'. There were several more boatloads to arrive in the Barossa from the same part of Prussia and neighbouring regions. Much of the information about the Barossadeutsch comes from Angela Heuzenroeder's definitive book, *Barossa Food*.

About half of those surviving that first voyage went to the Barossa Valley, took up land at what they called Bethany or New Silesia, and carved out those small, mixed farms so rare in Australia. They were followed by other families from other parts of Silesia, and what is now Poland. Earlier migrations of German people had settled in the Adelaide Hills. But the regional food culture and cuisine described as Barossadeutsch came from the Barossa Valley, where 'the original German culture remained strongest' in spite of a surrounding English-speaking community.

What's more, in the tradition of other expatriated food communities – Mauritian, Cajun – many of the recipes that arrived with the new settlers were adapted to incorporate local ingredients, most notably Rote grütze, a red berry dessert from Mecklenburg, Brandenburg and northern Germany. Traditionally made with red berries or gooseberries, the Barossa adaptation uses red wine grapes from the surrounding vineyards to replace the berries. Other adaptations include Silesian Streuselkuchen, which once again substitutes grapes – fresh sultanas – for fresh fruit; and Schlesisches Himmelreich, Silesian heaven, a savoury dish of smoked Speck, Backobst (dried apples, pears and prunes) and dumplings. The Barossa version substitutes pie-melons or stewed quinces for the dried fruit.

An interesting sidelight on the food of the Barossadeutsch is the contact of early German settlers with Indigenous Australians. Heuzenroeder writes that it was in the immigrants' nature to use wild foods in their homeland, and as a result they were vitally interested in what there was to forage in their new country. 'Aboriginal people showed them what they could gather, what was good food.' Plants pointed out to them included murnong, native cranberries (*Astroloma humifusum*), bitter quandong (*Santalum murrayanum*) and native currants (*Acrotriche depressa*), the last of which was used in making native-currant jam. This contact with and curiosity about the foods of their new land contrasts with that of the original non-Indigenous colonists who all but ignored those foods, except in times of shortages of their own.

Although 'All the elements were there in the Barossa to keep the original culture intact for a good long while', the many dishes created there neither broke out of the valley nor flourished as one would imagine such a vibrant food culture should have. The reasons for this are many, foremost being the influence of two world wars. As Heuzenroeder states: 'If any dishes were declining in popularity, the 1914–1918 World War and its aftermath sent them underground'. It was not a good idea, at the time, to show your German background. Surnames were anglicised, as were the names of dishes: the round yeast dough delicacy known in German as Berliner pfannkuchen became a Kitchener bun. The 1939–45 war would also prove to be a time for German Australians to duck for cover. Apart from the uncertainties of war, there was intermarriage with the locals.

'The English invasion into Barossa kitchens continued as, little by little, children in the third generation of Lutheran families began to marry partners outside the Lutheran church.' In introducing a list of local dishes in her book, Heuzenroeder wrote in 1999 that 'now is a good moment to look at a list of foods from the early communities that numbers of people make or at least remember today'.

One important name to emerge from the Barossa in the world of food is Maggie Beer. Although she is not herself of the tribe (she was born in Sydney, as Margaret Ackermann), her husband Colin Beer is, and Maggie is vitally interested in the produce of the region. Another Barossa name you may know is Schulz, the butchers who make the wonderful Schulz Bacon.

Developing Top End cuisine

Now for 'the bit'. I have to refer to one other minor and limited (in distribution) cooking style – hardly a cuisine – that has arisen in the Torres Strait Islands. This group of about 274 islands inhabit the 150 kilometres between Cape York Peninsula and Papua New Guinea. Most are recognised as belonging to Australia, while a few are administered by PNG. This is Australia's most porous border, and consequently its culture and cuisine are a mélange of Melanesian, Polynesian and British/Anglo-Celtic sources.

As Ron Edwards writes in *Traditional Torres Strait Island Cooking*: 'A Fijian or Tahitian would recognize most of the dishes, and their ingredients, but he would call them by different names'. He goes on to explain: 'As the Torres Strait Islands became a melting pot for a number of different cultures their cooks adopted a little of each regional style that seem appropriate, changing them here and there to fit in with the local tastes and available ingredients'.

The influences came from as far afield as the Philippines, other Pacific Islands, Malaysia via the bêche-de-mer and pearl shell fishers, the Asian storekeepers who followed the British, the Māori and those others mentioned above. But the recipes he collected are, Edwards writes, 'those of the Islanders, not necessarily of the Islands', and he doubts that any individual islander would claim to have tried them all: they were collected from many individuals. Nevertheless, these dishes and others from the Top End represent the kinds of dishes that should have, by now, developed in the rest of Australia, and it raises the question, once again: why didn't this happen?

We have to return to the gap between non-Indigenous and Indigenous Australians. There has been, over the years, very little mixing between the two populations, and so very little chance for a cooking style to cross the barrier, and become part of the non-Indigenous kitchen repertoire. We can compare that with the initial reception in America of Cajun and Soul Food: at first known and eaten only by their respective communities, but then breaking out and being adopted all over the USA and the world. The comparison is a little unfair, as those Torres Strait Islander dishes are far from the developed stage that Cajun and Soul Food were when they did break out.

Here also is the place to discuss Symons' contention that the main reason we have no cuisine is because we had no settled 'peasant' population 'who have demonstrated the advantages of tradition'. We did have such a settled population (although certainly not one that could be called peasant in any sense of the word). Indigenous Australians had demonstrated the advantages of tradition – and their food culture and foods had been developed – over millennia.

As I write this I'm also working on another book which will include domestic recipes using native foods. I've turned up such recipes from Indigenous families as spicy mussels with bush tomato and aniseed myrtle barbecue magpie goose skewers. I'm sure that over the 230 years of non-Indigenous occupation many other recipes have been developed, but we haven't asked because we have had very little contact. Just because Indigenous populations were forced off their lands didn't mean they stopped using native produce. And as time went on, they developed ways of using it in the non-Indigenous style of cooking. Now that is changing, we may well see such hybridised food cultures emerge.

The contenders

What of dishes or foods originating from the British/ Anglo-Celtic population?

I have already discussed Vegemite, but in a lovingly and meticulously researched book released while I was writing this, *Anzac Biscuits: the power and spirit of an everyday national icon*, author Allison Reynolds unravels the strands of the possible origins of this Australian favourite. She traces its provenance to five British contenders: Scots Oatcakes, the British Flapjack, Parkin, Ginger biscuits and Gingerbreads, and Scottish Parlies. Reynolds agrees with Santich, who stated in *Bold Palates* that 'British tradition provides no direct antecedents'. I was pleased to read in Reynolds' book that she had found ample evidence that women did send tins of Anzac biscuits to the Anzacs, something that had been questioned in recent years. More importantly for my story, the Anzac biscuit is not associated with a particular place.

Arguments about the provenance of these 'Australian' foods are widespread. At least two papers have been written on the Pavlova – was it invented in Australia or New Zealand?

Another book, *The Lamington Enigma: a survey of the evidence*, by Maurice French, concludes, over 280 pages, that 'The lamington, like the pavlova, was neither "invented" nor "created" in a particular place, at a specific time by a single person'.

In his book *Convicted Tastes*, Richard Beckett writes of the popular (and much reviled by what he calls the *beau monde*) staples of the Australian table, the emblematic quaternity – Lamington, Pavlova, meat pie and Vegemite. He laments that 'none of them had ever played an important part in past or present food styles of the country'. This is somewhat missing the point. The reason these foods are so often mentioned is that there is little else available to represent Australian food. Later in the book, he writes: 'to enshrine [the pie] as an absolute in national cuisine would be, by example, to judge British cooking on the number of jellied eels and whelk stalls, or Italian on the consumption of pizza'.

As much as I love Beckett's writing on food, here he muddles his own argument. The two foods chosen are excellent examples of regional dishes. Jellied eels, using eels from the River Thames, are representative of Cockney food; and the pizza, while it has been adopted by the world (and is regarded by Americans as theirs), has its provenance in either Naples or more broadly southern Italy. While neither could be 'enshrined' as absolutes in the cuisines of their respective countries and/or regions of origin, they are single dishes from a wide range representing the regional cuisines of those places.

Beckett does add two savoury dishes to the Australian repertoire: the spaghetti sandwich which, he claimed, understandably 'really did appal Europeans who took over food bars after World War Two'; and camp pie. This is the Australian name for beef tinned primarily for export, starting in the 1870s, to deal with the produce of excess herds of cattle; 'camp pie' was the tinned beef that remained at home. Beckett makes a mistake common to many when writing of 'regional food', conflating cuisine with produce. 'Australia taken region by region', he writes, 'still offers a lot to delight the palate'. He quotes from Donald Horne's book *Right Way – Don't Go Back* (1978), where Horne's partner buys shelled crayfish legs and claws, and eats them washed down with two bottles of West End beer in their Robe hotel room. This is produce, not cuisine: a regional cuisine is constructed using regional produce. As Italian restaurateur Beppi Polese said: 'it's not the ingredients that make the cuisine, it's the cuisine that makes the ingredients'. Polese cited pasta – which is, after all, only flour and water, sometimes with eggs.

In *Lily on the Dustbin: slang of Australian women and families*, Nancy Keesing proffers some micro-regional dishes. She records 'muttai' which, she says, is 'green corn boiled (often in corned beef water) and eaten on the cob, the name is certainly local to the New South Wales North Coast'. This was contributed by the poet Les Murray, who also contributed 'pommage', a coarse porridge of cracked maize. Keesing goes on to record dishes that are made of corned and/or smoked meat, which she says have several names, some regional. One, 'red flannel hash' from cold minced corn beef, and another, also from the New South Wales North

Coast, 'Yankee hash', the same as Red flannel but with an egg on top.

In seeking 'muttai', all that I could find was a variety of Indian egg curries – there is no muttai in the *Australian National Dictionary*. Neither the *Australian National Dictionary* nor any other recognises pommage (or pomage). Red flannel hash is, according to the *Simply Recipes* food and cooking blog <simplyrecipes.com>, 'traditionally made in New England [in the United States] for breakfast, with leftovers from a boiled dinner the night before, and gets its name from the somewhat obvious similarity of its colors to red flannel plaid cloth'. This would explain Yankee hash. Of those four examples, two are not to be found, one is a borrowing and the fourth a reference to the third. I'm sure that such dishes exist/existed in very small communities, but doubt that they represent regional cuisines, especially as they no longer exist.

When discussing the missing Australian food culture and recipes, the claim is often made 'but Australia is too young to have a food culture!'. But are we?

Recipes

COUNTRY WOMEN'S ASSOCIATION

....

LAMINGTONS

From the 1937 edition of the Coronation Cookery Book, *compiled for the Country Women's Association of New South Wales by Jessie Sawyer and Sara Moore-Sims.*

How many it makes, depends on the size of each square. But the regulation size according to the schedule of the RAS Perishable Cooking Competition is 1¼ inches (32 mm) square.

5 oz [142 g] butter

5 oz [142 g] sugar

1 oz [28 g] self-raising flour (or plain flour, add 1 tsp of baking powder)

2 eggs

4 tbsp milk

a few drops vanilla

1. Cream the butter and sugar, then add beaten eggs with milk and vanilla and last the sifted flour.
2. Grease a flattish dish and pour mixture into it and bake 30 minutes in a moderate oven.
3. Turn out into a cool place. Leave until next day, then cut into squares and ice with the following icing.

Icing
3 oz [57 g] butter
1 tbsp cocoa
8 oz [152 g] icing sugar
a few drops vanilla

1. Cream butter and icing sugar, add cocoa mixed with a little hot water.
2. Ice the squares [cakes] all over and then roll them in browned cocoanut [sic].
   To brown cocoanut: spread cocoanut on a shallow plate or tin and place in a slow oven for a few minutes.

Barossadeutsch

The recipes on the following pages are from Angela Heuzenroeder, Barossa Food, Wakefield Press, Kent Town, 1999 – the definitive book on the cuisine of the Barossadeutsch, Australia's only regional cuisine.

In an email, Angela also told me of a fascinating recipe that she had received from Pastor Juers of the Hoffnungsthal settlement: Roast kangaroo with bacon and garlic, a recipe that calls for steaming the kangaroo, similar to the dish Kangaroo steamer which first appeared in the 1920s. She said that she would rather offer her method of cooking kangaroo, which is:

to fry kangaroo steaks lightly dusted in seasoned flour, along with crisp curls of smoky Barossa bacon and chopped garlic. Then I remove them from the pan when the meat is still rare and add stock to thicken the sauce. Better than steaming the kangaroo. Quite delicious, in fact.

ANGELA HEUZENROEDER

....

ROTE GRÜTZ

Makes approximately 4 cups / Soak overnight

Pull berries from washed bunches of late-picked shiraz grapes. Boil the grapes for 10 minutes with cinnamon bark, a few slices of lemon and a little water. Let it sit for a while so that the colour comes out of the skins. Strain through a sieve, squeezing out as much of the juice as possible. At this point you can freeze the juice, ready for fresh batches of Rote grütz. Or proceed as follows:

To each 2 cups of juice add 1 cup of water, and sugar to taste (about 1 dessertspoonful). Measure the warm liquid into a saucepan and for each 500 ml of liquid, sprinkle on 2 tbsp sago. Allow to soak overnight. Next morning, simmer until sago is clear, about 15 minutes. Keep cooking time to a minimum to preserve the purple colour. Chill. It will keep for several days in the refrigerator, and the consistency will improve. Serve cold with runny cream.

8

STARTUP CUISINES AND FOOD CULTURES

A society's cookery is a language into which it
translates its structure, unless it reluctantly and no
less unwittingly reveals there its contradictions.

Claude Lévi-Strauss, *The Origin of Table Manners*

I've tried to leave the often perplexing but always
enlightening Lévi-Strauss out of this book. But the
Frenchman with (as *Nation* magazine put it) '… a sharp
eye for cultural patterns and a keen feel for the shape of
a story … a poet in the laboratory of anthropology' is
impossible to ignore. As was the above quote, to introduce a chapter on what I call startup cuisines. If I can
paraphrase, what I believe he is saying it is that food
is a code whose message is the structure of a whole
society and its relation to the outside world. While you

read this brief overview of a topic that could by itself fill an entire book, think back to that.

One reason advanced for non-Indigenous Australia's missing food culture is youth: we just haven't been around long enough. But in this chapter, I'll be looking at other nations, not much older than than non-Indigenous Australia, who have well-developed food cultures, cuisines and emblematic dishes that are unmistakable in their origins. Beginning with another settler nation, non-Indigenous North America.

In 'Eating American', the last chapter of his book *Tasting Food, Tasting Freedom*, Sidney Mintz recalls his answer to a question asked during a lecture on American eating habits: 'I did not think that there is such a thing as an American cuisine'. He spends the rest of the chapter proving it. But here, I want to provide some material evidence to cast doubt on his assertion. Although, in a sense, he is right. There is no 'American cuisine' – there are many American cuisines. And, as discussed at length by Harvey Levenstein in his book *Paradox of Plenty: a social history of eating in modern America*, an abundance of regional cuisines.

America, like Australia, is both multicultural and multiculinary, but in the USA there has been a merger of cuisines to create new forms. Just one of those cuisines, Cajun, has contributions from (primarily) the French, Native Americans, the Spanish, English, Africans, Germans and Italians. Similar merging has produced such undeniably American foods as the hamburger, the hot dog, and spaghetti and meatballs, an Italian-American invention. But first, a brief history of an American food cultural event that binds all those united states and their people.

'The roasted turkey took precedence ...'

On the last Thursday of November every year, Americans of all ethnic backgrounds, colours, religions – and lately, we must add, political persuasions – gather in their family homes to eat a ritual meal, comprising a mix of Native American and European ingredients, and latterly ingredients from newly arrived food cultures. Here, for example, is a brief description of one family's Middle Eastern Thanksgiving by Palestinian-American columnist Ray Hanania writing in the *HuffPost*, 'An American Arab Thanksgiving':

> We'll have the stuffed turkey, but oftentimes it will be stuffed with rice and minced lamb. We'll have grape leaves and zucchini (also stuffed with spiced rice and lamb), and tabouleh, a diced salad with burghal of cracked wheat. We have 'spheeha' (mini Arab pizzas) and 'kruss' (meat or spinach baked in triangular shaped bread).

This is a feast whose roots can be found, historiographical quibbles aside, in an expression of joy at bringing in the first harvest in a new land. Over the years it has transformed into a celebration of the idea of America, 'the land of the free and the home of the brave' as expressed in the American national anthem. America, like very few other countries (Liberia and Israel being two), was founded on an ideal. And that ideal is echoed in the culture of the annual meal known as Thanksgiving. Here is the basic historical version of how it all started.

On 16 September 1620, 102 passengers seeking religious freedom set off from Plymouth, Devon, and arrived at the mouth of the Hudson River in the *Mayflower* on either 9 or 11 November after a difficult and uncomfortable journey. They anchored in present-day Provincetown Harbor and arrived in Plymouth, in what is now Massachusetts, in December. After a terrible winter, they planted their first crops in the spring of 1621. 'On March 16', James W Baker wrote in *Thanksgiving: the biography of an American holiday*, 'a lone Indian entered the settlement and astonished the colonists by greeting them in English. This was Samoset, a Native Sagamore from Maine'. Samoset introduced them to Squanto, who also spoke English and who was to become the colony's translator and instructor in the planting of corn and other local resources. In autumn, 'the all-important corn harvest that would insure Plymouth Colony's survival proved successful, although some of the English crops were a disappointment'.

The claim for a first Thanksgiving in 1621 to celebrate that crop was not made until 1841 by Alexander
Young, author of the *Chronicles of the Pilgrim Fathers of the
Colony of Plymouth*. In that book, he published a letter
from the Pilgrim (and later third Governor) Edward
Winslow dated 11 December 1621. It described a
three-day event at the Plymouth Plantation, the dates
of which were not given. Winslow wrote:

> Our harvest being gotten in, our Governor sent
> four men on fowling, that so we might after a
> more special manner rejoice together, after we
> had gathered the fruit of our labours. They four
> in one day killed as much fowl as, with a little
> help besides, served the Company almost a week.
> At which time, amongst other recreations, we
> exercised our arms, many of the Indians coming
> amongst us, and amongst the rest their greatest
> king, Massasoit with some 90 men, whom for three
> days we entertained and feasted. And they went
> out and killed five deer which they brought to the
> plantation and bestowed on our Governor and upon
> the Captain and others.

In a footnote to Winslow's letter, Young claims this
as the first Thanksgiving, offering as support Governor
William Bradford's report that in the fall of 1621 the
settlers had accumulated 'a great store of wild turkeys,
venison, cod, bass, waterfowl and corn'. It must be said

that not all historians accept this event. Be that as it may, Thanksgiving survives.

In 1827, Sarah Josepha Hale published a novel, *Northwood*, in which she devoted an entire chapter to a Thanksgiving dinner: 'The roasted turkey took precedence ... yet the pumpkin pie occupied the most distinguished niche'. Using her fame gained from the success of *Northwood*, Hale began a campaign to make Thanksgiving a national holiday, a campaign that came to fruition in 1863 when, in the middle of the Civil War, President Lincoln proclaimed a day of Thanksgiving on the last Thursday in November beginning that year. 'I do', he wrote, 'therefore invite my fellow citizens in every part of the United States, and also those who are at sea and those who are sojourning in foreign lands, to set apart and observe the last Thursday of November next, as a day of Thanksgiving and Praise to our beneficent Father who dwelleth in the Heavens'. On 26 December 1941 – again in a time of war, indeed just 18 days after America's entry into the Second World War – President Roosevelt affirmed the fourth Thursday in November, for the first time making the date federal law.

The star of this national feast is the turkey, a native animal that defines Americans as Americans. Other native foods at the table were and still are pumpkins, as well as barberries. Here it is important to note that America, whose European history started just 181 years before Australia's – counting from the settlement of

Jamestown, Virginia in 1607 – has a unifying national feast, comprising native and European foods. A feast with a history that began with a meal shared by both European and Native Americans. While the Thanksgiving meal does not constitute a cuisine – nor did it help forge lasting convivial relations with Native Americans – it has insinuated itself into the DNA of culture and remains a foundation of America's national identity.

Immigrants who came much later readily joined in this foundational feast because it demonstrated their loyalty to their adopted country and their belief in the idea of American abundance. And while they added their own traditional foods to the feast, the turkey sat at the head of the table. Those same immigrants – and former slaves – also contributed to America's culinary traditions and cuisines. Perhaps the most pervasive, persuasive and deep-seated of those is Cajun.

Stirring the pot

The story begins with French colonists settling in Acadia in the colony of New France in eastern Canada in the first half of the seventeenth century. When the British went to war with the French in Canada, they began to expel the Acadians. Some went to Louisiana, which had been transferred to the Spanish government in 1762, and soon after became the largest ethnic group there.

Those early French settlers were peasants, whose diet in their homeland would have consisted mainly of soups and wholegrain bread, with little meat. Arrival in Canada changed their diet – pork, poultry, fish and wild game were added – but not their culinary traditions. They used two pots for cooking, a cauldron over the fire and a deep skillet, producing much the same dishes they had left behind, with different ingredients. But that seventeenth and eighteenth century Acadian cuisine bears little resemblance to its modern Louisiana descendant, except in cooking method.

In Louisiana, the Acadians turned to fishing and farming, including raising hogs and cattle. Dubbed Cajuns (from Acadian) by their neighbours, they took to salting pork, but continued to slow cook using their cauldrons, and from the eighteenth century through to the early twentieth their diet consisted of slow-cooked meat, corn bread and seasonal vegetables.

By 1900 one dish had emerged that could define Cajun cuisine – gumbo. It was first mentioned in 1803 by the French immigrant travel writer CC Robin. In *Stir the Pot: a history of Cajun cuisine* the authors, Marcelle Bienvenu and Carl and Ryan Brasseaux, write that:

> The popularity of Cajun gumbo, distinguished from its Créole counterpart by its use of both a roux base and okra ... was such that ... Louisiana Chief Justice Joseph A Breaux characterized it as the group's 'national dish.' The Cajun roux, the basic flavour that

enlivens many Cajun dishes, is French in name only, and consists of roughly equal parts – depending on the cook – of flour and fat (originally lard), cooked together to a light or dark brown. As the ingredients of the dish are cooked slowly together, in typical Cajun style, the roux produces an amazing depth and degree of flavor.

By the time of the Civil War, there were a number of varieties of gumbo all with the basis of roux, but with ingredients including onion, green bell peppers, celery, Andouille sausage (see on page 205), pork, chicken, crab meat, oysters and so on, depending on where and by whom it was made. For those interested in this fascinating cuisine and food culture I recommend *Stir the Pot*.

From these beginnings, Cajun cuisine has grown in strength and character, aided by such external agencies as refrigeration – which helped add seafood and freshwater fish to the list of ingredients – the improvement of the state highway system in the 1920s and 1930s, and the increasing affluence of the population with the expansion of the oil industry and tourism. In a relatively short time – and mostly in the twentieth century – a distinctive cuisine with eight regional variations and both domestic and commercial versions had arisen. The last major influence was the chef Paul Prudhomme who, in the 1980s, spearheaded its subsequent commercialisation.

Wrapped around Cajun cuisine is Cajun food culture. As argued in this book, there's more to food than what you put in your mouth: it tells us who we are and often where we stand in the pecking order. Bienvenu writes, for example, that 'Class also played a major role in shaping perceptions about beef and pork dishes ... poor Cajuns consumed "everything but the squeal" ... Affluent local families looked askance on such meals [of internal organs] and made pork pâté instead'.

Jambalaya is another dish, along with gumbo, identified as quintessentially Cajun. But jambalaya is the product of mutually reinforcing culinary traditions introduced into Louisiana from two different continents: France and Spain. Jambalaya is a naturalised version of paella. And although the exact date of paella's introduction to Louisiana is unclear, its traditional consumption is concentrated in the areas settled by Hispanic immigrants in the late eighteenth century. To further stir the pot, the colour of jambalaya changes according to where it is made. In rural south Louisiana it's brown, because the cast-iron cooking pots used there allow for more caramelisation of the sugars in meat and vegetables, which are absorbed by the rice in cooking. In New Orleans it's red, because of the traditional use of tomatoes in Créole cuisine, Créole being a close cousin of, but distinct from, Cajun. This cuisine and its culture arose around 1764, just twenty-four years before the European colonisation of Australia.

This occurred to me while on holiday in the

South Australian fishing village of Robe, immediately after reading American food writer Ed Behr's newsletter, *The Art of Eating*, on Cajun cuisine. Behr explains the theory and practice of Cajun ingredients and techniques, shows the derivation of the word *gombo*, dissects the racial mixes and the culture, and offers recipes for Chicken, oyster and sausage gumbo and Seafood gumbo.

When I arrived in Robe, a small – winter population around 1000 – and relatively isolated fishing village south-east of Adelaide, with the Coonawarra wine-growing region right behind it, I wondered whether there was some regional dish or cooking style. The village was established in 1845, mainly by Scots fishing families. Coonawarra, with its famous (for growing wine grapes) terra rossa soil, is good farming land, fish are bountiful and crayfish – now the main fishing industry – are still caught by locals, all of whom have a favourite spot to hang out a craypot. All this, I conjectured, should have resulted in at least one local dish.

We were invited to a cocktail party at the house of one of the oldest families in town. The other invitees were all well-established Robe locals, many with roots going back a century. I quizzed several of them on the subject. I found no such dish or style. By contrast, an online search uncovered *Louisiana Crawfish Recipes* <www.crawfish.org>, a compilation of almost one hundred recipes using the local freshwater crayfish.

This rich treasury of recipes, all of which fit within the general matrix of Cajun cuisine, is even more remarkable when we learn that, according to Bienvenu, 'Many, perhaps most, middle class prairie Cajuns did not eat them [crawfish] at all in the pre-World War II era, and those who did consume the crustaceans did not boast about it [as they were seen as food of the poor]'.

It's a long way from Cajun Louisiana to Philadelphia, Pennsylvania – and not just in distance – but that is where another emblematic item of American food culture was born.

Hamburger, hot dogs and Soul Food

The Centennial Exposition in Philadelphia opened on 10 May 1876, and showcased a wide variety of foodstuffs, many commercially processed, that went on to became mainstays of the American diet. One of these was the prototype hamburger, the hamburger steak.

The German restaurant at the expo served this hamburger steak as a patty on a plate, and the meat grinder – which made it quick and easy to mince the meat for the steak – was introduced both commercially and domestically at the same time and place. Hamburger steak was soon found on the lunch wagon menu: and because customers ate their food standing up, the steaks were placed between slices of bread or buns.

Nobody knows who was the first lunch wagon pro-
prietor to do so, but by the 1890s, as the 'hamburger-
steak sandwich', it had become an American classic.

By the early twentieth century, the name had been
shortened to 'hamburger' or 'burger'. Now it ranges
from the bland, cookie cutter item sold around the
world at McDonald's, to the $3000 creation of a Dutch
chef using Wagyu beef, lobster, pata negra (Spanish
jamón), foie gras, caviar, truffle and a bun coated in
gold leaf. The hamburger says America like no other
food – except maybe the hot dog.

Bruce Kraig is Emeritus Professor of History and
Humanities at Roosevelt University in Chicago. But
his claim to fame is as the foremost hot dog historian
in the world. In his book *Hot Dog: a global history* he tells
its story, another example of German butchery meeting American opportunism.

In April 1901, on a cold night at New York's Polo
Grounds, spectators were out to see the New York
Giants play. Although there are several versions of this
story, in 1935 the journalist Quentin Reynolds told
what has become the standard account. Harry Ste-
vens had the franchise to sell food and drinks at the
Polo Grounds. He had stocked up on ice cream and
soda, but recognised there was a need for hot food:
'Send round to all the butchers in the neighbourhood',
he told his son Frank, 'buy up all those German sausages you can, those long dachshund sausages – what
do they call them, frankfurters. Then hustle around to

the bakers in the neighbourhood and buy up all the rolls you can find ... And get some mustard!'. That night, the Frankfurter in a roll sold like ... hot dogs. In the Reynolds' version of this story, the renowned cartoonist TA Dorgan (TAD), 'delighted by the sight of a sausage-frenzied crowd' and thinking of a cartoon, reasoned that since the dachshund is a dog, why not call the new dish a 'hot dog'?

That these dishes, and, to a great extent, what is known in America as 'pizza pie', are American constructs is in no doubt. That they are a part of American food culture is similarly indisputable. But a difficulty arises when we try to describe them as 'American cuisine'. We can't go back to Revel's distinction that popular cuisine 'has the advantage of being linked to the soil'. None of those popular American foods are. Although it could easily be argued that, as America is primarily an urban culture – unlike the cuisines Revel analyses – the American versions are urban-based: their links are to the streets. As is the case with Soul Food which, although linked to the soil, came to fruition in the cities.

In *Paradox of Plenty*, Levenstein writes that 'The rise of black nationalism in the late 1960s had bought a new appreciation for the southern black culinary tradition, now called "soul food"'. And that 'On New Year's Eve, well-off urban blacks ostentatiously eschewed steak and roast beef for the ham hocks, peas and collard greens of their rural forebears'. Such cynicism can't deny the fact that from that time on, the street corners of African-American neighbourhoods were crowded with rib joints, chicken takeout stands and fish markets. Tracy Poe, in an article, 'The Origins of Soul Food in Black Urban Identity: Chicago 1915–1947', writes that 'until 1963, when Malcolm X recorded his life story for Alex Haley, there was no such thing as "Soul Food"'. As southern African Americans, however, began 'percolating' into the neighbourhoods of their northern brothers and sisters, they brought with them their 'southern rural culture', including music, language idioms and what became, eventually, Soul Food. A cuisine of nostalgia which, at the same time, represented many of the problems associated with African-American culture in the twentieth century, and was entangled with that complexity.

The food was an amalgam of their African past, their slave past, and ingredients found in the new land resembling the foods they had left behind (for example, the American sweet potato, which resembled the African yam), and others imported from Africa and cultivated on American soil (peanuts, known as *guba* on the west coast of Africa and as 'goobers' in America to this day, as well as watermelon and okra). 'Slave cooks', as Poe observes, 'created a new cuisine with the corn meal and cured pork that were the daily staples on the plantation'. And so was born not just a cuisine, but a distinctive and easily recognisable food culture, one that obeys Revel's tenet that a popular cuisine is linked to the soil. Africans also play a major part in our final startup cuisine, as do the French, the Indians and the Chinese.

Créole cuisine

Mauritius, the largest island of the Republic of Mauritius, lies some 2000 kilometres off the south-east coast of the African continent. In the space of 298 years it has developed a distinctive cuisine and a well-defined food culture. I could find little writing on this cuisine, and my knowledge of it derives primarily from two trips to the island, working in the kitchen with chefs, both domestic and commercial; from discussions with chefs, restaurateurs and cooks; and from *Exotic Cuisine of Mauritius*, the one authoritative book I could find.

The first trip was in 2003 to gather material for a story in *Australian Gourmet Traveller* magazine; the second, in 2006, at the invitation of the Republic of Mauritius, to attend the first International Créole Festival, a celebration of Créole culture, music and cuisine.

Prior to the arrival of the Portuguese, Mauritius was uninhabited. The Portuguese came and went several times between 1507 and 1513, but preferred Mozambique as an African east coast base. The Dutch first arrived in 1598, twice attempted to set up colonies (the second time in 1638), cut down most of the ebony, contributed largely towards the extinction of the dodo and left in 1710 – but not before naming the island after Prince Maurice of Nassau, the Governor of Holland at the time, and the pioneer of the Indian Ocean spice trade. They also brought the first sugar cane, as well as rabbits, pigs, deer, sheep and geese, and the first slaves from Madagascar.

In 1715 the French arrived, bringing with them their own slaves from Africa and Madagascar and extending the sugar plantations. As was the case with the slaves in other plantation colonies, the planters mixed individuals from different ethnic groups together, dissolving family structures. In 1810, the English beat the French in the battle of Grand Port and, later, freed the slaves. But then 'indentured' Indian labour arrived: indentured being a euphemism for a system tantamount to slavery. Along the way came the Chinese, many fleeing from the Opium Wars, who set up as traders. Today, just over 50 per cent of the population is made up of people from the subcontinent of India, 28 per cent are the descendants of Africans and Malagasy people, two per cent are of European descent and three per cent of Chinese descent. This multiplicity of ethnic origins, inter-ethnic marriage and reproduction has produced a heterogeneous people, which is apparent in the islanders' religious orientations, dress, architecture, music, cuisine and language. The one problem in this picture of inter-racial harmony is the disadvantage of the Afro-Mauritians, known as Créoles. But the term Créole is also used to describe the cuisine of the island. The word 'creole', with or without the accent, means people of mixed 'race' – as we saw it being used in Louisiana – but it is also used to describe the cuisine, music and so on of Créole people.

The dishes, ingredients and cooking methods used on the island betray the brew of ethnic influences. One example, rougail (or rougaille), is variously described as being Provençal, Caribbean, Mauritian or from the island of Réunion. *Larousse Gastronomique* says that rougail is 'a highly spiced seasoning used in the cooking of the West Indies and Réunion', and then gives a recipe that is entirely different from those I gathered in Mauritius.

In the Mauritian version, rougail is a fine example of multiculinary marriage: tomatoes with garlic, onion and turmeric (there called Indian saffron), chillis and curry leaves. This dish is not, as might be expected, cooked slowly, but briskly, almost at stir-fry heat, in a wide, open-mouthed cooking utensil, not unlike a wok, known locally as a caraille, more than likely a francification of the Indian vessel karahi. The local tomato used in the rougail is known to us as the Roma, but in Mauritius (and parts of southern France) is given its original French name, *pomme d'amour*, apple of love. So ubiquitous are sauces based on these tomatoes that there is a Créole expression for someone who is involved in many activities: that they are like *pommes d'amour* – into everything.

Vindaye is another dish that has moved from west to east. Vindaye is a Créolisation of *vin d'ail*, meaning a wine and garlic marinade. In the Mauritian version, the wine has turned to vinegar, as it usually did on the trip from France, and Indian saffron has been added, along with ginger, chilli and mustard seed. The vinegar/garlic mixture is also a method of preserving fish and meat. (I tried fish, venison and octopus.)

While in Mauritius I ate a meal with and cooked by Franco-Mauritian artist, chef and amateur culinary historian Jacques 'Vaco' Baissac. An account of that meal includes a perhaps apocryphal but telling tale of one dish, a Gâteau de patate douce, using African sweet potatoes.

'This pudding', Vaco explained, 'is originally African. I am sure a French planter tried it, and decided that it tasted like a marron – chestnut – purée, a dish he could not get in the tropics. And so, he had it dressed up with the egg white topping – and *voilà*! another basic dish entered the Mauritian repertoire'. In discussing this later in Australia with Australian chef Damien Pignolet, he opined that it would have reminded the French of a chestnut purée dessert called Mont Blanc.

Mauritian gastronomy evolved over a period of two-and-a-half centuries, from a modest start with the first French settlers and the help of African, Malagasy and Indian labour. Regional French recipes were adapted to the new environment, and tropical produce as well as introduced Asian and northern Asian spices were incorporated. The Indian immigrants, then the Chinese, contributed. And dishes were created that became, over time, pure Mauritian. In their book *Exotic Cuisine of Mauritius*, Philippe Lenoir and Raymond de Ravel write: 'The boredom spawned from standardization never remotely threatened Mauritian cuisine; it is noteworthy that dear Albion [England] never influenced, or made a mark on its style!'. The cuisine had evolved in about the same amount of time Europeans have been in Australia, and it betrays, like the layers of an archaeological dig, its origins.

The accident of English

Language runs through all these stories of culinary creation. The fusion of cuisines from French, German, African, Indian, Malagasy and Chinese cultures throw up words like gumbo, jambalaya, vindaye, rougail, hamburger and *guba* that overcome those differences and span the cultural and linguistic gaps. But for our first 230 years, we had no such gaps. British and Anglo-Celtic Australians spoke but one language (while Indigenous Australians spoke hundreds). Dealing more broadly with British/Anglo-Celtic culture in general, Julian Meyrick writes: 'The accident of English allows us to free-ride the cultural goods and services of the two international powers that have so far dominated our fate, Britain and the US'. He goes on to point out that unlike Israel, bilingual Canada – and I would add Mauritius and New Orleans – 'Our quest for independence did not involve the assertion of a separate linguistic identity with the result that we are a net cultural importer'.

Yet, curiously, we did transform the English we brought with us in ways that we did not do with the food. In *Australia's Many Voices*, philologist Gerhard Leitner points out that 'mainstream Australian English, the dominant variety of English, owes everything to Australia's Anglo-Celtic heritage'. Leitner also discusses the various pidgins and créoles that have formed since European occupation, the linguistic equivalent of cuisines.

Even within what he calls AusE (Australian English) there are regional variations in words, particularly those used to describe foods. For example, across Australia, the world 'rockmelon' describes *Cucumis melo*, but in south-eastern Australia it is often replaced with the word 'canteloupe'. Also, the large numbers of names for the simple Frankfurt – described as a small red sausage usually eaten with tomato sauce and mostly at parties. Responses elicited from a group of Australians when shown a photograph of this sausage by Leitner included: 'sausage, banger, cheerio, hot dog, saveloy, cocktail frankfurter, Frankfurt or frank'. Leitner goes on to source these names to their often quite specific origins. Yet in spite of the existence of an Australian English and the broad range of local words for foods, we persisted with our British/Anglo-Celtic culinary traditions, either from choice or, as Meyrick suggests, cultural inertia due to the 'accident of English'.

Did this change when the culture was invaded by predominantly southern European refugees from a war-torn Europe? Yes, but in much more complex ways.

Recipes

ROUGAIL SAUCE
Serves 4–6

From Mauritius. I devised this recipe after working in kitchens with local cooks and chefs and watching them prepare this sauce.

4 tbsp oil

1 onion, thinly sliced

2 tbsp turmeric

5 large cloves garlic, crushed

1 large knob ginger, crushed

750 g very ripe tomatoes, chopped

sprigs of thyme to taste

¼ cup fresh parsley leaves

5 fresh or dried curry leaves

6 long green chillis (or to taste), halved lengthwise and seeded

½ cup good chicken stock or water

1. Heat oil in a heavy frying pan (or caraille or wok) and cook onion, turmeric, garlic and ginger over medium

heat, stirring for 1 minute.

2. Stir in tomato, thyme, parsley, curry leaves and chilli.
3. Cook over high heat for 5 minutes, stirring to prevent the sauce catching.
4. Stir in stock or water and simmer for 5 to 6 minutes or until thick and bright red in colour.

Serve with/variations

As this is a base sauce, it can be adapted to many ingredients. It's the all-purpose sauce.

For example, if you have access to large, sweet onions, slice and fry 500 g slowly until transparent – or bake them whole until soft and then slice – and add to a rougail sauce. Or the same with 500 g thinly sliced scallions.

Cut 500 g of salt pork or pork belly into cubes, blanch in boiling water for 10 minutes, fry in hot oil, drain the fat and add the rougail sauce.

Serve with pan-fried chicken or sliced pork fillet, or pour over fried spicy sausages.

....

GÂTEAU DE PATATE DOUCE

Serves 6

The recipe given to me by Jacques 'Vaco' Baissac.

750 g sweet potato (the white-fleshed ones work better in this
dish than those with orange or yellow flesh, which don't
have the right 'chestnutty' texture)

125 g unsalted butter

125 g white sugar, plus 2 dessertspoons for egg white topping

2 egg yolks, reserve whites for egg white topping

2 tbsp dark rum

½ fresh coconut, grated (you can use a tough-fleshed coconut);
reserve some for decoration

1. Boil the sweet potatoes in their skins and peel while hot,
    removing any fibre.
2. Put them in the blender and purée while still hot.
3. Add the butter, sugar, egg yolks, rum and coconut and
    blend into the purée.
4. Turn into a dish and cool in the refrigerator for a few
    hours.
5. Remove from the fridge and mould into a smooth
    'mountain' shape.
6. Beat the egg whites until they peak, then add
    2 dessertspoons of sugar.
7. Spoon the egg white and sugar mixture over the gâteau,
    and fork into a fluffy shape. Sprinkle with remaining
    coconut.

8. Serve with chocolate custard poured around its base, or crème anglaise à la vanilla.

MARCELLE BIENVENU

....

CHICKEN AND ANDOUILLE GUMBO
Serves 6 to 8

This recipe is from Marcelle Bienvenu, Carl A Brasseaux and Ryan A Brasseaux, Stir the Pot: the history of Cajun cuisine, *Hippocrene Books, New York, 2008. With the kind permission of Marcelle Bienvenu, the lead author of* Stir the Pot *and a leading authority on and teacher of Cajun cuisine.*

Cajun andouille sausage is different from the French version, which is made from offal. It is a coarse-grained smoked sausage made using pork, garlic, pepper, onions, wine and seasonings. If you can't find it, substitute with a good-quality chorizo.

Gumbo filé powder is made from the powdered leaves of the sassafras tree and it was introduced into Cajun cuisine, according to Stir The Pot, by Native American groups. Substitute with thyme mixed with savory.

If you want to make this, I would suggest that you practise making the roux first. And while this recipe suggests a vegetable oil, try it with the same quantity of lard, the original fat used. It will require some practice.

1 cup vegetable oil [or 1 cup lard]
1 cup all-purpose [plain] flour
2½ cups chopped yellow onion

205

1 cup chopped green bell pepper

½ cup chopped celery

1 x 4–5 lb [2 kg] chicken, cut into serving pieces

salt

cayenne pepper

2½ quarts [2.5 litres] chicken broth

2 bay leaves

¼ tsp dried thyme

1 lb [500 g] andouille sausage cut into ¼ inch [½ cm]
    slices

2 tbsp finely chopped fresh parsley

2 tbsp finely chopped green onions [spring onion, or scallion]

filé powder [50 g]

1. In a large heavy Dutch oven or cast-iron pot, combine the
    oil [or lard] and flour over medium heat. Cook, stirring,
    until the roux becomes a medium-dark brown, the colour of
    chocolate, about 30 minutes.
2. Add the onion, bell pepper and celery and cook, stirring
    often, until the vegetables are wilted and slightly golden,
    about 10 minutes.
3. Season the chicken generously with salt and cayenne.
4. Stir the chicken broth into the vegetables, and then
    add the chicken pieces, bay leaves and thyme. Cook
    uncovered, for about 1½ hours, stirring occasionally.
5. Add the andouille and cook for another hour, or until the
    chicken is tender.

6. Remove the leaves and mix in the parsley and green onions. Ladle the gumbo into deep soup bowls over steamed rice. Pass the filé powder at the table to allow guests to add according to taste.

9

ENTER THE OTHER

Australia, having only one people, 96 per cent
British, has only one diet, steak, chops, beef,
mutton, potatoes and gravy (don't forget the
gravy), with suet puddings and slabs of cheese.
Every Australian home dinner is so amusing and so
very English. Our women can't cook and our men
do not know the art of good eating. There is no
epicurism in Australia, no fine sense of gastronomy
as the prop of happiness. There is not one first-
class restaurant in the Commonwealth so far.

George Meudell, *The Pleasant Career of a Spendthrift*

In 1929, Meudell, a banker, stockbroker, investor and
self-styled bon vivant published a book from which
the above epigraph is taken. It's a tale told with vanity,
pomposity and vigour of his travels, his impressions,

the famous people he met and, in large part, the meals he ate. Meudell is described in the *Australian Dictionary of Biography* as a 'passionate nationalist' and the inventor in 1882 of the slogan 'Australia for the Australians'. There is not much of the passionate nationalist in the epigraph at the head of this chapter. But there is much in the book for anyone interested in how non-Indigenous Australians ate in the late nineteenth and early twentieth century, especially in cafes, restaurants and clubs.

Meudell is a contradictory character. Australians are, he writes, '... a nation of crude raw people, the very antithesis of sybarites'. And then, a little further along:

And here is the right place to append the menu of the choicest dinner I have ever eaten during forty years of wandering up and down the world: Caviare, oysters on ice, lobster soup, schnapper with mussel sauce, filets of sole, sweetbreads Conti, supreme of chicken, Parisienne, saddle of mutton, English fashion, quail, omelette soufflé, chartreuse of strawberries, parmesan cheese straws, coffee ice, with wines en suite. That dinner was ordered carte blanche to be entirely made of Australian materials, bar the Russian caviare supplied by a general, and it was served at Scott's Hotel, Melbourne. This is said by the owner of a thousand menus gathered from a thousand hotel, ship and railway dining tables throughout the world.

Like Australia at the time, Meudell is hostage to an imported class system. The hereditary aristocracy of England was replaced by the colonial gentry, a class to which Meudell emphatically proclaimed his membership, a class often derided as the 'bunyip aristocracy', so-named for that mythical monster believed to inhabit inland waterholes. The English upper class fondness for French cuisine can be seen in the meal he outlines above. And it is an upper class meal: 'caviare', 'sweetbreads Conti', 'chartreuse of strawberries', with a nod towards the old country, 'saddle of mutton, English fashion'.

His contempt for the home cook – 'our women can't cook' – and the 'lack of epicurism in Australia' typifies the insecurity of the newly coined colonial gentry. And, until relatively recently, dining out in expensive clubs, hotels and restaurants in Australia was one of the perks of the 'upper classes' ('appanage' being Revel's word). I remember walking up to Kings Cross from our flat in Elizabeth Bay as a small boy and my father pointing out the site that had been the restaurant Kinneil, and mentioning that during the Second World War it had been reserved for officers. The democratisation of dining in Sydney had to wait until the post-war period. But upper class Franco-British food was not the only cuisine on offer at this time.

The other class (or tribe) to have their own haunts in both Sydney and Melbourne were the self-styled bohemians: artists, writers and, as Hal Porter described the clientele of Café Petrushka in Melbourne in 1937 in his book *The Paper Chase*, the 'famous, near-famous, flash-in-the-pan famous ... famous to be' and 'garrulous never-to-be-famous'.

Cafe society from around the mid-nineteenth century to the 1930s in Melbourne revolved around several such places: Molina's, Café Denat (whose French menu displayed the motto *Honi Soit Qui Mal Y Mange*), Café Latin, the Society, Café Florentino, Mario's and Fasoli's. Of these, Fasoli's, with its Italian-Swiss host Vincent Fasoli, was the most louche. Its habitués self-described as 'Fasolians'; they included the writers EJ Brady and Louis Esson, and the artist Percy Lindsay. Both wine and food here were Italian, spaghetti was made in house, and dishes might include a Spezzatini di vitello or an Osso buco.

Mario's was owned by Maria and Mario Vigano, wealthy Milanese refugees from fascism who had arrived in Australia in the early 1930s. They leased and eventually bought the old Melbourne Club Hotel, which became Mario's. One of their children, also Maria, married a Scottish engineer, and had a child, Mietta, who we'll meet later in this story. And although Mario's is no longer, Florentino, as Grossi Florentino, remains an important part of Melbourne dining. The Latin, as Marchetti's Latin, closed in 2001.

Sydney too had establishments catering to *la vie bohème*. In the period running roughly from 1890 to 1910, the local version of La Belle Epoque, Australian fare and wine was to be found at Adam's Café in George Street, and two Francophile offerings, the Diner Parisien in Hunter Street, but more importantly for rakish Sydney, The Paris House restaurant bistro and bar, which opened its doors in 1890 at 173 Phillip Street. First run by a Monsieur Desneaux, it came into its heyday under the leadership of Gaston Lievain, when it was described as Sydney's most glamourous restaurant.

While Sydney's early cafe life was mainly French influenced, there were also Italian and Greek cafes, restaurants and eating houses in Australian cities as early as 1903. But they were, for the main part, there for the Italian population. In Sydney, an advertisement in the Italian-language newspaper *Uniamoci* advertised the Cosmopolitan Dining Rooms of La Taverna, at 61, 63 and 65 Liverpool Street, which offered '*Buone comodità per Viaggiatori*' ('Good facilities for travellers'), with meals costing 6 pence, and weekly bed and board at 14 shillings. There were similar boarding houses run by Italians offering their residents Italian meals.

By the late 1920s, there were places like Ciro's, at 177 Elizabeth Street, advertising only in the Italian-language press. Many of the first cafes were started by Italians who had been working as waiters. In the late 1920s, brothers Guglielmo (William or Bill) and Edoardo (Edward) Vanzino, having worked at Sydney nightclubs Ambassador's and Romano's (see the Beppi Polese story on page 225) opened the Continental

Coffee Bar at 272 Victoria Street, in Sydney's Kings Cross, and served 'Coffee Made Fresh with our Specially Imported Express Hygienic Coffee Machine'. This could be the first espresso machine in Australia, beating the claim by Melbourne's Universita Bar restaurant by thirty years.

Apart from its ownership and coffee, it was a classic English tearoom, serving sandwiches, scones, cakes and bread rolls, malted milk, Oxo, Bovril, milk shakes and iced coffee or chocolate. By 1932, it was transformed into Van's Coffee Bar and Restaurant, and was serving fresh ravioli, gnocchi and other pasta.

Italians have long been prominent in feeding Sydney, but it was only after the post-war migration that many Australians began to eat the food the Italians ate at home, to take up the challenge of wine, olive oil and garlic. But before leaving these early Italians in Sydney, I have to mention a family whose last business I remember, and who had a profound influence on the way Sydney ate. When, after drinking beer in the Watsons Bay Hotel, I queued up to get my hands on one of Tony Marinato's prawn rolls on the wharf at Watsons Bay, I had no idea of the history of the place or the Marinato family.

In 1904, Michele and Rosaria Marinato opened the Watsons Bay Tearoom – later named the Continental Tea Gardens – at the Watsons Bay wharf. Once established, Michele battled for many years to get permission for outdoor dining. He was finally successful, around the middle of the 1920s. Al fresco dining at Watsons Bay was a first in Sydney and excited the wrath of the Health Department, until the Maritime Services Board – from which the Marinato family leased the premises – stepped in and gave it the nod.

Henry Lawson was an early customer, and in the 1930s Prime Minister Joe Lyons was a regular. When the tearooms grew into a restaurant in the 1950s, and expanded the offerings from pies, cakes and sandwiches to fried seafood, the Marinatos hosted such celebrities of the times as Rudolph Nureyev, Ava Gardner, Alfred Hitchcock and Liberace.

Nonetheless it was still BG Australia. The three Marinato sons, Vince, Tony and Michael, suffered the usual racist comments at school, but were on the receiving end of an additional insult because of the seafood their family restaurant served: 'ockie eaters'.

As a boy in Double Bay in the 1960s, I used to catch baby octopus with a mate and sell them to the local Italians. One day, my mate – like me, a skip (Italian slang for a non-Italian Australian, from the television show *Skippy the Bush Kangaroo*) – asked, 'What do the Italians do with them? Use them as bait?'. Being more sophisticated (my mother made Spaghetti bolognaise) I said, 'They eat them'. He made a face. 'Oh, yuck!'.

By the 1960s, a self-service bar was set up which produced 100 dozen prawn rolls each day. It was in the late 1960s I remember waiting for my prawn roll to be served by big Tony Marinato.

The Marinatos were responsible for more than just outdoor dining. In his book, *The Shop on the Wharf*, Vince Marinato claims his family introduced take-away chip containers, and were the first to bring an American soda bar to Sydney in 1910, to serve calamari, and to display fresh fish in tanks.

One early twentieth century Sydney restaurant, owned by Italians but not necessarily Italian, deserves a mention. In 1932, the Dungowan restaurant in Martin Place was leased by the brothers Aldo, Mario Pasquale and Aurelio Giovanni (John) Bottero, who retained the previous business name. Renowned at the time as a staff lunch and special occasion venue, it also had a dance floor.

In the early years, a Dungowan lunch consisted of Crumbed lamb cutlets with vegetables, a bread roll and butter, pudding and custard, tea or coffee, or Roast beef and Yorkshire pudding, Peach Melba and Crème caramel. Just before the Second World War, a dish of Grilled capsicum and fennel with a side of vinaigrette and ravioli entered the menu. And after the war, Chicken Maryland and Hawaiian salad with orange and pineapple slices was joined by ravioli, pasta al forno and frittelle. The last years of the Dungowan provide an interesting snapshot of mid-twentieth century Sydney. In 1957, it changed its name to Quo Vadis and became a nightclub, where big acts of the day like the Everly Brothers played.

Its final transformation was as a theatre restaurant, East Lynne, showing Victorian melodramas. Then, the private dining room was converted into Sydney's first Japanese restaurant, the Sukiyaki Room.

The invasion of the garlic munchers

In the introduction to my book *Wogfood: an oral history with recipes*, I tell a story of sitting next to an elderly Australian woman on a flight from Melbourne in the early 1990s, and her reaction to the in-flight meal presented to the author and the woman.

> I lifted the foil flap on my plate and on it was airline lasagne. I noticed my neighbour, having placed her bag beside her, cautiously lifting hers, peering in and poking at it apprehensively with her fork, as one would a slug in the lettuce. 'What's the mystery?' she asked, perhaps to no one in particular, but I answered anyway. 'Lasagne' I said, 'a layer of pasta, cheese, tomato sauce and probably mince.' She continued to poke at it before pushing it away with a sigh, adding 'I'm too old.'

None of the ingredients of the lasagne would have been unfamiliar to that woman – flour, water, eggs, minced meat, tomato and cheese. But it was the way in which they were constructed, put together and served that was foreign to one whose tastes in food had been set in the 1940s and 1950s. If the same ingredients had been presented as minced meat on toast with tomato sauce, sprinkled with cheese, it would have been accepted: same ingredients, different form. Lasagne Lady (or rather Anti-Lasagne Lady) had grown up in a curious food culture.

Rather than eating, as Waverley Root wrote in *The Food of France*, 'food [that] is a function of the soil', the foodstuffs she had grown up with were all brought in from somewhere else – the raw ingredients of her diet were exotic to the land she lived in. And the methods of cooking and assembling those foods were also devised elsewhere, in a country and culture that she only really knew second hand. As David Malouf writes: 'Yorkshire Pudding was Australian. It was what we had always eaten. What else could it be?'. So, confronted with lasagne, she was understandably confused. It was not food as she knew it. She confronted a food cultural chasm.

As commonplace and recognisable as the raw ingredients of the meal were, their cultural transformation rendered them inedible. In *The Consuming Body*, Pasi Falk discusses the food of others – in this case Italians – as opposed to our food. 'The general precondition for the other's food to be conceived of as edible for "us"', Falk argues, is the relativisation of their 'otherness' through a common denominator that puts us and them under the same umbrella; for example, as 'different kinds of human beings'. This 'food of the other' contradiction operated both ways in the post-war period in Australia.

The massive post-war influx of migrants and refugees from the social and economic chaos of Europe following the Second World War (between 1945 and 1975, citizenship was granted to over 960 000 of those we once called 'New Australians') brought with them more than their hard-to-pronounce names and impossible-to-understand languages. They brought their food cultures. They had no interest in what food we had here. And, at first, we had no interest in the food they brought with them. This initially caused friction. I collected many stories of these clashes of culinary culture for *Wogfood*.

This antagonism to otherness cut both ways. And it would appear that even as late as 1968, when a young Bill Marchetti arrived with his family at the Bonegilla migrant camp in north-eastern Victoria, the quality of the food had not improved: 'An army camp in a dustbowl ... The food was disgusting, unbelievable, army mess food. I remember walking past the kitchen and all you could smell was mutton, everything was mutton fat'.

But the membrane of separation between the two cuisines was beginning to dissolve. Rosa Matto's family arrived in the 1960s, and settled in the Adelaide suburb of Prospect which, unlike predominantly Italian

Thebarton, was mixed. The Mattos lived next door to a traditional Australian family. Rosa tells the story.

> My father hated the smell of lamb roasts – a lot
> of Italians do – I love them. On Sunday morning,
> all of Prospect would have this smell. My father's
> usual habit was to get up in the morning, open all
> the windows and go into the garden. On Sundays,
> he'd get up at the usual time, and shut all the doors
> and windows tight to keep the smell out. Our
> neighbours, the Greys – Aunty Bubs and Uncle
> Tom we'd call them – would always give me and
> my brother a roast potato which we thought was
> fabulous – my mother couldn't roast potatoes – but
> we weren't allowed to bring them inside, so we had
> to eat them in the garden.

Matto and her younger brother had made friends with the neighbours and had acquired a taste for their food. Rosa's father 'gave us the impression we [Italians] were better than anyone else when it seemed to me we weren't at all because all the things I longed for and wanted were all Australian and Anglo-Saxon'.

To go back to Falk, for the food of the others to be seen as edible, we have to shift our perception of the other so we see them in relation to ourselves. As Falk puts it, 'for example, as different kinds of human being'. Once Aunty Bubs and Uncle Tom were accepted as human beings, like Mama and Papa, albeit different, their food could be eaten. For others, it was too late: 'I'm too old', the elderly lady on the flight from Melbourne said, somewhat ruefully. She was too old for what I had called *Wogfood*, 'wog' being a word that a friend of mine told me she'd always thought stood for wine, olive oil and garlic. And so it does.

It is obvious that those who arrived here after the Second World War, preaching the gospel of wine, olive oil and garlic, did so to an empty church. That was about to change. But before we get to that change, I want to look at one anomaly.

The Chinese Paradox

Racism against Chinese immigrants to Australia began early. Its most obvious manifestation, the so-called White Australia policy (the Immigration Restriction Act), was enshrined in 1901 and was not repealed until 1958.

In 1937, two local officials in their report to the Board of Inquiry into Land and Land Industries of the Northern Territory declared that 'Our great ideal of a "White Australia" is worth living, striving and paying for'. But apart from the official slights, it was the daily indignities, the jeering of children, the petty restrictions that must have tried the patience of early Chinese Australians. Lo King Nam, whose ship's providoring business King Nam Jang, was based in The Rocks, told historian Shirley Fitzgerald that '[During the Second World War] ... all the Chinese were registered. We all had a badge with a number on it. To get rice, we had to go to a certain place to buy the rice and you had to show your registered number, otherwise you didn't get any'. Writing of the continued and highly publicised raids on the 'opium dens' of Chinatown in the late 1940s, Fitzgerald concludes that 'the negative outcome of the image of Chinatown was assured. Here was a place where the "otherness" of the Chinese was carefully and consciously linked to criminality and the underworld'.

How closely is this 'otherness' allied to visual appearance?

In her paper 'The Tyranny of Appearance', Carole Tan notes that it is easier for a new migrant of European appearance to be accepted as a 'real Australian' than a Chinese Australian whose family had been here for decades. 'The insidious effects of facialisation/racialisation on people of Chinese descent in Australia is referred to as "the tyranny of appearance" by William Yang', she wrote. Is this the source of the Chinese Paradox?

We rejected the Chinese, yet ate their food. To refer back, again, to Falk, the precondition for the 'other's' food to be conceived of as edible for 'us' is the 'relativisation' of their 'otherness'. How did we relativise the otherness of the Chinese? The Chinese, as a racial group, have been in Australia since the 1840s, when they were imported as indentured labourers to make up for the lack of workers after the end of transportation. And even earlier, as recorded by Annette Shun Wah and Greg Aitkin in *Banquet*. Mak Sai Ying (later John Shying), who arrived in 1817 or 1818, was the licensee of a public house called The Golden Lion in Parramatta – and the first Chinese landowner in Sydney.

In the 1850s, thousands arrived to mine the gold at Ballarat and Bendigo. The first Chinese restaurant, owned by Chinese butcher and eating-house owner John Alloo, opened on the goldfields in Ballarat around 1855, serving both Chinese and Australian meals. Since then, the Chinese restaurant has proliferated across the country to the point where, according to Shun Wah and Aitkin in 1999, there were 3000 of them. And we ate their food – albeit a heavily Westernised version of it – without fully accepting them as equal human beings. Chinese food wasn't restricted to eating out. The cookery editor of *New Idea* magazine, Anne Marshall, told journalist Cherry Ripe that in the 1970s when she published Chinese cookery supplements – which she did twice a year – they pushed weekly sales figures up by 50 000.

The complexity of our relationship with the Chinese is displayed in this anecdote told to Shun Wah and Aitkin by Chinese-Australian cattle breeder Peter Young.

One Tamworth restaurant had a special line in feeding drunks. It was the only restaurant open after the pubs shut. It seemed okay to the customers to play up in a Chinese restaurant, because they were Australian and the owners were Chinese, so they would be as obnoxious and abusive as possible. Funny the people who ran the place didn't seem to mind. The cook would come out with the chopper and threaten the customers throwing food. It was all part of the show. There was a kind of a stand-off. The drunks didn't want the Chinese restaurant to close down or there'd be nowhere to eat, and the Chinese didn't want the drunks to stop coming because they were a good source of money.

The Chinese perspective can be imagined. The *gweilo* (foreign devils, as they called us) were uncultured drunks, but they spent money. And they could be controlled by the appearance of the chopper, which confirmed for the drunken Australians the latent brutality of 'the heathen Chinese'. Settled to mutual advantage.

More others

But the Chinese weren't the only ethnic group to have restaurants here prior to 1945.

Like the early Italian restaurants in Sydney, those

of the Greeks, on the whole, served Australian food, hiding their own food or serving it only to Greek customers. Xenos Café (now restaurant) in Crows Nest first opened in 1969, and even then, on the conservative lower north shore 'if there was a whiff of garlic anywhere near the place', founder Peter Xenos told me, 'they wouldn't come in'.

They couldn't come in when the doors were locked.

As Lex Marinos recalls in his memoir of his grandfather, 'The second world existed when the shop was closed'. It was then that the local Greeks – other cafe owners, family and friends – would produce their own food. 'Lamb baked with garlic and oregano. Cabbage rolls. Spinach and beans in olive oil ... Food that we ate. Food that was never on the café menu. I thought it was our secret food.' But the other element of the Greek cafe was its introduction of American style – not just in food like the hamburger, and beverages like the soda fountain with its milk shakes and spider sodas – but in their streamlined art deco architecture. In country and city, the Greek cafe or milk bar provided a curious amalgam of Hellenic Australian and American culture. One-time waitress Mary McDermott reminiscences that 'Greek cafes were a little bit of Hollywood glamour, a little bit of American life ... That's why there were called the Niagara, the Monterey, the California and the Golden Gate'. Many of these Greek cafe owners had worked in America before coming to

Australia and had brought these design ideas with them.

The Hellenic Club in Elizabeth Street, Sydney – long known as the Purple Greeks because of the chairs – had dished out souvlaki and slow-cooked lamb on the bone since 1956. I ate there frequently with my mother in the early 1970s. It is now closed, their website says, temporarily, but the club has financially backed a modern Greek restaurant, Alpha, and that will probably be the new site for the club restaurant.

Another Sydney institution, this one still going, is Beppi's, an Italian restaurant in east Sydney, opened by Beppi and Norma Polese in 1956 (now, since the death of both Beppi and Norma, run by their son Mark). Beppi and Norma continued to run it as St James Café, an eating house for local Yugoslav workers, until 1960, when the restaurant turned Italian with the arrival of the chef Giuseppe Arena. Beppi introduced the diners of the day to such exotic foods as mussels (which he and Norma originally gathered themselves from the harbour), calamari and baby sardines. When I interviewed him for the book we wrote together (*Beppi: a life in three courses*) he told me that he had developed a technique for making his British customers try these foreign foods.

> I had a special way of doing this. When they asked me what it was they were being offered and I told them, they'd say, 'oh, I don't want that.' And because

I had that experience of being rejected when they
asked 'what is it?' I'd say 'you try it, then I tell you.'

This was the difference. The post-war wave of
migrants – perhaps because of their numbers, which
emboldened them – set out to convert their new neighbours to their food cultures. As one post-war Italian
migrant (who wants to remain nameless) said to me 'I
could never understand why the Australians thought
they were better than us when their food was shit!'.

And more of the same

On the other hand, there was one other group of
migrants who came in their thousands after 1945 who
could not be described as 'the other', and whose food
culture fitted right in. Indeed, for many of them, the
food they found in Australia was better than any they
had ever known: these were the British migrants who
arrived under the assisted passage schemes, the first
of which began in 1947. They were known, colloqui-
ally, as '10 pound Poms' because that is what they paid
per head for passage; at one time children under 18
came free. The desire was, post-Second World War,
and with the White Australia policy still in force, to
'stock' the country with good British stock. In 1946,
Arthur Calwell, first minister in the new Ministry of
Immigration, argued that for every foreign migrant

there will be 'ten people from the United Kingdom'. It didn't work out like that. By 1951, they settled for 50 per cent, which was only achieved in the 1960s, the peak years. The peak year was 1969, when almost 80 000 Britons migrated. Even so, about 1.5 million people emigrated to Australia from the United Kingdom between 1945 and 1982. So successfully did they merge that they have been called 'Australia's invisible migrants'. And, as such, they played no part in the multiculinary revolution that was taking place.

Yet another post-1945 influence on Australian food and food ways came directly from America with the soldiers on leave during the Second World War. Disparagingly described as 'overpaid, oversexed and over here' they brought with them cigarettes and chocolate bars – in short supply for the locals – and less obvious influences. Norman Lee was born in 1913 on the first floor of a building housing the tea and feng shui shop Live Craft Centre, which closed in 2017. Lee lived in and around Sydney's Chinatown for all but sixteen of his ninety-three years. Speaking of Dixon Street during the war he said:

> There were cook shops back then, they didn't call them restaurants. It was good food, genuine stuff. Most of the customers were Chinese, only the Australian drunks came then … When the Americans came over during World War II, they would bring their Australian girlfriends here. The girls liked the

food and brought their families, and after the war the Chinese restaurants began to boom.

Another American influence was coffee replacing tea after dinner. And although this coincided with the influence of Italian coffee, following the introduction of the first espresso machines, most of the coffee first drunk – and still drunk – in Australia was instant, product of the invasion of multinationals such as Nestlé: Nescafé first arrived in Australia in 1936. Domestically, the immediate post-war years in the *Australian Women's Weekly* saw a vogue for 'American' food sensations such as mixing sweet and savoury: Casserole tongue with raisin sauce and Pineapple Swiss liver are among the recipe suggestions.

Little is left in the domestic sphere of the predilection for American combinations and dishes, although some sources believe that the barbecue came here as an American invention. This is perhaps true of the word (originally a Spanish word, *barbacoa*, of Caribbean origin), but the idea of cooking outdoors was around long before. As noted already in this book, colonial Sydney loved to cook outdoors, something they couldn't do with such regularity in England. The *Australian National Dictionary* supports that assertion by not listing the word barbecue, and only giving 'barbie' (the earliest citation being 1976) – being of such cultural significance it has entered the language as 'a few snags short of a barbie' (meaning a not very bright individual).

Of greater importance than any American domestic dish was the gradual insinuation of convenience foods – cake mixes, packaged sauces, TV dinners – and supermarkets, undoubtedly as a result of our adoption of American marketing and retailing. The supermarket had enormous influence on the quality of the food that we ate, but little on the culture. As Symons wrote, 'supermarkets prefer longer life, which tends to lower quality … They prefer hard tomatoes and frozen chickens … food becomes cheap, so cheap that it's hardly worth eating'.

Cheapness, in a land without the criteria of an established regional or national food culture (excellence, faithfulness to tradition), often becomes the only criterion, just as the indicator of a good meal might be its size – a steak so big it hung over the edges of a plate was, and often still is, the measure of 'a good feed'. At this time in the USA large corporations like Kraft were buying up successful ethnic food companies. These corporations proceeded to sell, via the supermarkets, a mix of products and brands that included frozen and canned facsimiles of the foods from cultures which had begun to have some influence on Australian eating habits. But as far as both domestic and commercial cooking was concerned, these food cultures were kept in silos.

It was around this time that a new cuisine crept into the Australian lexicon: continental. In a 2003 *Quarterly Essay*, 'Made in England: Australia's British Inheritance', David Malouf wrote:

There was an intermediate period in the '50s when food was represented on menus all up and down the country by T-bone steak, often in the form of 'Steak and the Works' which in Brisbane at least meant spaghetti, chips and salad (nothing more transitional, surely, than this early version of fusion). The first clear move from an entrenched English style to a rather eclectic 'something different', half Italo-American, half Central European, and the first timid indication we were ready to break away and experiment.

That 'something different' fusion – seen mainly as a mixture of dishes other than the traditional British/Anglo-Celtic on menus of the period – was soon being called 'continental'. In the *Daily Mirror* in June 1963, in the column 'Goings on About Town', the pseudonymous Elizabeth Pitt (disclosure: my mother) described the food at Milano's as 'good continental food'. In an essay, 'Food as Nostalgia: eating the fifties and sixties', food historian Jean Duruz writes of a dessert 'served in a "continental" cafe in Newcastle in the early 1960s'. There were, as well, continental delis, continental cakes.

It was a grab-bag word meaning any foods from the cuisines of the 'New Australians' who had recently appeared, in droves, in our midst – French, Italian, Greek, Polish – who weren't, well, British. And in a way, the use of 'continental' implied, with absurd

geographic illogic, that Australia was in as close a relationship with continental Europe as England.

The word 'fusion' used by Malouf is not quite
correct. It was, rather, a jumble, as can be seen on
the two following menus from that period found in
the Ephemera Collection of the State Library of New
South Wales. Note the cultural naïveté of 'Spaghetti
Italienne':

*Dinner for State Parliamentarians NSW in the
Parliamentary Refreshment Room 9th October 1951*

Soup.
Potage Tyrolienne
Fish.
Fried Filet of Bream
Entrées.
Victoria Steaks and Onions
Tomato, Eggs and Bacon
Spaghetti Italienne
Cold Joints.
Oxford Brawn
Devon Sausage
York Ham
Corned silverside
Ox tongue
Pickled Pork
Hot Joints.
Roast beef au jus
Roast Seasoned Veal

Poultry.
Boiled Fowl and Ham, Parsley Sauce, Vegetables in Season
Sweets.
Baked Caramel custard
American Fruit Slice and Custard Sauce
Vanilla Ice Cream
Fruit
Cheese

Civic Luncheon
at the Oaks Hotel Albion Park
to commemorate
The Centenary of Local Government in the
Municipality of Shellharbour
Saturday 10th October 1959

Entrée:
Indian Curry and Rice
Curried Chicken and Rice

Main Course:
Cold Chicken
Cold Leg Ham
Roll and Butter   Mayonnaise
Salads in Season
Pickles   Nuts   Sweets

Enter the other

Sweets:
Fruit Salad and Ice Cream
Wine Trifle Jelly
Tea or Coffee

In the domestic sphere, there's very little evidence of American influence, but some for continental food. In the *Australian Women's Weekly* book *Picture Cookery*, published in 1952, apart from American meatburgers there is little change from the cookbooks of the 1930s and 1940s, with four mutton dishes and each of the chop dishes specifying either lamb or mutton. As was the case pre-war, there was an enormous number of cake, biscuit and sweet recipes: 67 pages of them. Other indications of the time included instructions to boil baby carrots for twenty minutes, and older specimens for an hour; and the advice that 'Poultry requires to be hung for at least 2–3 days after being killed'.

In a later but undated edition of *The Australian Women's Weekly Cookery Book* (dated circa 1956 by long-term food director, Pamela Clark) compiled under the guidance of food editor Leila Howard (nom de plume of Betty Dunleavy), there are clear signs of American and international – or perhaps continental – influence. Among the American dishes, recipes for Oysters Rockefeller and Chicken Maryland (complete with corn fritters and fried bananas) and Prawns jambalaya. It's interesting to note that the urban *Australian Women's Weekly* cookbook is so close, in many respects, to the rural CWA, even at this relatively late stage, and not as suggested earlier in a nostalgic way: this was the food that was being eaten.

In the impressively comprehensive but often culinarily naïve International Dishes section we find recipes from the following countries (numbers indicate how many recipes): Austria 7; Brazil 1; Ceylon 1; China 8; Czechoslovakia 1; Denmark 1; France 9; Germany 2; Greece 2; Holland 5; Hungary 3; India 1; Indonesia 4; Italy 1 (zabaglione); Japan 1; Norway 1; Pakistan 1; Russia 3; Spain 1; South Africa 1; Thailand 1.

Australia, today, is undoubtedly a multiculinary society, as reflected on our tables. We have learnt to identify the individual countries within the 'continental'.

Recipes

RECREATION OF THE MARINATO PRAWN ROLL

Makes 4 rolls

Here, I've combined two foods of others: my recreation of the wonderful prawn rolls from the Watsons Bay wharf on crisp white Vietnamese rolls which, in turn, are a legacy of the French occupation of Vietnam. As if that's not enough, the method of boiling prawns was gifted to me by a Spanish friend, thus even further compounding the multiculinarity.

16 medium-sized green prawns

300 g whole-egg mayonnaise (better if you make it yourself)

2 tbsp lemon juice

2 cloves garlic, crushed

2 tbsp chopped chives

Tabasco sauce to taste

salt and cracked black pepper

4 crisp, white banh mi rolls from a Vietnamese bakery

butter

watercress or sliced baby cos

1. Boil the prawns, but have ready a large bowl full of iced salted water. As soon as the prawns have cooked (turned pink) throw them in the iced salted water. Then drain and peel. (This method of boiling fresh green prawns ramps up their flavour.)
2. Place the mayonnaise, lemon juice, garlic, Tabasco and chives in a bowl, add prawns, salt, grind black pepper over the bowl and toss to coat the prawns.
3. Split the banh mi rolls, butter them, and fill with prawn mixture and either sliced cold cos lettuce or springs of watercress.

ROSA MATTO

....

LA RIBOLLITA

Serves 4 / Soak overnight

Rosa's recipe (with bay leaves) for Tuscan bean soup – a winter soup. Here, Rosa introduces the recipe:

Regarded by many as a quintessential cucina povera recipe from the area around Pisa, Firenze and Arezzo, it belongs, more broadly, to the tradizione invernali contadina toscana (Tuscan peasant winter tradition.) The name ribollita refers to the fact that housewives made this soup in vast quantities, usually on a Friday. Over the next few days, the soup would be reheated (ribollita/re-boiled) many times.

When you discuss la ribollita with una toscana, you will be told – amongst other essential details – that the il cavolo nero, essential to this dish, as is its less glamorous cousin, the savoy cabbage, must be picked after it has experienced the first winter frosts. In this way, the leaves are more tender.

250 g dried cannellini beans, soaked overnight (or use
  2 tins beans, drained, but I don't want to know about it)
3 tbsp extra virgin olive oil
1 onion, finely chopped
1 carrot, finely chopped
1 stalk celery, finely chopped
2 thin leeks, finely chopped

1–2 bay leaves (add these at your peril)

1–2 cloves garlic, mashed to a paste with salt

1 sprig of rosemary, finely chopped, plus extra

2 large potatoes, peeled and cut into small dice

200 g chard, or silverbeet or spinach

200 g savoy cabbage, cut into fine strips

200 g cavolo nero, taken off the spine and cut into strips

vegetable stock, if necessary

salt and pepper

1. Cook the beans in cold, unsalted water (I add a clove of garlic and a bay leaf) for about an hour or until the beans are tender. Do not throw out the water, this will become our 'stock'.

2. In a large, heavy-bottomed saucepan, heat the oil and sauté the onion, carrot, celery, leeks and bay leaves (if you dare). Allow them to soften completely without taking colour. Now add the garlic and rosemary and stir for a minute. Add the potatoes, chard, savoy and cavolo nero. Completely cover with stock or even water and allow to cook for an hour or so.

3. Meanwhile, mash half the beans to a chunky purée. At this point, add the mashed beans, whole beans and all their cooking liquid. Allow to simmer for another hour. Season well with salt and pepper and perhaps a little chilli, if you like.

4. Tradition dictates two things from this point. The soup should be allowed to 'season' overnight in the fridge and served the next day, heated and poured over toasted,

stale bread. Ideally, the bread should be the close-textured, saltless Tuscan variety but a good loaf of Italian bread will do. (I like to rub the hot toast with garlic but then I'm going to hell for sins committed against *la vera cucina toscana*.)

4. Garnish with fresh rosemary leaves and a drizzle of robust extra virgin olive oil. (Do not serve with parmesan unless you want to join me in that 'other place'.)

BEPPI POLESE

....

BEPPI'S CUTTLEFISH (SEPPIE)
Serves 2 as a main course, 4 as a starter

From Beppi Polese with John Newton, Beppi: a life in three courses, *Murdoch Books, Sydney, 2007.*

As Beppi explains in the introduction to the recipe: 'Once customers are familiar with calamari, they should have no trouble with seppie – which makes a lovely stew with peas'.

1. Clean 500 g of cuttlefish (remove the bone for your budgie, throw away the beak and the insides, and keep only the hood and the legs for yourself). Slice the hood into strips.

2. Brown 2 chopped onions for 5 minutes, then add rosemary and the sliced cuttlefish. After 10 minutes add chopped parsley, 3 crushed anchovies, a soupspoon of tomato paste and a can of tomatoes (or 3 chopped fresh tomatoes).

3. Add half a glass white wine and half a glass water or fish stock.
4. Simmer for 30 minutes until the sauce is reduced and the cuttlefish is tender.
5. Add 100 g fresh peas and cook for 5 more minutes. Serve with mashed potatoes or polenta.

10

THE MULTICULINARY
SOCIETY EMERGES

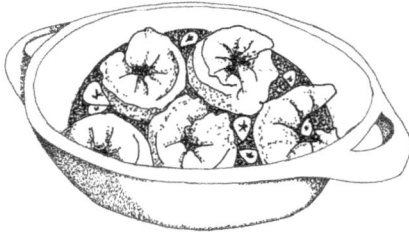

I wish to use the word 'multiculinarism' in a
strong sense – to point not just to the presence
of many cuisines but to the awareness of other
cuisines, to mutual comparison and influence. And
multiculinarism, in this sense, has the consequence
of raising our consciousness of food.

Anthony Corones, 'Multiculinarism and
the Emergence of Gastronomy'

Spanish food has provided me with any number of
intense gastronomic experiences, mostly pleasurable,
some palate-shaping. My first was in Sydney's Liverpool Street at a restaurant called the Costa Brava, in
the early 1970s.

It arrived at the table, innocently enough, in a tiny brown earthenware bowl, sizzling, straight from the oven. Prawns floating in olive oil and more garlic than my dear mother would have used in a year. And chillis, tiny, red and potent. The dish was listed as Garlic prawns or, as I later came to know it, Gambas al ajillo. Wow! Holy planets aligning! Where had this been all my life?

Later, having gone back many times for this devilishly heavenly dish, I developed a ritual for eating it. First, I dipped bread into the sizzling oil and mopped it up with as much chopped garlic as possible, which also helped cool the oil. Then I ate the prawns which, far from being overwhelmed by the garlic, were catapulted to another flavour level. And then if I was still feeling bold, I'd bite into one of the tiny chillis – and reach immediately for the water carafe.

Here the garlic was used, not as the *Australian Women's Weekly* suggested in 1983, 'with discretion', but as an assault on the senses the like of which I had never experienced. Much later, I read that the celebrated Spanish writer Julio Camba said that garlic was the axis of Spanish cuisine. After my first trip to Spain, I was able to verify that first hand. For me that dish heralded the beginning of the post-garlic (PG) epoch, the epoch of big flavour, the end of plain – or, if you prefer, bland. All around me, there were monumental changes taking place on the Australian table.

In a peevish but not entirely inaccurate attack on British food, French historian Jean-Louis Flandrin said of the British diet that it passed directly 'from Mediaeval barbarity to industrial decadence'. If that was the case, then the Australian diet passed from eating to fill the belly to eating for pleasure, from eating in badly to eating out well, all the way to fully fledged, joyfully promiscuous multiculinarism within the space of a decade, from the 1960s to the 1970s.

In that decade, as a nation, Australians woke up to food.

It moved from the edge of our consciousness, from being something that was, for the majority, prepared by the 'little woman' or an anonymous chef in the kitchen (remember the fat bloke in the grubby white jacket?), to a source of curiosity, pleasure and status. This change did not happen on the stroke of midnight 1969, nor did it happen across the country. At first, it was a big city revolution – rural Australia had to wait a decade or so.

The 1970s was a decade of astonishing economic, political, social and technological change. Snapshot. There was Germaine Greer on the front page of *The Weekend Australian* of 16 January 1972, 'bra-less and busty' as described by the journalist (some things never change, journalistic prurience being one of them), launching her book *The Female Eunuch* in Australia. In the same issue a story on Nixon's imminent visit to China. Another headlined, 'Eton Head defends pot and permissive society'. By December of that year there would be a radically new government led by Gough Whitlam, the first Labor government for twenty-three years.

Among many reforms in this period was the formal abolition of the White Australia policy in 1973, in 'colourful' Al Grassby's time as the Minister for Immigration. (The Spanish-Irish Grassby wore what were seen by the conservatively dressed men of the 1970s as garish ties and shirts, and was criticised and lampooned for doing so.) Grassby became the champion of multiculturalism after delivering a speech, *A Multi-Cultural Society for the Future*, on 11 August 1973. This was a manifesto presented as a basis for migrant settlement, welfare and social-cultural policy, and went against prevailing public opinion. Contemporary opinion polls suggested that about 90 per cent of Australians were opposed to multicultural ideas. Hand in hand with this commitment to multiculturalism goes a commitment to multiculinarism because, as Corones writes, 'cuisine cannot be separated from culture' – and vice versa.

Another crucial element in this cultural and economic mix was the extraordinary rise in income and affluence in the post-war boom. Between June 1960 and June 1970, according to the Australian Bureau of Statistics (all figures quoted here are from the ABS), gross disposable income rose by an astonishing 700 per cent. This is the background against which Australian society went through major social changes and saw the birth of the consumer society. It was the side effects of increased spending power that had the greatest effect on our eating habits.

I have already quoted Michael Freeman writing on high cuisine in China during the Sung Dynasty, proposing that such a cuisine 'requires a sizeable corps of critical, adventuresome eaters, not bound by the tastes of their native region and willing to try unfamiliar food'. In the 1970s, all but one of those criteria were present among urban Australians, who were beginning to eat out regularly. The missing attribute was 'critical', and that was about to be redressed.

In *Cooking, Cuisine and Class*, Jack Goody writes that the cuisines of the major societies of Europe and Asia were shaped firstly, by those societies practising intensive forms of agriculture and secondly, by the employment of writing for a number of purposes – not just economic and administrative, but literary and 'practical'. I'd like to suggest a 1970s Australian variation on the Goody duality of plough and pen: jumbo jet and typewriter. In *Wogfood*, I quote chef Bill Marchetti as saying: 'My big hero in this story is the Boeing 747. All of a sudden everybody could afford to get on a plane and fly to wherever they wanted and taste the food there'.

'Australians were curious and they wanted to travel'

The first Boeing 747-238B, popularly named the jumbo jet, went into service in Australia for Qantas in September 1971. And jump on jumbos we did, going to discover the other, coming home with a broadened perspective on food and wine. And going not just to Europe. In her memoir, Australian chef Stephanie Alexander writes of her trip to Bali: 'Roadside stalls sold the delectable *babi guling* (roast suckling pig) to locals – and I was quick to taste it too, carrying my portions away inside folded banana leaves'.

It was around this time that I also took my first trip out of the country, also to Bali, and discovered that kitchens were not all white-tiled and scrubbed clean, and that durian fruit smelt foul and tasted sublime. So many of us were making that pilgrimage that, by 1984, the band Redgum could have a hit song with 'I've Been to Bali Too'.

In his memoir, Australian chef Tony Bilson writes, 'Australia in the 1970s was ready for change … Australians were curious and they wanted to travel'. Bilson, with his then partner Gay, made a first trip to France in 1976, visiting, with introductions, some of the finest restaurants. They were just three of the eight million (out of a population of 13.5 million) short-term resident departures recorded in the 1970s: that eight million also included those who departed more than once.

But the majority were Australians leaving for the first time, to smell, taste, sip and savour the planet and arrive back home hungry. Hungry for more of what they had tasted. In addition to those travelling in comfort, there were also those who took off on the 'hippie trail' overland to Europe, which meant passing through Asia and the Middle East, where they also sampled the cuisines. In this way, we were, from quite early on, softened up for multiculinarism.

From beer-swilling barbarians to winos

The other great change on the Australian table that began to take effect in the 1970s was the appearance of table wine – and for much the same reasons as the culinary changes. The first known record of grapes having been planted in Australia comes from Watkin Tench, who wrote that on 24 January 1791, 'two bunches of grapes were cut in the Governor's garden from cuttings of vines brought three years before from the Cape of Good Hope'. Like most early plantings, they didn't thrive. The first commercial vineyard was planted by John Macarthur at his property Camden Park, which played a vital role in the fledgling wine industry via its importation and distribution of vine cuttings throughout New South Wales and the Barossa Valley in South Australia. By 1853, Camden Park listed some 33 grape varieties for sale. However, table wine remained a minority drink until the PG seventies.

It was immigrants from Switzerland and Germany who were responsible for the early growth of the Australian wine industry, particularly in the southern regions of the country, in areas such as the Barossa in South Australia and the Yarra Valley in Victoria. By the turn of the nineteenth century there were vineyards in many of today's viticulture areas, but it's fair to say that right up until the 1960s the majority of Australians looked on wine as 'plonk'.

This was about to change: through the influence and enthusiasm of wine lovers like Melbourne's Jimmy Watson, Sydney's JK 'Johnny' Walker, surgeon and winemaker Max Lake, art dealer and wine judge Rudy Komon, and English-born wine educator Len Evans. With their help and guidance, Australians slowly – then rapidly – transformed from what Komon labelled 'beer-swilling bloody barbarians' into enthusiastic wine drinkers.

When Evans joined the Australian Wine Bureau in 1965 as its first director, Australians were drinking 'just over five bottles per head per annum of which four were fortified', the fortified being what was known as 'fourpenny dark' cheap Australian port, the preferred beverage of impoverished drinkers. By 2015, Australians were consuming 23.8 litres of wine per capita.

Developing our *Essengeist*

We returned from our travels and began eating – and drinking – out, partly to rediscover the food and wine we had encountered. The first restaurant guides and reviews began to appear. And, for the home, thanks largely to Charmaine Solomon's million-copy-selling *The Complete Asian Cookbook*, we bought woks in their thousands.

It was also the decade when food and cooking shows first appeared on our televisions. Graham Kerr's *The Galloping Gourmet*, produced in Canada, ran on Australian television from 1969 to 1971. For a viewing public who had most likely never heard of, let alone tasted, such dishes, he cooked Huevos rancheros, Jamaican pepper pot and Gâteau St Honoré.

Bernard King's pioneering *King's Kitchen* began in 1972, finishing in 1983. King was a flamboyant showman who, according to his obituary, 'pioneered television advertorials in Australia, doing whatever it took to promote sponsor-supplied products, even if it meant cooking a whole fish in saccharine-sweetened grapefruit-flavoured soft drink'. He wasn't the last to take the tasty dollar.

Although Kerr and King and television food shows generally didn't reach the audience numbers and obsessive following of the early 2000s, it was then that we began to develop our distinctive Australian *Essengeist* – a way of eating – browsing across cuisines both at home and out. *Essengeist* is a word that I have coined to describe our 'style' of eating. I borrowed it from the German word *Zeitgeist*, meaning the defining spirit or mood of a particular period of history as shown by the ideas and beliefs of the time, *zeit* meaning time and *geist*, spirit. I checked this coinage with a German-speaking friend and he said it would make perfect sense to a German.

Our *Essengeist*, eating spirit, describes our way of eating – across many cultures – with everything borrowed and nothing created or transmitted. It is what we have instead of a food culture, what I have called mongrel cuisine.

In a few restaurants of the 1970s – at Mietta's, Hermann Schneider's Two Faces, Cheong Liew's Neddy's, and others – there was an *Essengeist*-like cross-cultural blending of ingredients and techniques.

At Mietta's in Brunswick Street, North Fitzroy, in 1974, restaurateurs Mietta O'Donnell and Tony Knox introduced what was most likely the first mixed menu in Australia. One menu grouped together the following dishes, side by side.

Old English (eg Saffron and honey chicken, Gammon bacon)
Classic Escoffier (eg Fricadelles, Blanquette de veau)
Italian (eg Osso buco, Bollito misto)
Cantonese (eg Steamed chicken and Chinese sausage, Hoi sin pork, Beef stir fry with oyster sauce Land onions) Indian (eg Spiced mushrooms, Lamb shanks, Vindaloo)

Elizabeth David provincial (soups and desserts mainly)
Middle Eastern (eg B'stilla and Muhallabia)

At his South Yarra restaurant Two Faces (1960–87), German-born chef Hermann Schneider was the first in Australia to use Chinese vegetables – bok choy, snow peas, and soups with Chinese soup melons – in a European context.

In Adelaide, Chinese-Malaysian chef Cheong Liew was cooking food at Neddy's which he said, in his book *My Food*, drew on experiences 'from my life and work in Greek, Indian, South East Asian, French and Chinese kitchens. Dishes from that time and place included Warm Salad of Moreton Bay Bugs with Toasted Salted Fish and Rhubarb Tart with Clove Cream and Chocolate Figs'.

This bold experimentation was to become our only claim to a cuisine, later dubbed Modern Australian or Mod Oz, a cuisine I'll analyse in a later chapter. But there were other forces helping shape the way we ate in the 1970s.

Recipes

....

GARLIC PRAWNS (GAMBAS AL AJILLO)

Serves 4 as a large main, or 8 as a starter

This was the dish that marked entry into PG Australia and my initiation into a Spanish obsession, as described by Spanish novelist Julio Camba: 'Garlic and olive oil are a national vice, used by the Spanish to frighten off witches and foreigners'. Sadly, I have been unable to find the original Costa Brava recipe and so, rather than attempt a poor copy, I have used the same ingredients but cooked them in my own way. The amount of garlic and chilli I leave up to you – I have indicated minimums.

150 ml extra virgin olive oil (preferably Spanish)

1 head garlic, cloves sliced thinly

1 kg medium-sized sea-fresh green (raw) prawns, sprinkled with
     coarse salt and left for 15 minutes

4 bird's-eye chillis, sliced finely, seeds removed (unless you
     want extra heat)

a good handful of finely chopped flatleaf parsley

1. Heat the oil in a large heavy pan or wok. Your oil needs to be hot, but not quite smoking. Speed is of the essence with this dish.
2. Add the garlic. Stir well and quickly. Do not allow to brown.
3. Add the prawns. Keep stirring. Everything should be cooking quickly, the oil bubbling.

4. At the exact moment that the prawns are cooked (a
    matter of judgment: they are now pink and still resist
    the teeth – about 4 minutes over a hot flame), turn off
    the flame, throw in the parsley, spoon it through, and
    transport to the table at a run.

To serve
To be eaten instantly, from small bowls, with plenty of the oil
and garlic and chunks of crusty bread for mopping up.
Better have a second kilogram of prawns handy to avoid riots
when the first lot are finished.

CHRIS MANFIELD

....

TEA-SMOKED YELLOWFIN TUNA WITH SWEET AND SOUR CUCUMBER AND FENNEL

Serves 6

*Chris Manfield has for many years been one of our boldest,
sauciest (and I don't mean tomato) and most innovative chefs.
She is a spice mistress, and while she no longer has a restaurant
she writes (eight books so far), teaches and leads tours to her
beloved India and beyond.*

*The best way to smoke your eggplants is over a flame, either
on the barbecue or directly on the stove top. At a certain point
they'll yield a smokey flavour.*

6 x 120 g pieces of belly tuna, 2 cm thick
2 continental cucumbers

1 fennel bulb, sliced into very fine rounds

2 small eggplants, smoked, peeled and sliced

1 tbsp red onion, finely diced

2 tbsp pickled ginger, drained and sliced into fine julienne

2 tsp sweet basil leaves, sliced finely

2 red radishes, sliced into fine julienne

12 small radicchio leaves

18 witloof leaves

Tea and spice smoking mixture
1 tbsp Chinese Oolong tea leaves

1 tbsp Chinese jasmine tea

2 pieces dried tangerine peel, broken up

2 tbsp raw jasmine rice

2 tbsp brown sugar

3 whole star anise

2 tsp Sichuan peppercorns

3 pieces cassia bark

Sweet and sour dressing
100 ml vegetable oil

pinch dried chilli flakes

2 small garlic cloves, sliced finely

60 ml light soy sauce

100 ml cider vinegar

150 ml sugar syrup

1. To make the tea and spice smoking mix, combine the ingredients.

2. To make the dressing, heat the oil in a saucepan with the chilli flakes and garlic over low heat until the garlic becomes golden but does not burn. Add the soy sauce, vinegar and sugar syrup and bring to the boil. Remove from heat, allow to cool, then strain and store in the refrigerator until ready to use.

3. To smoke the tuna, line a large wok with aluminium foil and place over high flame or heat. Lay a sheet of baking paper across a steamer tray that fits neatly into the wok. Be sure to leave some air holes along the sides of the tray when putting in the paper, or the smoking will not be as effective.

4. Lay the tuna pieces over the paper, making sure they do not touch. It may be necessary to do this process in 2 batches to ensure even smoking.

5. Sprinkle the tea mixture over the base of the hot wok. When it starts to seriously smoke and begins to burn at the edges, place the steamer tray over it and cover with a tightly fitting lid. This must be done under an effective exhaust vent or you will smoke and smell the place out.

6. Smoke for 4 minutes, take off lid and turn the fish over and replace lid. Smoke for another 2 minutes, then remove the tray immediately from the heat. Fold the burnt foil over on itself and discard outside straight away. Throw these burnt offerings in the bin when they have cooled down.

7. Take the tuna off the tray and allow to cool slightly, so that it is cool enough to handle.

8. Slice the tuna, going with the grain. It should be cooked on the outside and very pink and rare in the centre. Smoking for too long produces a bitter, high tannin taste in the fish.

9. Peel the cucumbers and shave into long strips with the peeler, discarding the core of seeds.

10. Pickle the cucumber shavings and the fennel slices in half the sweet and sour dressing for 3 minutes only – any longer and the cucumber will start to disintegrate.

11. Put the tuna into the remaining warm sweet and sour dressing with the smoked eggplant and marinate for 1 minute. Add the remaining ingredients to the cucumber, as well as the tuna and eggplant, mix thoroughly to ensure even distribution, and pile carefully onto serving plates. Serve immediately.

11

CRITICS AND DICTATORS

Australians, who have only comparatively recently
become converted to the delights of the table are
still wandering in a gastronomic no-man's land.

Margaret Jones, *Sydney Morning Herald*, 1970

Prior to the 1970s, apart from recipe books, there was
very little writing about food. Restaurant reviews, such
as they were, were short puff pieces in newspapers to
accompany advertising, the earliest form of advertorial.

One of the notable exceptions to this lack of culinary literature was the curious *Oh for a French Wife* by
Ted Moloney and Deke Coleman, with illustrations
by George Molnar, first published in 1952. While not
quite the Antipodean Brillat-Savarin, it was a light-
hearted if determinedly Gallic attempt at imparting
recipes (supplied by four French wives), accompanied
by Lloyd Ring 'Deke' Coleman's essays, such as 'How

Can You Cook with Air?', touching on the importance of air to the cooking of omelettes; the 'Philosophy of Frying'; and 'Observations on the Sense of Taste'. That they read more like advertising copy than serious gastronomic analysis was because Coleman was in his working life managing director of the J Walter Thompson advertising agency. His coauthor, Ted Moloney, also worked for J Walter Thompson.

It is perhaps not entirely coincidental that so many restaurant critics and writers on food worked in advertising. These include not only Moloney but also Margaret Fulton, who had worked at J Walter Thompson with Moloney and Coleman (who hired her), Leo Schofield, Terry Durack, Jill Dupleix and this writer. Much of the work of advertising is carried out over lunch, and for many the food became more important and interesting than the work.

By the 1970s, the media were beginning to take notice of what the *Sydney Morning Herald* called, in a story by Margaret Jones, 'The Dining Out Boom'. This story analyses the genesis of and the possible directions being taken by this phenomenon of the times. 'The dining out boom', Jones wrote, 'is probably the biggest thing which has happened to Australia recently outside uranium shares'. To support this contention she provided figures (unsourced but probably from the Restaurateur's Association, whose chairman, Jacob Gobes, she quotes in the story). In New South Wales in 1950, there were 99 licensed restaurants; in 1960, 230; and in

1970, 551, of which 359 were in the metropolitan area. If reliable, those figures represent a significant 420 per cent increase in just twenty years.

Jones was a reputable journalist, but her figures are difficult to verify. Statistics from the industry peak body, the Restaurant & Catering Industry Association of Australia, don't go far enough back. By comparison, in 'Feeding the Public Stomach: dining out in the 1970s with restaurant critic Leo Schofield' Melissa Harper writes that 'at the beginning of the decade (the 1970s), Australia had 1000 licensed restaurants and by its close that figure had climbed to over 3000'.

Jones wrote that the future of the restaurant business in Australia depended on whether we 'go European' – lingering over the meal with wine – or 'go American' – fast food, self-service, no frills. This depended much on the young, who preferred self-service, simple menus and fast eating. As evidence of what was then 'fast eating' she cited the Cahills Brass Rail chain of restaurant wine bars. Cahills used to be, she writes, 'quiet places full of ladies in flowered hats eating ice cream cake served by haughty waitresses in black dresses'. The chain changed dramatically to themed self-service in the 1960s, and by 1970 its restaurants were flourishing. By the end of the 1980s, Cahills had disappeared. A significant event in the tussle between American and European was the opening in 1971 of the first McDonald's in Australia, in Yagoona. This dichotomy – fast or slow, European or American – continues today: we only need look at the alarming proliferation of hamburger joints as I write this in 2018.

Jones raises the issue of class in the development of dining-out culture by reporting that while 'Most of the credit for the gastronomic revolution must go to the migrants, who introduced the native-born to a whole alphabet of delights, from avocados to zabaglione ... Some of the credit for changing the habits of the working-man is also claimed by the clubs'. She quotes the executive director of the Registered Clubs Association, Jerry Shaw, as saying: 'They taught him [the club member] to drink wine and to look for an entrée before his main course'. Clubs drew their members from a different socio-economic level to that of the more expensive restaurants. And it is true that the 1970s saw the dawn of the democratisation of Australian dining. Before the Second World War and through the 1950s, eating out was the preserve of the middle and upper classes.

In 1996, I interviewed Lina Holderegger (then eighty-six years old), who had been the owner of The Chalet restaurant in Circular Quay – which opened in 1948 and closed in 1979 – and also her long-term employee Trixie Rule. When asked about the clientele, Rule said they were made up of 'woolbuyers, shipping people, bank people, a fairly good class of people'. Customers included stockbroker Sir Reginald Reed and Marcel and Nola Dekyvere, then the leading lights of 'Sydney society'. Rule told a story that epitomised the social rules at the time.

One night this fellow banged on the door and he
was like a hobo and he said I want to eat here, and
I said I'm terribly sorry you can't, we're booked up.
I said if you're coming here you have to book a table
and have a collar and tie and a suit. One night there
was a table booked for one. The door opened and in
walked this fellow. With a suit and a collar and tie.
He ate a lot and we thought my goodness he's not
going to pay, but he came up to the counter and paid
and said I've never had such a delightful meal. He
never came back again.

Rule then went on to recount that 'when Barry
Humphries was in Sydney every night he'd come in
with his old mac on'. The dress code was flexible.

By the mid-1950s, writes Margaret Fulton, 'Australians were becoming food conscious. With post-war
travel the well-heeled were able to eat in restaurants
like the Tour d'Argent in Paris ... in London's Savoy
or New York's Plaza'. By the 1970s, the not-so-well-
heeled could afford – and were being encouraged – to
eat in a rapidly growing number of restaurants by a
fledgling corps of critics. Leo Schofield's guide *Eating
Out in Sydney, 1976*, for example, lists over 160, all of
them considered by this Petronius of the public palate
to be good enough to review.

The clash of the critics

In the introduction to his *Eating Out in Sydney, 1976* Leo Schofield wrote: 'Avoid the cliché dishes. Disparage the garlic prawn. Sniff at steak. Hiss and boo the Idaho potato and the Forbidden apple'. It is vintage early Schofield, elitist and proscriptive and educational. Forbidden apple was an industrial dessert served by most Italian restaurants at the time, and the 'Idaho potato', which was not from Idaho, was a crisp-skinned baked potato, often filled with sour cream.

It was a menu cliché at the time. Elitist he may have been, but we needed him.

There is no doubt that the reviewers had an enormous influence on what we ate, how we ate it and how we used restaurants. Until the advent of Schofield, Sam Orr (*nom de plat* of journalist Richard Beckett), Len Evans and Peter Smark, the only experience of eating out for most Australians would have been the local Chinese, the Greek cafe and post-war 'chophouses' such as the New York in Kellett Street, Kings Cross. From 1953 until it closed in 2010, the New York fed its clientele – comprising mainly locals without kitchens and transients in boarding houses – the kind of food they would have been used to at home. In other words, it was eating out not for pleasure but for sustenance.

In 2006, I reviewed the New York restaurant for the *Sydney Morning Herald*. One of my companions for the meal was ex-restaurateur Gay Bilson. On the way out, she said: 'I walked down Oxford Street, Paddington, today. It occurred to me that all the shops and cafes and restaurants were designed for the same people. This place', she indicated the New York, 'is for everybody else. I hope your story doesn't ruin it for them'. It didn't, but nevertheless, it closed a few years later – 'everybody else' had moved out of the inner city.

The critics heralded the new age of restaurants as entertainment, and taught us that there is more to the restaurant than sitting at a table and ordering a meal. They taught us the rules. The restaurant is one of the most complex and difficult of our public spaces, and it was the restaurant critic who guided the trainee restaurant-users of the 1970s through its nuances of manners, behaviour and conduct. And Australians took their advice seriously – sometimes too seriously.

This was the case even as late as 1993, as I discovered when I reviewed a new restaurant in Bondi. As was my habit, I rang the chef to discuss the meal I had eaten with him. He pleaded with me not to review him. When I asked why, he told me: 'because your readers will come waving your review, demanding to have what you had which will probably be out of season, swamp me for three months and I'll have to hire staff, then they'll go, never to return'.

The dangers of a review were not all directed one way. Reviewers could close restaurants as well as fill them. Writing in the *Sydney Morning Herald* in 1979, Marie Toshack claimed that Leo Schofield 'had his

life threatened' after one review and that 'he took the
threat seriously enough to go overseas till the temperature cooled'. Not quite, Schofield told me. 'I did have
a death threat but certainly didn't take off overseas.
Just didn't visit that particular restaurant, now gone, in
Crown Street.'

Beginning in the 1970s, restaurant food, the restaurants themselves and the conversation around them
generated by the critics became important elements in
the urban social mix. More than that, in part due to
our increasing familiarity with the restaurants and their
food, they (the critics) became important contributors
to what I have already called our *Essengeist* and the move
towards an Australian style of cooking. Two critics in
particular tell the story of that time. Their 'literary'
personae could not be more contradictory: the suave
opera buff adman Leo Schofield and the garrulous, bib-
ulous journalist Sam Orr.

Leo Orr Sam, take your pick

Schofield, as previously noted, worked in advertis-
ing, although he had served briefly as a cadet at the
Sydney Morning Herald in the 1950s. His first review, for
Café Florentino in Melbourne, was published in *The
Sunday Australian* on 23 May 1971. This new career
came about because he was the creative director at the
Jackson Wain advertising agency in Sydney and

The Australian was one of his clients. When the paper decided to publish a Sunday edition, Schofield was asked by the editor to contribute a restaurant column. It was not the first. In 1966 the *Sun-Herald* and the *Financial Review* had both instigated food pages, and Ted Moloney occasionally wrote restaurant reviews for them. Schofield, because of his engaging and entertaining writing style, was immediately popular. From 1984 he wrote restaurant reviews and the column 'Short Black' (originally written by Jenna Price) in the *Good Living* section of that paper. Also in 1984, Schofield established the *Sydney Morning Herald Good Food Guide* with coeditors David Dale and Jenna Price, and remained editor until the ninth edition was published in 1993.

Schofield was the food critic that Sydney needed. While Sydney was gradually overtaking Melbourne as the financial capital of Australia, Melbourne was the more sophisticated and 'cosmopolitan' city (given its earlier commercial start, with the discovery of gold in the 1850s and the subsequent property boom, and then – much later – the mining boom of the late 1960s). Schofield, wrote Melissa Harper in 'Feeding the Public Stomach', 'saw his role as a pedagogical one … to inform readers about good places to eat, to warn them about bad and indifferent restaurants, to encourage diners to broaden their food education, to try new cuisines and to define and explain good (food) taste'.

He not only exposed readers to his own preferences – for vegetables served separately, for example

– but along the way educated them on how and what to eat. Although his first reviews were self-indulgent and self-aggrandising, they did evolve, over time, to become genuinely informative. At the earlier self-indulgent end, on 21 May 1972 in *The Sunday Australian* he told his readers: 'Le Trianon has been around for a long time. Madame Angela Rezzonico opened the place in 1958 and what a shock to Sydney's system it was'. Schofield wrote, in his review, that 'The idea of eating in pleasant, well-decorated surroundings obviously hadn't occurred to anyone since 1770'. Readers were then given the name of the new manager, Andre Villnave (but not the chef), after a digression on recent changes in Kings Cross. The restaurant was at first empty but for Schofield and his female companion, who regaled him with stories about her past husbands. In between this chatter his readers learnt a little about the food – but not a lot. He chose Ouefs sur le plat Meyerbeer because he is 'an opera nut', even though Meyerbeer is not his favourite composer – much on Meyerbeer – and it was a disappointing dish. He concludes: 'we folded our serviettes like the Arabs and crept away ...'.

By 1976, in a review for Le Catalan in *Eating Out in Sydney*, he has begun the job of teaching his readers: 'the openers, at the time of writing, included a splendid Fenouil au Jambon (layers of fennel and ham in a creamy sauce baked in white Pillivuyt bowls'. This at a time when fennel would have been difficult to find and ham would have been served, more often than not, in a tomato and iceberg lettuce salad, and Pillivuyt bowls only just in the stores. In the notes at the front of that guide, under the heading SPECIALTIES, he writes:

> Nothing is more depressing for an enterprising chef or restaurant proprietor who has evolved a series of interesting house specialties, than to find customer after customer ignoring them and ordering an unimaginative meal of oysters, steak and cheese-cake which could be as easily prepared at home. In this guide we have listed the specialties of each restaurant, and we urge customers to try them. Only if diners are adventurous in their eating can we foster better culinary standards in Australian restaurants.

He was on a crusade, dragging the people of Sydney along with him. His credo, spelt out in the first edition of *Eating Out in Sydney* in 1974 (which sold out), was that 'honest food presented with style in agreeable surroundings … simplicity of preparation and presentation, value for money and freshness are of prime importance'. As Harper wrote: 'His reviews produced an influential discourse about restaurant dining, about where and what to eat and why it mattered, and played an important role in fostering a community of gourmets'. And, I would argue, eventually lifted the restaurant game. If the customers were being educated, the restaurants could not get away with inferior food and service. But there's more than one way to review public food.

The first restaurant review by Sam Orr appeared in *Nation Review*, an iconoclastic and irreverent but predominantly political journal, on 21 March 1971 (two months before Schofield's first review in *The Sunday Australian*). In achieving the balance between cogent criticism and straight-out entertainment, Orr invariably opted for the latter – mixed in with a large splodge of vulgarity. He was, as described by Richard Walsh in *Ferretabilia* – his compilation of articles from the *Nation Review* after its demise (the slogan for the paper was 'lean and nosy like a ferret) – a 'big bluff bearded man, always handsomely turned out in a well-tailored suit, occasionally boasting a flamboyant handkerchief in the breast pocket'.

Beckett/Orr gave us the restaurant as a site for bad behaviour, rarely good food, and always copious quantities of alcohol. His first offering, a review of a Russian restaurant called Berioska (in Melbourne, where the *Nation Review* was published), was described by Richard Walsh as not yet showing signs of his 'rumbustious persona'. It does, however, display his characteristically opinionated aggression by stating that the only two cuisines that matter are French and Chinese, followed by: 'It is an undisputed truism that most of Melbourne's restaurants are fairly bad' and that is why 'it is with a feeling of distaste that I have embarked on this, a plain man's guide to Melbourne restaurants'.

The 'guide' eventually spread to Sydney, but the choleric copy did not abate. By 19 April 1973, Orr had become, in a letter to the editor, 'Orrful Sam' – and reading the offending review of Melbourne's Bistro Alexander it is easy to see why. In a style much later made popular by London's AA Gill, Orr spent 75 per cent of the review on other topics – the state of restaurant criticism and food writing in Australia for example – before launching into an excoriation of everything about the restaurant: from the 'totally tasteless dish of overcooked and what appeared to be thawed Taiwan shrimp', which on second thoughts he decided 'tasted like cardboard', to 'jam rolls in various stages of disintegration, all topped with foam cream'.

Beppi's was the subject of a typically scathing and violent review from Sam Orr in the early 1970s, in which he lashed out at the food, the service and anything else that got in his way. A careful reading of this curiously dissenting opinion on a much-loved restaurant of the time uncovers a possible reason. Mr Beckett was known to like a drink, and it was not unknown for him – by his own admission – to over-imbibe while he was eating a meal in a restaurant that he was reviewing. This appears to have been the case at Beppi's. 'For some reason', he wrote, 'the waiters decided I was not drinking wine and wouldn't give me any and my business manager had to snatch the wine bottle off an adjacent table to refill the glasses'. It is easy to reconstruct the ugly scene. An increasingly tired and emotional diner's incessant demands for wine are politely ignored by the perennially professional waiters at Beppi's – attempts at persuading him to drink water prove useless – until his male companion – also perhaps the worse for wear – grabs a bottle of wine from diners at an adjacent table (it's a wonder a brawl didn't break out) and they proceed to guzzle it. This would not have been well received, and as a form of retribution he lashes out in a review headlined:

BEPPI CAN STUFF HIS ARTICHOKES.

Beppi framed the review, and hung it under the Gold Fork award he had recently received with the added instruction:

WE SAY – SAM ORR CAN STUFF HIS OWN!

While Schofield was teaching us about new foods, new ingredients and how to behave properly in these new spaces, Orr was appealing to our larrikin instincts and confirming for us that most of them were second rate and service was, invariably, 'abominable'. They balanced each other out: Schofield the sophisticate we wished we were; and Orr the barbarian we feared we were – and secretly relished. We were in transition. But these weren't the only two reviewers at this time, only the most read and noticed.

In an article, 'Writing About Food', in *Quadrant* in 1977, the novelist and gastronome Marion Halligan reviewed the reviewers – Moloney, Schofield, Johnny Walker, Smark and Orr – and found them wanting. While acknowledging that 'Several decades ago, this article could not have been written', Halligan asks: 'Where is our Brillat-Savarin, our Carême, our Dumas – the philosopher, the cook, the man of letters to provide us with this food for thought? The answer is, he doesn't exist'. Halligan goes on to compare the domestic crop unfavourably with French critics like Robert J Courtine. While her criticism of the critics is justified, the comparison of French criticism with the brash, new, feeling-their-way-in-a-new-environment Australians is a little premature. For all their faults, they were performing a service: familiarising us with what would become a vital element in the development of our *Essengeist*. But she did point out one curious omission from these first attempts at restaurant criticism.

'A great chef', Halligan writes, 'is one who has made his dishes so much the expression of his own individuality that they are recognisable anywhere as his'. To illustrate this, she quotes from a restaurant review in the French women's magazine *Elle*, whose 'pretensions to intellectuality are very mild ... yet it runs a critical ... restaurant column of real seriousness'. The review discusses the career and cuisine of a chef (Bernard Loiseau), which 'encapsulates what is lacking in Australian food writing ... Notice how it places the chef ... His teachers, his previous experience...'. In hardly any of the early reviews of Australian restaurants, either in newspapers or guides, were the chefs mentioned by name. They were still at this time, and on the whole, anonymous toilers in the hidden 'empire of smoke'. Indeed, it was not until 1995 that the *Sydney Morning Herald Good Food Guide* added the names of chefs to their restaurant listings.

In a tragically ironic postscript to this story, Loiseau shot himself in 2003 after losing a Michelin star. Death by critic? Proof of the deadly seriousness with which the French take their gastronomy. Meanwhile, in the domestic kitchen, other influences were at play.

The magazines: kitchen dictators

To a great extent it was the women's magazines, two in particular, that decided what was cooked in the home, introducing new dishes and new cuisines, although this was tempered by another powerful negative influence: husbands. In 'Eating the Other', Susan Sheridan notes '... men tend to exert a conservative influence over the family's diet', giving several examples of women who prefer 'foreign' foods but can't get their husbands to accept them; for instance, '"he doesn't like anything Chinese or foreign"'. Although Sheridan was writing of the 1960s, this constraint was echoed even in my 2013 interview with a cohort of CWA women, one of whom said, 'I like stir fries but when I try something, my husband says you know savoury mince would be nice – it's nice on toast'. The difference being that today's CWA wife fought back. 'I gave him savoury mince on toast ten nights in row. That got him over it.'

But with increased affluence, travel and availability of ingredients, the influence of the magazines began to make inroads on the domestic kitchen, eventually dragging the husbands along.

Perhaps the most influential at that time we are examining was the *Australian Women's Weekly* (*AWW*). As Sheridan says: 'The major influence on a magazine's representation of food and cooking, apart from its advertisers, is its Cookery Editor, whose role it is to introduce new food ideas while at the same time keeping up the supply of recipes for familiar/family food'.

Pamela Clark was a long-time food director, and then editorial and food director, cookbooks, at the *AWW*. She first joined the magazine in 1969, left in 1973, returned in 1978, and left finally while this book was being written. When I interviewed her in 2013, she told me that when she first arrived, Ellen Sinclair 'had only been here a couple of years … [but] was never recognised as the food director until [editor] Ita [Buttrose] arrived'. Until then the kitchen had been run under a fictitious name, Leila C Howard, in reality Betty Dunleavy. I asked Clark how the *AWW* reflected and influenced the way we ate in Australia at that time.

I guess we got a feel for what people were eating –
we used to have a hell of a lot of contact with our
readers either by mail or by telephone – we had
a lot of phones and they were always ringing and
people were always talking to us and telling us what
they wanted – and they wanted vol au vents and
comfort food. Vol au vents were pretty fancy, as
were Indonesian prawn puffs and Dutch bitterballs.
These sorts of things were common because the
women weren't going to work and they had the
time. French onion dips made using [Continental
brand] French Onion Soup powder, salad cream,
fondues, mulligatawny soup, short soup, long soup
– Australian adaptations of Chinese soups – and
soufflés because they had the time to and because it
was clever: it was showoff food. The wives were at
home and the husbands would have dinner parties.

In 1978 the *AWW* published a Chinese cookbook.
Clark said: 'A home economist came and worked for
Mrs Sinclair, and she was half Chinese and had worked
in the restaurant business. She went into restaurants
and watched them cook, and came back to the [*AWW*]
kitchen with the recipes'. Some of the recipes in that
Australian Women's Weekly Chinese Cooking Class Cookbook
(credited to food editor Ellen Sinclair) were:

- Spring rolls
- Gow gees

- Ham and chicken rolls
- Dim sims
- Long soup
- Short soup
- Szechuan soup
- Prawns on toast
- Crab in ginger sauce
- Garlic pork rashers (2 cloves)
- Sweet and sour pork (canned pineapple)
- Steamed pork buns (cha siu pau)
- Lemon chicken
- Braised duck
- Chicken chow mein
- Beggar's chicken
- Billy Kee chicken [from a section named Restaurant Dishes, which included the recipe at the end of this chapter, from the Four Seas in Redfern; Flower blossoms from the Dixon in Chinatown; Stuffed chicken wings from The New Dynasty in Cremorne; Sizzling steak from The Golden Lily in Malabar; Honey prawns from Dragon City in the city; Pork chops with plum sauce from Rose Bay Chinese; Chicken hotpot from The Eastern in Circular Quay; and Toffee apples from the Peking Palace in Cremorne.]

I remember Billy Kee chicken from the Tai Ping restaurant, which used to be on Campbell Street, a restaurant I first visited as an eleven-year-old boy with my parents. I didn't know that it had been named for fashion designer Jenny Kee's father. 'Every Thursday', she wrote on the SBS website, 'he cooked for his mates at the Tai Ping opposite the Haymarket corner of Dixon Street. Years later, the Tai Ping named a dish in his honour – Billy Kee Chicken'.

'By this time', Clark said:

> we were dictating [tastes]. The Chinese book was
> Mrs Sinclair's decision. She loved Chinese food.
> We always went to Chinese restaurants – her
> sister lived in Hong Kong and she went there for
> holidays. We were setting the [culinary] agenda
> because we got confident. The minute these books
> would hit the streets they would sell out. We'd
> have newsagents ringing up and pleading for more.
> The demand was incredible. We had the market to
> ourselves – there was only Bay Books and Margaret
> Fulton.

Unlike Betty Dunleavy, who was a home economist, and Ellen Sinclair, a writer, Margaret Fulton was a trained chef, having studied French cooking at East Sydney Technical College under Jules Weinberg. While the circulation of *Woman's Day* was lower than that of *AWW*, the readership was a little more sophisticated. When I asked Clark who they saw as the reader of *AWW* she said: 'They say our reader lives at Eastwood and Ryde. Our books don't sell as well in the eastern suburbs (of Sydney). Middle Australia is who we're aiming at'. Fulton, on the other hand, travelled widely, ate in all the best restaurants, and brought recipes from her travels back to Australia and shared them with her readers.

In her 1999 autobiography *I Sang for My Supper*, Fulton recalled that at the time she joined *Woman's Day* in 1960 her editor, Joan Reeder, 'encouraged people to travel, enjoy good food, good wine, live life to the full and bring back results to match for the magazine'. And with her training as a chef, she was able to speak to chefs on an equal footing, resulting not only in good features, but also in books like *Superb Restaurant Dishes*. While Ellen Sinclair was publishing Chinese restaurant dishes, Margaret Fulton was meeting Alex Cardini Jr, the nephew of Alex Cardini Sr, the originator of the Caesar salad (named for his brother Caesar) in Mexico City, and bringing back the original recipe. Early in her career at *Woman's Day*, and perhaps because of her stint at J Walter Thompson, Fulton understood the importance of mixing celebrity with food and wrote cover stories telling of her cooking with Graham Kennedy, and Bob and Dolly Dyer, among others. It was the *AWW* that retained the larger circulation and had, perhaps, the greatest influence as a magazine on domestic cooking. On the other hand, *The Margaret Fulton Cookbook*, published by Paul Hamlyn in 1968 with a first print run of 100 000, had a wider and longer lasting influence.

As did Charmaine Solomon's first book, *The Complete Asian Cookbook*.

It was first published in 1976, republished in 2011, and has sold well over a million copies, not just in Australia, but globally. But here, it was revolutionary. When I go into a home kitchen for the first time, I always look through the cookbooks. And there it is, sauce-splattered and battered like all well-used, well-loved cookbooks.

Charmaine worked as a journalist in her birthplace of Sri Lanka. Although she always claimed that she taught herself cooking in Australia to while away the lonely hours while her husband Reuben was playing in jazz bands (he was a clarinettist) – which is no doubt true – her food credentials begin in Sri Lanka. Her father's first cousin, Hilda Deutrom, wrote the first cookery book published there, and Solomon worked with Deutrom on 'bringing it into the fifties'. In 2008, she told an interviewer for *The Australian* how she was approached while working as a journalist on the *Ceylon Daily News*. 'One day the women's page editor said she wanted me to do a cookery column. I said, "But I can't cook!" and she replied, "Well, you'd better learn then." So I started a food column called Oceans of Notions. It was very popular.'

She and Reuben came to Australia in the late 1950s. As she wrote in *Charmaine Solomon's Family Recipes*, because the White Australia policy was still in force, 'I had to prove to authorities that I came from Dutch Burgher stock and was not Sinhalese (which seems incredible to me now)'. Reuben, as a Sephardic Jew, had no such problem.

Then, in 1964, she entered a national contest, the *Woman's Day* Butter White Wings Bake Off and came second: in some reports she won it, but in that interview in 2008 she said she came second. Of little moment, because that was when Margaret Fulton, hearing Solomon was a trained journalist, rang her and asked her to join *Woman's Day*. And later, Margaret's publisher, and then Margaret, urged her to do a South-east Asian cookery book.

It was the right time. We'd been to Asia, we'd trekked overland, and Charmaine gave us the recipes from 13 countries, from India to Japan, to help us recreate our taste memories. That publisher, Paul Hamlyn, was canny. The right book at the right time. If Margaret Fulton reintroduced us to great European cooking, Charmaine blew our minds with dishes like Ooroomas badun (Fried pork curry), Rendang daging and Lut tze mun ngap (Braised duck with chestnuts), dishes that just ten years before we would have run a mile from.

And not only did she give us the carefully crafted recipes, but also instructions on serving and eating, as well as the right utensils, and a larder for each nationality's food. I'll be bold and predict that this book will stay in print for decades to come. If any individual is responsible for our multiculinary culture, it is Charmaine Solomon. On behalf of all who cooked from her wonderful first book, I thank her.

Recipes

AUSTRALIAN WOMEN'S WEEKLY

BILLY KEE CHICKEN

Serves 3–4

From the Australian Women's Weekly Chinese Cooking Class Cookbook: *food editor Ellen Sinclair; Pamela Clark running the Test Kitchen, published 1978.*

Although in the book the recipe is credited to the Four Seas Restaurant in Redfern, which is no longer there, I remember it from the Tai Ping in Campbell Street, Chinatown – which is where Billy Kee first cooked it and like the Four Seas also, alas, no longer.

750 g chicken (without skin)
2 egg yolks
oil for deep frying
¼ cup tomato sauce
¼ cup dry red wine
½ tsp Worcestershire sauce
salt and pepper to taste

1. Cut chicken into serving-sized pieces, cut meat away from bones (or you can use boneless chicken also).
2. Chop chicken into small pieces. Add to lightly beaten egg yolk: mix well.
3. Heat oil in pan or wok, deep-fry chicken in batches until lightly browned. Remove from pan, drain well.
4. Drain oil from pan. Add to pan combined wine, tomato

sauce and Worcestershire sauce. Stir over heat until sauce boils. Add chicken pieces, mix well, allow to heat through. Season with salt and pepper.

MARGARET FULTON

....

CAESAR SALAD

Serves 2 as a light meal, 4 as a side salad or first course

From Margaret Fulton, Superb Restaurant Dishes: over 200 delicious recipes to cook at home, *Octopus Books, Sydney, 1982. Introducing this recipe, Margaret wrote:*

There are many versions of Caesar Salad, but this is the original and authentic one – prepared for me in Mexico City by Alexander Cardini Jr, the nephew of Alex Cardini Sr, who actually created the salad. Garlic and anchovy croûtes, coddled egg, lemon dressing and freshly grated Parmesan are all essentials. The lettuce is not tossed in the dressing, but gently rolled to avoid bruising.

1 cos lettuce (sometimes called romaine)
4 canned anchovies, drained
1 clove garlic, crushed
8 slices of French bread
1 egg, at room temperature
salt and freshly ground black pepper
juice 1 lemon
3 tbsp olive oil

1 tsp Worcestershire sauce

3 tbsp freshly grated Parmesan cheese

1. Separate lettuce leaves, wash carefully and dry. Place in a
   plastic bag and chill.
2. Mash anchovies with garlic and spread the mixture on the
   French bread slices (these are now called croûtes). Bake
   in a slow oven (150°C) until crisp and dry. Allow to cool.
3. Gently place the egg in boiling water for 60 seconds
   only.
4. Arrange the lettuce in a large bowl, season with salt and
   pepper and break the coddled egg over.
5. Combine lemon juice, oil and Worcestershire sauce in
   a small bowl and beat with a fork until thick. Add to the
   salad with cheese and croûtes.
6. Gently roll lettuce leaves in dressing until each leaf is
   glistening. Serve at once.

12

MOD OZ: THE CUISINE THAT NEVER WAS?

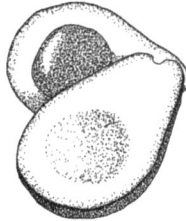

To eat Australian food is to be Australian, to be non-traditional, to be innovative, open-minded and sophisticated. However, unlike some hybrid forms such as Australian music that have erupted 'naturally', Australian food is orchestrated. The conductors have been the chefs in the fine dining restaurants in tandem with food producers.

Danielle Gallegos, 'Cookbooks as Manuals of Taste', in *Ordinary Lifestyles*

We all have different tastes. Some people like Indian, some people like Chinese. Some like a bit of everything. We've just learnt to use flavours, as have most of the chefs. I just use what's available. I'd say that was bloody Australian.

Joan Campbell, *Bloody Delicious*

The bunyip is a mythological Australian animal whose presence sorely taxed the early European inhabitants. On 11 February 1847, the *Port Phillip Herald* wrote, in a satirical mode, that 'Naturalists of every grade have, since the plantation of the Australian colonies, been racking their brain with fruitless researches as to the existence or non-existence of the supposed amphibious monster y'clept [called], amongst many other designations, the Bunyip'.

By the 1980s we had a modern bunyip in our midst, what has been called Australian cuisine, or Modern Australian cuisine, or simply Mod Oz. Although it was not categorised as such until 1993, its ingredients were assembled in the 1970s and placed in the oven in the 1980s, but only in the public sphere. Modern Australian cuisine is the creation of chefs, not cooks. What exactly was it that prompted us to reach out for such an ambitious construction as a national cuisine at that time?

If the 1970s was the decade during which Australians took off en masse in giant silver birds to discover the rest of the world, and began to adjust their way of life to incorporate their discoveries – including the way they ate and ate out – the 1980s was the decade in which they began to assert themselves and to believe they could compete with and even beat the best in the world. Our much-admired national trait of egalitarianism gave way to triumphalism and nationalism. The election in 1983 of the Hawke Labor government coincided with that national mood of optimism and brashness. As Frank Bongiorno wrote in *The Conversation*:

> During that golden period of about 18 months after the 1983 election as the drought broke, the recession ended and Australia II triumphed in the America's Cup ... Hawke did not just ride the wave of national pride and optimism during what Jim Davidson has aptly called the 'Age of the Winged Keel'. He embodied it.

Winning the America's Cup in 1983 was a massive boost to national confidence and pride, and it could be argued helped that confidence to slip over into hubris. The headlines of the day convey the often humorously over the top general mood.

On 28 September 1983, the *Sydney Morning Herald* ran with the headline: 'The biggest thing since peace in 1945: triumph unites nation'. Really? On the same day, *The Australian* proclaimed: 'Yes we can do anything if we try.'

The day of the win, the country ran out of champagne.

It was no accident that the hero of this saga was neither the boat nor its skipper – John Bertrand in case you'd forgotten – but the owner, Alan Bond, a symbol for this decade of overreach. The discourse was entirely masculine, as were the larrikin capitalists. In *Making It National*, Graeme Turner noted that 'The story of Bond and the America's Cup … is that of the self-made Australian armed with determination and ingenuity taking on the world and winning'. It is not a little ironic that this 'self-made Australian' was born in Hammersmith in London.

Something radical happened in the Australia of the 1980s. Political debate morphed into a continuous discourse on economic management, the start of an era in Australian politics that is with us still. During the first half of the 1980s, the businessman, until then a grey individual in a grey suit, emerged as a celebrity. A prime example is the aforementioned Alan Bond, a sign writer in the 1950s, then a property dealer who branched into the media, gold and beer. And Christopher Skase, a former *Australian Financial Review* journalist who became a resort builder and the owner of a media group.

Others included Robert Holmes à Court and John Elliott. By the end of the decade all had crashed and burned in spectacular fashion.

But while they remained airborne, it was a heady time – its code name, 'the excessive eighties'. The very rich were very rich indeed. In 1976, Leo Schofield's *Eating Out in Sydney* listed 160 of the city's best restaurants. By 1984, in the first edition of *The Sydney Morning Herald's Good Food Guide*, Schofield wrote in his introduction that he and his coeditors had chosen 400 from some 2000. 'The high-livers [in the 80s]', Bruce Grant observed in *The Australian Dilemma*, 'are not music-lovers or theatre-goers but they eat frequently in fashionable restaurants and drink good (occasionally imported) wine'. The other decade-defining event of the 1980s was the Bicentenary, the high point being 26 January 1988.

Celebration of nationalism

The Bicentenary was one more in a seemingly never-ending series of largely unsuccessful attempts to define Australia and what it means to be Australian. According to the Bicentennial Authority's booklet, *How to Make It Your Bicentenary*, its aim was:

> To celebrate the richness and diversity of Australians, their traditions and the freedoms they enjoy.
>
> To encourage all Australians to understand and preserve their heritage, recognize the multicultural nature of modern Australia and look to the future with confidence.

How were we to achieve this? The Authority told us to 'Plant shrubs, hedges and trees ... make community litter bags ... bake an Australia-shaped cake for a raffle ... Plan to have a meal from a different culture once a month'.

In addition to hedges and Australia-shaped cakes, a new $1 billion Parliament House was built, roads were pushing further into the interior and a highway completed that almost circumnavigated the continent.

In 1986, the Sydney chef Tony Bilson was approached by the government architect, Andrew Andersons, to help design some of the government catering outlets in time for the Bicentennial celebrations. These included the Hyde Park Barracks, the Centennial Park Café and East Circular Quay (which he eventually took over with restaurateur and property developer Leon Fink and opened as the first Bilson's).

At the top of the Bicentennial agenda was the 'forging of a nation' and, alongside this, developing, creating or uncovering a national character. It was an ambitious project. Whereas the 1888 Centenary as conceived by Henry Parkes was designed to 'commemorate the establishment of British rule in Australia', by 1988, as the jingle jangled, it was 'Celebration of a Nation'. If, in celebration, a society is committed to the telling of a story about itself, what story should we choose? Perhaps we shouldn't be trying. As Frank Moorhouse once wrote '... Perhaps we should go with the synthesis instead of painfully pursuing a unique nationalism'. This attempt at the construction of a nation was highly problematic, if not, like the tycoons, overreaching, but something was going on – and food had to be in it. And, as it turned out in the long run, it was indeed a synthesis.

The 1980s was the decade that ushered in the kind of jingoistic boosterism that gave us 'C'mon Aussie

C'mon', which led to the more aggressive 'Aussie Aussie Aussie, Oi Oi Oi'. Along with this aggressive nationalism came the – at first embryonic – desire for an Australian cuisine.

It had to happen. Having only recently discovered the power of food, the chefs and restaurants that had become the hangouts for these newly enriched and flashy business nabobs had to shove their way to the front of the queue, waving the flag for an Australian national(istic) cuisine. They didn't know what it was, but they had to have one.

Chef Neil Perry was at the time at Bluewater Grill. The *Sydney Morning Herald Good Food Guide* in 1988 called his food 'a more modern kind of food, somewhat Californian in style, involving lots of grilling and a slew of oriental influences'. This is a close description of a cuisine that did not yet have a name, nor even codified components. But in the 1980s it was busy being born. And its birthplace was in the newly minted food guides.

We needed guidance. We got guides.

Any examination of the birth of Modern Australian cuisine must take into account the publication of *The Age Good Food Guide* in 1980 and then *The Sydney Morning Herald Good Food Guide*, first published in 1984. In

introducing the Melbourne guide, editor Claude Forell
wrote:

> Why *The Age Good Food Guide*? Several reasons.
> One is THE AGE POLL finding that dining out
> is a more popular leisure activity than going to
> parties, football or cricket, the races, the cinema,
> theatre or concerts. Another is the bewildering
> proliferation of restaurants. Victoria now has nearly
> 300 licensed (to serve liquor) restaurants and 1500
> BYO (bring-your-own liquor) restaurants. Most are
> in metropolitan Melbourne and new ones seem to
> spring up every week.

In that first edition, the majority of the restaurants awarded two and three hats were French. This
accorded with the index by cuisine, with the largest
category being French, followed by International. Rita
Erlich, who was to become Forell's coeditor in the
second edition and continue so for fifteen years, wrote
of the 1980s: 'It was the decade of more BYOs than
licensed restaurants, and the time the licensing laws
changed to allow for bars and cafes to serve alcohol,
with or without food'. This was a pivotal point in Melbourne having the jump on Sydney at the time.

The first edition of *The Sydney Morning Herald Good
Food Guide* was a natural progression of Schofield's *Eating
Out in Sydney*, and marked the beginning of his long
relationship with Fairfax. Schofield's introduction,

unlike Forell's examination of the local scene, took the form of a Q&A (written by Schofield). The first exchange was:

You must have a wonderful life, eating out all the time.

Well, it's not all beer and skittles you know ... problems with weight ... nice just to have a chop occasionally, something simple. You can get awfully bored with French food.

In this way Schofield set the tone for a more relaxed and chatty guide than Melbourne's. In the first guide, three hats were given to Berowra Waters Inn and Reflections and two hats to Bagatelle, Claude's, Glenella, Imperial Peking Harbourside, Pegrum's, Rostbif, Suntory and Taylor's. Of those, seven served French-based cuisine, one Italian, one Japanese and one Chinese. Those serving French would acknowledge, as Gay Bilson later noted in *Plenty*:

An indebtedness to European cuisines, especially French ... informing the use of Australian produce ...

It would not be too great a generalisation that most accredited, self-consciously, culinarily explorative restaurants of the early eighties fitted into this category.

By far the largest category in the index is French, followed by Italian.

The introduction to edition two of the Schofield-edited guide begins with a stern admonition: 'Sydney restaurants need to pull their socks up'. It goes on to list hiked prices, indifferent pasta served by indifferent waiters, and other gastronomic sins – ending with the stern warning that 'Short-term economies and profit-maximising scams can only lead to long-term oblivion'. He argues that Sydney diners-out know good value and can spot rip-offs which, he concludes, has perhaps 'led them to patronise the Vietnamese and Thai restaurants that have proliferated throughout last year, and whose popularity shows no sign of abating'. In 1985–86, three hats were awarded to Berowra Waters Inn, Reflections and Suntory and two to Bagatelle, Barrenjoey House, Glenella, Imperial Peking Harbourside, Pegrum's, Perry's and Taylor's – much the same line-up, with the addition of Neil Perry's first inner-city appearance at Perry's, in Paddington (formerly Le Café, first under the leadership of Patric Juillet). And while Gallic influence continues at the core of most of the (non-Japanese or Italian) menus, Perry has already begun his quest for an Australian style with (from the review) 'a salad of yabbies and avocado in a hazelnut oil mayonnaise'.

Closer inspection of this second edition uncovers a curiosity. Perry's is listed in the 'Index by Cuisines' as Modern, and there is no index listing for Modern

Australian – but there are two restaurants listed in the body of the guide as Modern Australian: one being September in Surry Hills, of which Schofield wrote, 'Revolving fans and Victorian furniture suggest Somerset Maugham, but the cuisine is modern [no upper case] Australian'. To support this, he lists 'king prawns coated in crushed pine nuts' and 'boned chicken breast stuffed with camembert and baked in puff pastry'. The other restaurant described as Modern Australian is Bennelong, the food of which, Schofield (or the reviewer) complained, 'tends to combine too many disparate flavours, one example given being 'a cold cake of scallops, salmon and pickled walnuts'. In the index, both of these restaurants and 12 others are listed merely as 'Australian'.

In the next edition, 1986–87, Bennelong, The Pitts in Pitt Street and EJ's in Canberra are listed, again in the body of the guide, as Modern Australian. There is still no listing for Modern Australian in the index. It does indicate that the idea was in the air as early as 1984, when the 1985–86 book was compiled. What was curious was that a listing under the heading of Modern Australian in the index had to wait. But what is the story of the genesis of this nebulous, chimerical style?

Who put the Mod in Mod Oz?

The Australian tendency to argue about the existence of Modern Australian cuisine is well known, and it was noted in the waspish assertion in *Food Cultures of the World Encyclopaedia* (edited by Kenneth Albala) that 'the slippery nature of food and eating in Australia and the debate itself, probably is the essence of Australian food culture'. This exercised many minds in the late 1980s and through the 1990s.

In 1995, a debate was held at the Treasury Restaurant in the InterContinental Hotel in Sydney. The question was: 'Is Australian Cuisine Possible in a Multicultural Society?'.

For the affirmative, food writer Jill Dupleix, restaurateur Victoria Alexander and chef Neil Perry; for the negative, chef Tony Bilson, food writer and broadcaster Lyndey Milan and me. During the course of the debate, two arguments set the boundaries, Dupleix asserting that it was 'a glorious new way of cooking that is sweeping all other cooking under the carpet', and Bilson slyly suggesting that it exists 'only because Neil Perry said it does'. While the affirmative won on audience applause, a member of the audience approached me later and whispered that our argument was better – however, he'd been frightened to appear 'un-Australian' and so cheered loudly for the affirmative.

As we have seen, the first serious 'cuisine' in Australia in the nineteenth century was French, its ascendency lasting well into the 1970s. In an article in the *Australian Financial Review*, chef Stefano Manfredi wrote of the time: 'I remember a lot of mousselines and bavarois and turned vegetables and rich sauces like beurre blanc'. Two important restaurants of the decade in Sydney, Tony's Bon Goût (Tony and Gay Bilson) and Le Café (Patric and Chrissie Juillet), were run by chefs steeped in the French method. Underlining the persistent Francophilia of the era, in his book *Advanced Australian Fare* Melbourne restaurant critic Stephen Downes cited as examples of the emerging Australian style two dishes from Le Café in the 1970s: a Loin of lamb with wild garlic purée and a sauce containing Volnay, and a Fish and shellfish broth containing Meursault – both white wines from Burgundy. By 1976, a review by Schofield of Tony's Bon Goût (which opened in 1973) told his readers to 'Forget the aspics, the decorated foods, the chaud-froids. Today's food is different – less got-up, less complicated, letting the ingredients speak for themselves'. But before examining the components of Modern Australian, I want to explore one more dimension of the French–Australian nexus.

Nouvelle Oz

Once, when asked by a journalist who was the most influential cook in Australia, Tony Bilson replied 'Michel Guérard', one of the founders of the nouvelle cuisine. Later, in an interview, Bilson defended that position, noting that he 'was using him [Guérard] as a metaphor, because that revolution [nouvelle cuisine] was the most influential thing that happened in French cooking internationally. That's the basis of the contemporary aesthetic, internationally'.

A detour into the history of nouvelle cuisine and its influence on modern cooking in general, and Australian in particular, is necessary. *Larousse Gastronomique* tells us that nouvelle cuisine was 'A movement in cookery, started in 1972 by two food critics, H Gault and C Millau, with the aim of encouraging a simpler and more natural presentation of food'. The principles are 'absolute freshness of ingredients, lightness and natural harmony in the accompaniments, and simplicity in the cooking method'. Two examples quoted were Guérard's Aubergine purée cooked in saffron-flavoured steam, and Alain Senderens' Calf's sweetbread in a sea-urchin cream.

The timing was significant. It was 1972, giving a couple of years for the news (and the chefs) to travel. Some chefs in Melbourne and Adelaide especially were beginning to break out of the rigid mould. Nouvelle cuisine gave the professional chef and restaurateur permission to go somewhere else. Chefs need no longer be merely the faithful servants of convention, recreating dishes from a stern and unvaried canon, but instead could become artists, using produce as a palette, creating new dishes, new combinations of flavours, based on the classic techniques and dishes of a variety of national and regional cuisines.

This admission of other cuisines was something that had not been done in France since the brilliant and perhaps self-aggrandising Carême claimed to have invented modern French cuisine, having 'borrowed nothing from anyone'. Even if that claim of Carême's was a boastful exaggeration, the freedom to borrow and *acknowledge* it was one of the great liberating effects of the nouvelle cuisine. In particular, it was the addition of elements and techniques – and the aesthetic – of Japanese cuisine. More than anything, it is this openness to the influence of other cultures – at first, especially, eastern – that is one of the hallmarks of modern Australian cooking. But could the components of Modern Australian cooking be codified?

Mod Oz codified

In 1994, I was asked to join a group of Australian food professionals – an industry reference group – as a representative of the food media, to help develop a course to be taught in TAFE (Technical and Further Education) Colleges around Australia. It was to be called Australian Contemporary Cuisine (ACC), and it was the vision of one man, Graham Latham, who from 1973 to 1995 had been the founder and principal of the Regency Hotel School in Adelaide. Latham was imported to Sydney to run Tourism and Hospitality for TAFE, which he did from 1995 to 1997.

In that short time, he devised and implemented this ground-breaking course.

The industry reference group was charged with making the course happen and developing a structural definition of the Australian cooking style in the late twentieth century. The course was inaugurated in 1997. And Latham was relieved of his position the same year. 'TAFE didn't believe in the concept', Latham said. 'The managers [at TAFE] were trained in the old Swiss and German hotel traditions. Their ideas were deeply entrenched, and the course never got out of being peripheral. By 2000 it had arrived at the guillotine'. I asked Latham why he had not called it Modern Australian Cuisine. 'It [Contemporary] implied a more sophisticated approach. I thought at the time the word "modern" was a little jaded. I was trying to be conscious of where we were and where we were going.'

It appears he was right. Contemporary it is today. While the course was decapitated, the style itself, whatever it was or was called, captured the attention of the world.

If you were to look for a structural definition of the Australian cooking style in the late twentieth century, you would start with the curriculum we hammered out over three years of meetings and subcommittees. Let me outline the relevant modules in the curriculum (leaving aside the technical ones like Basic Accounting

Practices). It was a one-year course, open to all students who had completed the Commercial Cookery Grade 3 certificate, or its equivalent:

Specialty desserts
Advanced Fish & Shellfish Skills
Malay, Nonya & Indonesian Skills
Japanese Skills in Australian Cookery
Native Australian Cookery
Indian Skills in Australian Cookery
Guangdong Skills in Australian Cookery
Thai Skills in Australian Cookery
Gastronomy
Technology in the Kitchen
Research & Development New Recipes
Master Chefs in the Kitchen
Italian Skills in Australian cookery
French Skills in Australian Cookery
Middle Eastern Skills in Australian Cookery
Australian Contemporary Commodities
Wine & Wine Service
Responsible Service of Alcohol
Wine Knowledge
Wine – Sensory Evaluation
Wine & Food Philosophy

Latham and his team were prescient enough to include Native Australian Cookery but, curiously, it was almost entirely missing from the critical discourse at the time. Indeed, when it did come up, many critics and commentators were likely to dismiss it as 'tourist food'.

This was one of the reasons that spurred me on to champion native produce and the few cooks persisting with it, and eventually to write *The Oldest Foods on Earth*.

Meanwhile, unburdened by any native produce, Australian chefs were following Australian businessmen (and it was mostly men, both in business and as chefs) onto the world stage, with considerably more success: 'I have been given an insight into the food of the millennium', wrote an English journalist, 'there was no flash of lightning or crystal ball involved. It simply involved a trip to Australia'. In 2000, the highly respected journalist RW 'Johnny' Apple wrote in *The New York Times*:

Between carrying on about Ian Thorpe, the young swimmer with feet almost as big as a kangaroo's, and marveling at Sydney's magnificent harbor and opera house, the writers and broadcasters covering the Olympic Games have somehow found time to rave about the food and wine they have discovered in Australia.

And in 2004 in the *Guardian Weekly*, Veronica Horwell offered:

The real missionaries for fusion's casual freshness were a new international catering corps of Anzacs … the antipodean recruits' active approach suited the Californian styles, which they loosened up, jettisoning the waffly philosophy and the footnotes; then, as vineyards spread across Australia through the 1980s, Sydney rather than San Francisco became a leading model for good times, while culinary hands with Oz experience could work their way around the world's kitchens.

In 1996, André Cointreau, the owner of Le Cordon Bleu International, claimed: 'Ten years ago, I thought it was going to be Tokyo. But now, in my opinion, it is Sydney making the kind of synthesis that was made in Paris 100 years ago'. Synthesis is the correct word – not fusion – but it was not the kind of synthesis made in Paris 100 years ago. If Cointreau was alluding to Antonin Carême, his construction of French cuisine was in direct contrast to Modern Australian.

Carême 'frenchified' foreign dishes to make them more palatable to French tastes and attainable for French chefs. The synthesis that Cointreau alluded to had more in common with a far more ancient cuisine: Roman. Like Australia – but here via immigration rather than conquest – Rome's market offered foodstuffs from the length and breadth of the then known world (its empire). When the Romans conquered Africa, that country's flora and fauna were imported for Roman cooks to experiment with. After conquering the western Mediterranean, they took control of the trade routes to India and China and so added spices to the mix. With its diversity of culinary influences and ingredients, Rome was a closer model for Mod Oz than was France. But we have assimilated them in an entirely different and more conscious way.

Australia, since 1945, has been a multiculinary society, the opposite of which is a monoculinary society. As Corones points out: 'Within monoculinary societies, food is not usually "conscious", or reflected on, because a food tradition, no matter how highly articulated, is handed down from generation to generation uncritically'. In such a society, the only variations from the unquestioned monotony of an unvarying diet are seasonal. For example: 'To eat bread and olive oil is a daily habit of most of the inhabitants of the archipelago [the Balearic Islands]', writes Tomás Graves in his book *Bread & Oil*. The romantic notion promulgated in countless books on Mediterranean food ignores or glosses over this dietary uniformity.

Surrounded as we are, and have been for some fifty years, by an ever-increasing variety of cuisines and ingredients, many of us have become acutely aware of and knowledgeable about the foods we eat.

In the midst of this culinary plenty, our chefs have created a style of cooking that skitters across a large number of cuisines. I use the verb skitter deliberately, because nothing permanent has been created, only innumerable dishes, most of which disappear from the menu within a week.

Very few of those chefs have arrived at the state where they 'realise that food is more than just feed [and] ... begin to become sensitive to the philosophical dimensions of it, to the idea that is not just recipes that make a cuisine but principles'. Corones illustrates this by citing the Chinese principle of 'fan-ts'ai', with 'fan' being grains and starch foods and 'ts'ai' vegetable and meat dishes. With that principle in mind, Corones suggests, a Chinese cook could enter an American kitchen containing either Chinese or American ingredients and prepare a meal whose 'Chineseness' would increase with the right ingredients but still be, essentially, a Chinese meal. At least in the 1980s, we had not yet reached that stage, and I am inclined to agree with Corones, almost thirty years later, that 'There is little sense then in talk about an Australian cuisine if we mean by it the single cuisine of all the people. Given time, perhaps the various cuisines will mingle and blend, but we would lose a great heritage in the process'.

That great heritage being our 'very Australian way' – to borrow a phrase from comedian John Clarke – of assimilating those multiculinary influences that surround us. (The full quote from the brilliant and sadly departed Clarke was: 'Australia is not the only country to be obsessed with sport, but it is the only country called Australia to be obsessed with sport. And it is obsessed with sport in a very Australian way'.)

As Albala and others have observed, we are also obsessed with our food in that very Australian way …

And defined

For a project in the late 1990s, I asked a number of Australian chefs: 'If you were to open an Italian restaurant in Frankfurt, you would know, more or less, what to serve: a French restaurant, the same. But what would you serve at an Australian restaurant in Frankfurt?'. Frankfurt was chosen because it is a large, cosmopolitan city, which had a similar mix of 'ethnic' restaurants to Australia. At the time, there was no Australian restaurant in Frankfurt.

Here are a few of the responses:

Peter Conistis: Firstly I'd use whatever produce I could find there. Australian cuisine is a lot to do with whatever you can find. If I was going to do a Mod Oz restaurant – whatever that is – it would be a mixture of Mediterranean and slightly Asian influences using whatever was at hand.

Christine Manfield: Exactly what I'm doing here [at her Kings Cross restaurant at the time, Paramount]. What's happening in this country is great diversity. And that's the positive thing we have to play on. What David [Thompson], Tetsuya [Wakuda], Neil

[Perry] etc are doing is their personal interpretation –
but it all fits under the umbrella of Australian cuisine.
It's not slavishly copied from somewhere else, it's not
definitive, and it's not the only food experience you'd
get if you came to Australia. We have that freedom
because we haven't been bound in by strict rules that
define the way a cuisine develops.

Sean Moran: I'd draw on Anglo-colonial history, it
would be along those lines, with maybe an Italian
flavour to it, but definitely using Australian produce.

Tony Bilson: I wouldn't [open an Australian restaurant
in Frankfurt] because the term Australian restaurant
would only be a marketing term and have no real
cultural relevance outside of Australia. That is not to
say that some other enterprising soul might make it
relevant.

It's interesting to note that since I asked those questions, where none of the answers mentioned anything
Indigenous, there are now three Australian restaurants
in Frankfurt, and Bilson was right. Most definitely
marketing, not much 'Australian'. In Kakadu's, there's
Cranberry kangaroo; at Down Under, Emu burger and
Banjo Paterson chicken wings; and at Yours Bar, one of
several around Germany, all themed, this one Australian, with Uluru and boomerangs galore, on the menu
– The Aboriginal grill delight.

So then, if the Modern Australian chef was not creating an easily identifiable, exportable new cuisine, what was she or he doing?

I call chefs cooking in this territory – high tables – contemporary food bricoleurs. Bricolage is, I believe, the right term for Modern or Contemporary Australian, especially as the word is used in the arts to signify the creation of a work or works from a diverse range of materials at hand. The word was first used in this sense by anthropologist Lévi-Strauss, for whom it was an attempt to reuse available materials in order to solve new problems.

The Modern Australian chef casts about for ingredients and techniques – neither difficult to find in a multi-culinary Australia – which can be used in ways that they would not have been used in their original context, to create dishes never before seen and (in most instances) never to be seen again. But along the way, something of the personality of the chef is revealed. As Lévi-Strauss writes: 'the bricoleur [gives] an account of his [her] personality and life by the choices he/she makes ... he always includes some of himself [herself]'. Whatever else it is, Modern Australian cooking is a chef-creation, and has arrived from 'the top down, not the bottom up'.

For it to become *the* food chosen by people for self-identification, all groups in Australia would need to become equal stakeholders. That is clearly not the case. And the same journalists who created Modern Australian then attempted to eradicate it.

As a separately indexed category, Modern Australian first appeared in *The Sydney Morning Herald Good Food Guide* in 1994 (it had been named before, as we saw above, but not indexed), the last issue to be edited by Schofield and Michael Dowe (Dowe joined Schofield in the 1989–90 edition as coeditor). There was not, according to Schofield, much serious deliberation before adding it. In an email to me he wrote: 'I recall that Michael and I had a discussion about this. There was much talk about categorisation – Greek, Italian etc – and we needed a name to describe the local style, often a hybrid, that had evolved and emerged in force at the time'.

By 2000, it was far and away the largest category in the guide, with over 130 entries and at least that many in 2005, the year before it disappeared from the Sydney edition.

The attempted assassination of an affectation

The editors during that period, Matthew Evans and Simon Thomsen, replaced it with Contemporary in 2006. In an interview at the time, Thomsen said they (he and Evans) 'decided that Modern Australian cuisine did not exist. It was merely an affectation'.

The Age Good Food Guide introduced the description under the editorship of Sally Lewis in 2003, and replaced it with Contemporary when editors Necia Wilden and John Lethlean took over in 2007. Lethlean later told me: 'Modern Australian didn't seem to me … to mean that much in the sense that it was being used in the *Guide* for so many different cooking styles. Contemporary seemed to cover it much better'.

If journalists thought they had done away with Modern Australian cuisine/cooking, they overestimated their influence, as is often the case. The style, if not the name, lives on. Go to Google, type in Modern Australian cuisine, and you will get (as I just did) over two million references. And at the end of this exploration, I now offer two possible definitions of (Modern) Australian cuisine (cooking).

Defining the indefinable

Firstly, from food writer Jill Dupleix in 1995. 'Australian cuisine', she wrote, 'is the cuisine of honesty and of democracy. It's like an oyster, a hidden treasure waiting to be opened, and while waiting creating a luminous, precious pearl through the simple art of internal friction'.

But let me offer a more precise and less ardent definition of Australian haute cuisine – or high cooking:

The cuisine of chefs working in Australia who create it daily. A largely rootless 'personality-cuisine' born not of the anonymous creations of mysteriously dispersed dishes, but from the hands and minds of talented individuals working with an ever-increasing range of materials.

These can be chosen at random or filtered through a chosen but not imposed set of traditional technique and ingredient sets using 'bricolage'.

It differs from French haute cuisine in that although individual chefs may have been trained in the French method, or may have been influenced by nouvelle cuisine, they are not within the sphere of influence of either, nor indeed do they obey any rules at all, but are out on a distant planet.

As Marieke Brugman wrote in an essay, 'Food in Australia or Australian Food?', 'Sometimes isolationism creates a particularly open-minded curiosity'. But did it ever 'trickle down' to the domestic kitchen? Only in small ways.

Lebanese-born anthropologist Ghassan Hage tells a story from the western Sydney suburb of Westmead, where a Lebanese family introduced their Anglo-Celtic neighbours to Lahmeh w'snoobar, a mixture of minced meat, onions and pine nuts. The woman of the house thought this was the best minced meat she had ever tasted, so she used it in making meat pies.

Whatever Mod Oz is or was, it doesn't appear on home tables or even what I call low tables, those places most Australians who eat out, eat out at: the cafes and mid- to low-range restaurants.

Dishes like Deep-fried whole King George

whiting with Thai dressing, corn and potato fritters (Neil Perry, 1989), or Jasmine tea smoked ocean trout, snow peas, zucchini, ginger and chilli vinegar (Luke Mangan, 1995), or Rockpool of shellfish and seaweed in a chilled fish consommé (Janni Kyritsis, 1995) are unlikely to roll out of a home kitchen near you – with the usual exception.

At the end of the 1990s, I ate a meal at the home of a friend who could only be described as a 'foodie'. His life was consumed by reading about food, eating at the best restaurants, and cooking. His obsession informed the meal. It began with plates of oysters delivered that afternoon by one of the growing number of seafood brokers supplying the white tablecloth trade, Sydney's now defunct Flying Squid Brothers, who made home deliveries for special customers. That was followed by Deep-fried harbour prawns, a recipe taken from Armando Percuoco of Buon Ricordo restaurant in Sydney's Paddington. Next, an assembly of buffalo mozzarella, radicchio and cold roast veal from a menu at Ecco – a small Italian restaurant then in a hotel in the suburb of Five Dock; followed by a Fennel risotto, the recipe of another guest who had imported it from the Villa d'Este on Lake Como in northern Italy; followed by an assortment of French and Australian cheeses from Simon Johnson, provedore to the restaurant trade. This reverence for our high-level chefs was reflected in cookbooks – and, later, television.

Recipes

TONY BILSON

....

CODDLED SALMON WITH RED WINE SAUCE

Serves 6

From Tony Bilson's Fine Family Cooking, HarperCollins, Sydney, 1994, this recipe exemplifies his French-based take on Mod Oz. Tony introduces the recipe with these words:

> We call the fish 'coddled' because, just as a coddled egg is never boiled, and is cooked at a lower temperature than a boiled egg, the same technique is used to cook the salmon to prevent the protein hardening. By cooking the salmon at a low temperature, the protein remains soft and when you eat the fish it literally melts in your mouth. Goose or duck fat is available in tins from specialty shops. If it is unavailable, you can substitute a good quality extra virgin olive oil. I use a domestic deep-fry set on the very low setting. Experience will tell you the method that suits you the best.

4 cups (1 litre) goose or duck fat
6 x 200 g pieces of the best fresh salmon, skinned and
   de-boned

Sauce
1 tbsp butter

½ cup mirepoix [a dice (6 mm) of equal quantities onion, carrot and celery which is lightly sautéed in butter or oil. It is used for flavouring stocks or braised dishes]

4 golden shallots, chopped

bones and the head of the salmon

1 tbsp tomato paste (purée)

2 cups (500 ml) red wine

2 thyme sprigs

1 bay leaf

½ tsp black peppercorns

½ tsp truffle essence (optional)

100 g butter, diced

salt and freshly ground black pepper

Spinach
1 large bunch English spinach

2 tbsp butter

1 garlic clove, crushed

salt and freshly ground black pepper

To make the sauce
Melt the butter in a frying pan or skillet over a medium heat and cook the mirepoix and the shallots until they are lightly golden. Add the fish bones and increase the heat so that some caramelisation occurs in the pan. Add the tomato paste (purée) and stir until the mixture begins to stick to the pan. Add the red wine, the herbs and peppercorns and

continue cooking until the mixture is reduced by half. Strain the contents of the frying pan or skillet into a small saucepan and skim any fat from the surface. Reduce to about $1/3$ cup (100 ml) liquid, add the truffle essence and then, still over a medium heat, whisk the butter into the sauce.

Taste for salt and adjust the seasoning if necessary.

To cook the spinach
Trim and wash the spinach, then blanch it in boiling water for 1 minute. Refresh it under cold running water. Melt the butter in a saucepan, add the garlic, and cook gently for 3–4 minutes, turning slowly with a wooden spoon until heated through. Season as desired.

To cook the salmon
Heat the fat in a deep saucepan or deep-fryer so it is tepid (70°C). Lower the fish into the fat and cook for 12 minutes. Take a piece of fish from the pan and test to see if it is cooked. You should not be able to see any raw fish; it will be pink, translucent and tender when cooked.

To serve
Spoon some of the spinach into the centre of the heated serving plate and make a bed for the salmon. Drain the salmon on paper towels (absorbent kitchen paper) and place in the centre of the spinach. Spoon over some of the sauce and serve.

NEIL PERRY

FRIED FLATHEAD FILLETS WITH TURMERIC POTATOES AND TZATZIKI

Serves 6

From Perry's first book, Rockpool, *William Heinemann, Melbourne, 1996.*

Of it he says: 'The potatoes are served warm and the tzatziki gives the fish a real Mediterranean flavour. These potatoes are delicious with salad, and the tzatziki, paired with hummus and flat bread, makes a great starter at picnics'.

Tzatziki
1 cucumber peeled, seeded and finely shredded
200 ml fresh farm yoghurt
2 cloves garlic, crushed
1 bunch mint leaves, shredded
lemon juice
sea salt and freshly ground black pepper

Turmeric potatoes
2 small onions, finely diced
3 cloves garlic, crushed
60 ml olive oil
sea salt
2 tbsp ground turmeric
1 kg desirée potatoes, peeled and sliced
200 ml cream (35 per cent butterfat)
freshly ground pepper

Beer batter
350 ml plain flour
355 ml beer

Fish
vegetable oil
4 × 200 g flathead fillets
seasoned flour
lemon wedges
sea salt

To make the tzatziki: salt the cucumber for 1 hour. Drain and add the yoghurt. Add the garlic and mint to the yoghurt mix. Season with lemon juice, salt and pepper and refrigerate until needed.

To make the turmeric potatoes: first preheat the oven to 180°C. In a large frying pan cook the onions and garlic in the olive oil until soft but not coloured. Add the salt and turmeric, and cook for 3 minutes. Add the potatoes, cream and pepper, and toss for 1 minute. Transfer to a baking tray and place in the preheated oven for 30 minutes or until the crust is golden brown.

To make the beer batter: add enough flour to the beer to give it the consistency of pouring cream. Mix it with a chopstick (it shouldn't be completely smooth), allow to stand for 10 minutes in the refrigerator, then add some ice cubes – the batter seems to turn crisp in the hot oil better if it is cold.

To cook the fish: heat the vegetable oil to 180°C in a large pot. Lower the heat if necessary: don't let the oil get hotter as it will burn and darken the fish too much. Dust the fillets with flour and dip in the batter (fry 2 at a time so the oil temperature doesn't drop too much). Carefully put them into the oil and cook for about 5 minutes until the batter is golden brown. Remove with a slotted spoon and drain on kitchen paper while you cook the rest.

To serve, place a spoonful of potatoes in the centre of the plates, pour over the tzatziki and top with a fish fillet. Serve immediately.

LEIGH STONE-HERBERT

SUSHI SCALLOPS, MARINATED IN LIME, WITH AVOCADO AND TOMATO DRESSING

Serves 6

Stone-Herbert's Sydney restaurant Rostbif (1982–85) was an early pioneer of the Mod Oz style and won two hats in the first edition of the Good Food Guide. *From a very young age Leigh worked in the garden and behind the scenes at his father's country house hotel Gravetye Manor in West Sussex. After Cambridge, he went to France to work with chef Jean-Marc Reynaud in Châteaubourg; he then returned to England to work with the Roux Brothers and other English restaurants, before coming to Australia and working at Berowra Waters Inn. Leigh sent me the recipe introduced with this amusing Schofield anecdote and a comment on the times.*

This was one of our top sellers at Rostbif, and regarded in those days as pretty radically different. Leo Schofield once dryly said to me, 'So you grill your oysters but serve your scallops raw do you?'. This version is a very early one, probably the first, from 1982 I would imagine.

Today it is easy to purchase very fresh, beautifully cleaned, ready to eat, sushi-grade scallops from the fish markets or even suburban wet fish shops. 'Back in the day', we had to search out scallops in their unopened shells and do all the work ourselves. Whatever, the scallops must be very fresh and meticulously cleaned as they are to be eaten raw.

24 sushi grade scallops

Avocado mash
1 avocado
1 fresh jalapeño chilli, de-seeded and very finely sliced (reserve some for tomato dressing)
salt crystals/flakes and freshly ground black pepper
juice of 2 fresh limes (reserve some for scallops)
Tomato dressing
2 very ripe tomatoes, of the finest quality
a nib (clove or to your taste) of fresh garlic
a few leaves fresh basil
extra virgin olive oil

1.   Start by making the avocado mash, by skinning the avocado and removing the stone, then mashing the

avocado in a shallow bowl with the back of a fork. It should still have some 'lumps' or texture.

2. Carefully stir in some of the sliced jalapeño, salt and pepper and lime juice to achieve your preferred taste. Remember that scallops are a very delicate flavour, so be careful not to produce too powerful a flavour in the avocado mixture. Set aside under food film in a cool place.

3. Next coarsely cut up the tomatoes and machine-blend with the nib of garlic, some chopped jalapeño and basil leaves, until you have a smooth purée. Pass through a fine sieve to remove any skin and pips, then whisk in enough olive oil until you have the texture of a dressing – less than half the volume of the tomato. Season to taste with salt and pepper. Set aside at room temperature.

4. Cut each scallop into 2 equal discs and lay them out on a couple of ceramic plates. Do not lay them on any metal surface; this will taint the scallop flavour. When you are about to serve, squeeze a little lime juice over *all* the scallops, then sprinkle with a few crushed salt flakes.

5. Our presentation was a small spoonful of avocado flattened in the middle of the plate, then the 8 discs of marinated scallop fanning out over a third of the plate, with the tomato dressing thinly covering the rest of the plate. Towards the end of the eighties we would sprinkle some smoked paprika finely over the shoulder of the plate – à la mode! Ah, the eighties ...

13

CHEFS LEAP FROM PAGE TO SCREEN

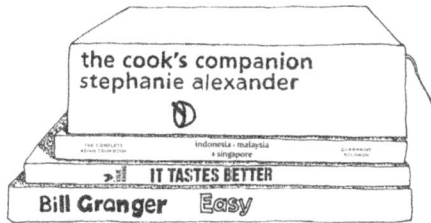

the cook's companion
stephanie alexander

indonesia · malaysia · singapore

IT TASTES BETTER

Bill Granger   Easy

Cookbooks, which usually belong to the humble
literature of complex civilizations, tell unusual
cultural tales. They combine the sturdy pragmatic
virtues of all manuals with the vicarious pleasures
of the literature of the senses. They reflect shifts in
the boundaries of edibility, the proprieties of the
culinary process, the logic of meals, the exigencies
of the household budget, the vagaries of the
market, and the structure of domestic ideologies.

Arjun Appadurai, 'How to Make a National Cuisine:
cookbooks in contemporary India'

The 1990s saw a cornucopia of celebrity chef
cookbooks.

Just as a chef didn't exist if he or she wasn't on
television in the 2000s, so in the 1990s the cookbook

was the proof of the pudding maker. Cookbooks were, on the whole, aimed at the urban, the leisured and the affluent. Those with access to the often-esoteric ingredients, the time to cook and hunt for those ingredients, and the skill and the kitchens that enabled them to cook from the recipes. Australian food at the high level was (and still is) the realm of the upper middle classes – but we will see how television may have challenged that class domination to some extent. But first, let's rewind a decade and briefly survey a selection of 1980s cookbooks, because taken together, the cookbooks of the 1980s and 1990s reflect the changes taking place in a society in culinary and cultural flux.

The vast majority of the almost 700 Australian cookbooks published between 1980 and 1989 were authored by women. The most prominent and multi-published names on the list were Margaret Fulton, Charmaine Solomon, Jacki Passmore, Beverley Sutherland-Smith and Tess Mallos, all of whom worked either in magazines and newspapers or wrote cookbooks and food articles. This is the era before the masculinisation of the cookbook, before the emergence of the 'celebrity chef', most of whom are male. There was not one book by a restaurant chef, and only two by television chefs: Peter Russell-Clarke and Gabriel Gaté. In the 1980s, we still took our kitchen cues from women.

Of the rest, many were concerned with health: losing weight, diabetes, vegetarian cookery and so on.

Several were published by food and food industry associated companies, like *The Comalco Alfoil Nostalgia Cookbook*, compiled by the *AWW*'s Betty Dunleavy. At the end of the decade, in 1987 and 1989, two books were published that looked forward to one of the movements of the next two decades: *Bush Food: Aboriginal Food and Herbal Medicine* by Jennifer Isaacs, and *The Bushfood Handbook: how to gather, grow, process & cook Australian wild foods* by Vic Cherikoff.

If the mainstream cookbooks of the decade were either retrograde, conservative or 'ethnic', the *Australian Women's Weekly Dinner Party Cookbook No. 2* (1983) included some 'creative' recipes worthy of the best restaurant menus of the time. These included Avocado with jellied gazpacho; Oyster vichyssoise; and, in an all-Japanese menu, a variation on the traditional Tonkatsu (Breaded deep-fried pork cutlet) – Eggkatsu, made using beef.

These Australian 'variations' on classic dishes recall a passage in Gay Bilson's book *Plenty*, commenting on the conversation between an Australian food journalist (disclosure: me) and Singaporean chef and cookery teacher Violet Oon. The journalist asked Oon if she was considering opening a school in Sydney, to teach us how to make (the Nonya dish) laksa so our chefs could 'fiddle' with it. 'Fiddling with the traditional foods of our Asian neighbours might just be the best definition of what some commentators hopefully call "Australian cuisine"', wrote Bilson.

Such experimentation or 'fiddling' is not exhibited in the only two books that I could find published for the Bicentenary: *The Australian Gas Cookbook: the Bicentennial edition* and *The Terrace Times Minimum Effort Maximum Effect Bicentennial Cookbook* (both 1987). They, and especially the first, contain nothing remotely fiddled with or fused, although the second wanders further afield in terms of cuisines, going as far as Poland, Russia and Moldavia. But by the end of the decade, change was in the kitchen.

The 1990s ushered in the 'celebrity' chef cookbooks, with the first publications by Serge Dansereau (Kable's), Neil Perry (Rockpool), Liam Tomlin (Banc), Bill Marchetti (Marchetti's Latin), Philip Johnson (e'cco), Greg Malouf (O'Connell's), Stefano Manfredi (The Restaurant Manfredi), Jean-Paul Bruneteau (Riberries), and Armando Percuoco (Pulcinella).

Hard to ignore that most of the chefs from then (and now) are blokes. In 1978, in Anthony Blake and Quentin Crewe's *Great Chefs of France*, ten were men, with one … femme. Then in Mietta O'Donnell and Tony Knox's *Great Australian Chefs* (1999) – a series of essays with recipes – about the same ratio: 52 chefs, four female. If you did a count in 2018, it would be about the same. The nurturing women of the 1980s gave way to the brash blokes of the 1990s. But then, professional chefs in hotels and restaurants have always been mostly male, a gender imbalance that shows no sign of disappearing.

It was also the decade in which we began to scrutinise the food our chefs were cooking, with books like O'Donnell and Knox's *Great Australian Chefs; The Food of Australia*, a collection of recipes from Australian chefs compiled by Stephanie Alexander; and the celebratory *Australia the Beautiful Cookbook* by Elise Pascoe, with a foreword by Cherry Ripe; and, in 1999, to review the decade, *Australian Food*, with a long, reflective introduction by Alan Saunders on the nature of Modern Australian cooking.

Three notable books published in the 1990s (by women) were *The Cook's Companion* by Stephanie Alexander, *New Food* by Jill Dupleix, and *Bloody Delicious* by Joan Campbell. Alexander was a restaurateur/food writer; Dupleix a food journalist; and Campbell – a one-time caterer, food editor at *Vogue*, and eventually food director of all *Vogue* publications – was an irascible style-setter and much more. Dupleix's book achieved impressive international sales, a first for an Australian cookbook. The differences between these books were stark. The Alexander book was a scholarly, meticulously researched and produce-based compendium of information and recipes, all information, little polemic. *New Food*, on the other hand, was an enthusiastic and colourful (predominantly orange and yellow) celebration of the new-found freedom of the (Modern) Australian chef translated for the domestic cook. It contained a credo that proclaimed that the reader should 'Buy only what is fresh and in season ... Have fun (and) Buy the

best quality food you can and do less to it'. And Campbell's is an eclectic mix of the modern and the country
traditional. Like its author, the book was a one-off: she
was in her eighties when it was published.

But the celebrity chef cookbook phenomenon had
to wait until the new millennium to take off. Television
was the next stop for these chefs, fast emerging from
the kitchen and embracing the word 'celebrity' in their
titles. And, sorry to harp on, but all were men.

Where did the term 'celebrity chef' originate?

In 2013, I asked British food historian Paul Levy
that question:

> I don't actually know, though I'm pretty sure I used
> it myself – as a pejorative term – in *The Observer* in
> the '80s or early '90s. I've had a quick trawl through
> the *Foodie Handbook* [*The Official Foodie Handbook* by
> Ann Barr & Paul Levy, 1984], which seems to be
> carefully avoiding using the expression … I very
> much doubt that there is a single source for the
> coinage, as once one started speaking and writing
> about 'celebrities', 'celebrity chef' was inevitable,
> and I imagine dozens of writers coined it all at
> once. And there's the additional problem that the
> first uses of the expression may well have been on
> TV, and not in print. In the UK, for example, there
> were food 'magazine' programs on the BBC from
> the early '80s.

The 2000s (or the noughties as this decade was dubbed) saw the beginning of the domination of these television celebrity chefs/cooks/hosts/restaurateurs as authors, and the birth of cookbooks themed around television cooking shows. Among the authors were Gary Mehigan, Matt Preston and George Calombaris, Jacques Reymond, Pete Evans, Matthew Evans, Lyndey Milan, Bill Granger (not actually a chef), Kylie Kwong, Curtis Stone, Miguel Maestre, Ed Halmagyi, Peter Kuruvita and the first of the *MasterChef* books, *MasterChef Australia: the cookbook*, which was published in 2009: at least 12 more have been published since. At time of writing (late 2018) Wikipedia lists around 54 television food shows, some long gone. Of those television food shows, none had the impact of *MasterChef Australia*.

MasterChef: cooking or competing?

A few statistics. In its first year, 2009, each episode of *MasterChef* averaged 1.42 million viewers, peaking at two million a week for the final weeks. The finale of the first series began with 3.47 million viewers and soared to 4.11 million for the last half hour. The first series was the most watched show of 2009. On 16 June 2009, a story on news.com.au reported that 'cooking schools have been flooded with students eager to learn how to simmer, marinate, braise and sizzle like the contestants on Channel 10's reality hit *MasterChef'*.

Since 2009, there have been several spin-off shows: Celebrity, Juniors, All-stars and Professionals, and a magazine that came and went. Ratings, although down, are still impressive. In 2017, 1.060 million watched the season premiere, and 1.303 million the finale. In 2018, only 890 000 watched the season premiere, about the same number watching each night as of June 2018.

While there is no doubting the commercial success and viewer popularity of this show, what of its wider influence? Presenter Matt Preston said in an interview, 'the purpose of this show is to pull as many people as possible over to our side and to show them there is value in cooking, that you can create great food in short periods of time'. In the same interview, presenter Gary Mehigan said:

> When a six-year-old bounds up to me and says,
> 'I made ganache on the weekend with mum,'
> I almost want to burst into tears. [I'm] looking
> at this little kid who is so excited because she's
> seen you on TV and her mum went and bought
> couverture. I mean, I didn't know what couverture
> was until I was 17. I didn't know there was good and
> bad chocolate. I think that is an amazing influence.

Those two statements epitomise the contradic-tions to be found within this show and its relation to food culture. Preston sees it as influencing quotidian food; Mehigan was overwhelmed by a child making ganache, hardly a daily food item. In discussing this show with students while teaching my course Writing About Food, one of those students said she believed it was influential because her husband, who had previously had no interest in food, had become 'really interested in plating' (that is, how restaurant chefs present food on the plate) after watching the show. But is *MasterChef* a cooking show? Gay Bilson thinks not:

> Like most television shows, MasterChef and its
> offspring are first and foremost entertainments
> devised around the advertisements that will pay for
> them … As an entertainment, MasterChef has an
> edge because it is a competition, a sport; not any
> old gladiatorial sport, but culinary gladiatorial sport
> – a home-grown version of Japan's Iron Chef.

And, in so far as it is a cooking show, it is a restaurant cooking show. Bilson again:

> In the episode of Celebrity MasterChef I watched,
> a woman cooked lamb cutlets with Moroccan
> spices and suitable accompaniments. She stacked
> the three cutlets on top of each other at semi-
> rakish angles and then dribbled something extra
> on the plate. The panjandrum declared the dish
> 'very chefy' and, peering over his paper-towel

cravat, he said to the cook, 'You have an artist's eye. Beautiful.'

The show is primarily cooking professionally, in competition with others. As Peter Naccarato and Kathleen LeBesco write in *Culinary Capital*, it is 'less about demonstrating the feminine attributes assigned traditionally to the mother and hostess and more about embracing the masculine traits of strength, vigour and authority'. Although the *MasterChef* phenomenon is now shown in around 40 countries, I believe this type of programming resonates in the masculinist Australian setting, presenting a way of giving men permission to move into a traditionally feminised workspace – the kitchen – and to take over domestic duties usually assigned to women. It would be comforting to think that shows like *MasterChef* give women the opportunity to break into the (paid) public kitchen and out of the (unpaid) domestic one. But a quick flick through the pages of the restaurant guides will show that the vast majority of chefs are still blokes.

What's more, according to Rebecca Swenson in her paper 'Domestic Divo?': 'By supporting hegemonic masculinity rather than a domestic masculinity, competitive contests counter constructions of cooking as nurturing, democratic and family-centred labour'. And remember, even when the presenters (blokes all) urge the contestants to cook for Mum ... it's still a contest.

Bilson points out that 'Restaurant food makes up only a tiny percentage of food consumed in this country. Television's endless parade of food programs gain audience in inverse proportion to the number of people who handle real food and cook good meals'. But, the important question is – has *MasterChef* had or will it have any real and lasting effect on what Australians eat in the home? In 2010, social researcher Rebecca Huntley began sceptically:

> Look at kids who are aged seven to nine now: will they be living on two-minute noodles in 10 years' time or cooking good meals? … Mothers should seize upon this show to teach their sons to cook. As long as everyday cooking is something that mainly women do, all the MasterChef shows in the world aren't going to change the reality for them, for whom cooking is a difficult, stressful, chore-like task.

Three years later, research by her company found that 'of 1000 Australians [polled] 61% … felt that watching the show had encouraged them to be more creative when cooking meals at home'. This prompted her to post, on her blog, a piece entitled 'I Heart Master-Chef' with this comment: 'I was slow to become a fan of *MasterChef* but by mid-series, I was a full-blown devotee; ironically, perhaps, we planned our evening meals around the show'.

In a small book published in 2014, *Does Cooking Matter?*, Huntley recounts an interview she conducted with Calombaris, Mehigan and Preston. At the outset, she wrote, 'I had to keep reminding myself: you are here as a journalist and not a groupie'. Later, I like to think that the journalist peeped out when Preston posited that children asked their mums 'do we have to have sausage rolls, can't we have a soufflé?'. Huntley added, 'I considered for a moment how many mums would be truly delighted to be making a soufflé on a Tuesday night after a long day at work, but I kept a lid on my cynicism'. Perhaps she shouldn't have.

My own research, TableWatch, nowhere near as extensive, does not indicate that there is huge support for *MasterChef*, or that the show has any great influence on cooking in the home. Of the 50 people I interviewed by phone (in five capital cities: Sydney, Melbourne, Brisbane, Adelaide and Perth), 12 said they watched it, 29 didn't watch it, and only three said they had cooked anything from it (one: 'my wife might have cooked something from it'). One person told me: 'It's influenced the way I would like to cook'. Another that her husband watches, 'but he doesn't cook, just likes to watch the shows'. Another's husband asks her, after watching the show: 'to do certain things and I say no, that's not going to happen'. One woman told me she and her husband loved *MasterChef*, never cooked from it, but they 'record it and we sit down when the children have gone to bed and watch it. It's quite relaxing'.

One said, 'in a sense I might be more experimental, I'll give it a go if I see something', and another said it made her daughter 'a bit more adventurous'. Nine of those interviewed watched *My Kitchen Rules*. Other shows mentioned were Jamie Oliver, Iain Hewitson, the *Barefoot Contessa* (Ina Garten), Luke Ngyuyen, Peter Kuruvita and *The Chef and the Cook* (Maggie Beer and Simon Bryant). One person said, 'I like to watch a lot of the shows on Channel 2, a bit more exotic than *MasterChef*'.

There were a number of negative comments concerning *MasterChef*, specifically: 'they've taken the fun out of food, it's become a competition'; 'I'm not sure they love cooking for the sake of cooking'; 'I don't like those other shows [*MC* and *MKR*] they're horrible'; and 'I'm not mad on *MasterChef*, to me they're rather pompous'.

While recognising that this is a tiny and statistically insignificant sample, my observation suggests to me that these responses are typical, although there is no doubting the broad-ranging influence of *MasterChef* as entertainment.

In an interview with Huntley, presenter Gary Mehigan recounted the following story. 'It has crossed a strange number of demographics. I was in a traffic jam – they were digging up Burnley Street in Melbourne – and this big hairy-arsed guy with his stop sign sees me and yells "Yah, MasterChef!" and all the guys down the line did the same thing.'

Television cooking shows and magazines like *Australian Gourmet Traveller* in general have had some 'trick-ledown' effect as shown on one episode of the satirical show *Kath & Kim*, which offered an acute observation of Australian suburban society of its time. Kel Knight, Kath Day-Knight's husband, is not just a butcher, as his online profile attests: 'As a purveyor of fine meats, I'm always in search of the perfect gourmet sausage, so if you want to discuss your recipes with me, just waltz on down to my butcher shop and have a yarn – don't be backward in coming forward!'.

The shift in Australian culinary culture – magazine- and television-driven – is clear when even a 'bogan' like Kel Knight has become a 'gourmet'. In one episode, Kel is inveigled by his wife-to-be Kath to go out on a buck's night before their marriage. But Kel has different plans. He and Brett Craig, Kath's daughter Kim's estranged husband, go to a local restaurant. We first see them eating squid with linguine and drinking 'a Riesling, Cockfighter's Ghost 2000, it makes the spaghetti taste better, that's the trick with matching your wines', as Kel puts it to Brett. When Brett toasts to 'our wild buck's night', Kel corrects him: 'our wild night of degustation'. Kel represents one kind of Australian infected by the media 'gourmet' culture. For Kel, gastronomy is still a foreign culture, one he is copying based on what he has seen on television and read in magazines and is interpreting for the less sophisticated Brett. But it is his hobby rather than an embrace of food culture. This, I think, is relatively common. This is a 'fan-based' food culture and, as such, could be switched off when something newer comes along.

But Kel got one thing right. The effect of wine on food. I once took the winemaker, flavour researcher and gastronome Max Lake on a review of a burger joint in Manly. He arrived with a very good bottle of Burgundy from his cellar. At the end of the meal, he said (like Kel): 'You'll notice, Newton, that the wine improved the food. It's never the other way around'.

More generally, there appears to be a dichotomy between the food we eat at home and the food we read about, watch on television and – if we can afford it – eat at restaurants.

Recipes

STEFANO MANFREDI

PANNA COTTA WITH MANGO CHEEKS AND PROSECCO

Makes 7 standard dariole moulds

A dish from Italian-Australian chef Manfredi, who leapt into print in 1993. This was served at his restaurant bel mondo in 1997. In sending me this recipe, Stefano prefaced it with this tale of its conception.

This was a dish I created to straddle the two cultures I inhabit or, more precisely, that inhabit me. It's fruit, jelly and custard, a dessert for an Australian summer where mangoes define the season. I grew up with jelly at friends' places so I thought that prosecco jelly could be what we regress to when grown up. Suddenly my Italian is showing with panna cotta binding as a more suitable stand-in for the much-loved custard.

2 mangoes

Panna cotta
375 ml cream
90 g sugar
50 g caster sugar
1/2 vanilla bean, seeds scraped
3 x 'titanium' 5 g gelatine leaves, soaked in 1 tbsp cold water
375 ml buttermilk

Bring the cream, sugar and vanilla to a simmer, stirring so the sugar dissolves. Stir in the gelatine. Add the cold buttermilk. Strain into a jug, then set into moulds and refrigerate.

Prosecco jelly
50 ml water
750 ml prosecco
1 tsp sugar
3–5 gelatine leaves

Bring water, prosecco and sugar to the boil. Add gelatine and dissolve. Pour liquid into a container to set.

Assembly

Cut cheeks from mango. Peel and cut into 8 equal portions (eat one). To release the panna cotta from the mould, dunk the mould into a container of hot water. Upturn the mould onto a plate and delicately place mango portions around the panna cotta. Place cubes of jelly around the plate.

CALLAN SMITH

JAPANESE-INSPIRED SALMON TARTARE

Serves 2

Smith was eighteen when he was accepted as the youngest-ever contestant on MasterChef, appearing in series 9. His recipe arrived in a very precise MasterChef recipe form, whose instructions I've incorporated. Callan told the following story.

I was nine years old when *MasterChef* was first introduced to the Australian TV scene and gee how it has changed and morphed into what it is today. Not only has it changed as a show but it has become a medium to educate, encourage and inspire everyday Australians as well as people from around the world. As well as trying to find Australia's best home cook *MasterChef* is designed to provide Australians who love to cook an opportunity to learn and develop.

My Judge's Audition dish, Japanese-inspired salmon tartare, is a prime example of how cooking over the years has changed. Tartare and raw meat and fish dishes have been around for a very long time and for me it was about how I could take a culture and a cuisine and combine them with my love of molecular 'outside the box' cooking. The result is a salmon tartare served with a ponzu sorbet, yuzu air and wasabi caviar, with the aim of making each mouthful fresh and vibrant, reflecting the combination of tradition and modernisation found in Japan.

(Where you see 'canister' of oil, Callan means any tall container that can hold the oil and allow the wasabi to drop through it.)

Ponzu sorbet
½ cup caster sugar
½ cup water
¼ cup soy sauce
⅓ cup lemon juice
⅓ cup lime juice
3 tbsp rice wine vinegar

Wasabi caviar
20 g soy sauce
10 g wasabi paste
70 g water
0.9 g agar agar powder
2 cups vegetable oil

Sesame tuile
30 g plain flour
1 tsp caster sugar
½ tsp sea salt
30 g butter, melted
1 egg white
½ sheet nori, ground
3 tsp dry bonito flakes

Salmon tartare
350 g sashimi-grade salmon

Pickled vegetables
½ cup rice wine vinegar
2 tsp caster sugar
1 tsp salt
2 cm ginger, crushed
1 clove garlic
1 small telegraph cucumber
½ small red onion

Yuzu air
½ cup yuzu
2.5 g soy lecithin, powdered
½ cup water

Garnish
Micro shiso leaf

Preheat oven to 170°C. Turn on ice cream machine to chill according to the manufacturer's instructions. Place canister of oil for the wasabi caviar in the freezer.

For the ponzu sorbet
Combine sugar and ½ cup water in a small saucepan, place over low heat to bring to boil. Once boiling, remove from the heat and add remaining ingredients. Stir well until fully combined then set over an ice bath to cool. Once cool, transfer to pre-chilled ice cream machine and churn until set, about 35 minutes. Once set, transfer to the freezer until needed.

For the wasabi caviar
Combine soy and wasabi in a small bowl and stir in until well-combined. Set mixture aside to cool slightly.

In a small saucepan place 70 g water and bring it to the boil. Add the agar agar powder and whisk while the water is boiling for 2 minutes. Remove from the heat and whisk into the bowl of soy–wasabi mix. Set mixture aside to cool slightly.

Transfer mixture to a large syringe. Remove cold oil from freezer and carefully drop small droplets of the mixture into the oil, moving the syringe in a circular fashion as you drop the liquid into the oil. Strain the pearls through a fine sieve to remove oil and rinse under cold water. Set the caviar aside in a bowl until ready to plate.

For the tuile

Line a baking tray with baking paper. Combine flour, sugar, salt and melted butter in a small bowl and mix well until smooth. In a separate bowl, whisk egg white until foamy, then add to the bowl of batter and whisk until smooth.

Spread batter thinly onto the pre-lined baking tray in 5 cm wide rectangular strips. Top with ground nori and bonito flakes then bake in the preheated oven until golden, about 6–8 minutes. Remove from the oven and set aside until needed.

For the salmon tartare

Trim salmon fillet of any excess fat and then cut into 5 x 5 mm cubes. Place in a bowl, cover with cling film and set aside in the fridge until required.

For the pickled vegetables

Combine vinegar, sugar, salt, ginger and garlic in a small saucepan over medium heat and bring to the boil. Once boiling, remove from the heat and set aside to cool slightly.

Meanwhile, place finely diced cucumber and onion in a bowl. Once the pickling liquid has cooled, pour over the diced vegetables and set aside to pickle until needed.

For the yuzu air

Combine yuzu juice, soy lecithin and ½ cup water in a narrow canister. Use a stick blender to blitz the liquid until a foam forms on the surface, about 4 minutes.

To plate

Place 6 cm wide chef's ring moulds in the middle of each serving plate. Divide the salmon tartare between the moulds and gently press down with the back of a spoon to compress and level the surface. Top the salmon with some pieces of pickled onion and cucumber, then gently remove the mould. Add some wasabi caviar to the top of the salmon, then top with a few micro shiso leaves. Skim some of the yuzu air from the canister and spoon onto the plate, close to the salmon tartare. Add a tuile to one side of the plate. Finish with a small scoop of ponzu sorbet on top of the salmon.

14

AUSTRALIA'S TABLES:
HIGH, LOW AND HOME

The single most important ingredient in the
Australian restaurant kitchen today? A passport
... I love this restaurant [The Bridge Room]. It's
hospitable, mature and adventurous, in a grounded
manner. You know, the phrase 'international cuisine'
used to be the kiss of death for a restaurant;
suddenly, it makes a whole lot of sense.

John Lethlean, restaurant critic, *The Australian*

In this chapter, I examine the food we are eating currently on three tables: the high and low public tables,
and the domestic table. I also investigate how and why
– regardless of our lack of a food culture as traditionally
defined, or of a clearly delineated national or regional

cuisine – some of us do eat contemporary food as fine as any in the world: those fortunate enough to be able to afford a place at our high public tables. Let me begin with a discussion of the chef at the restaurant mentioned above, The Bridge Room, Ross Lusted.

Lusted's career began in Australia, where he worked at – among other places – Sydney's Darley Street Thai, whose head chef, David Thompson, is today a world-renowned authority on the food of Thailand; and Rockpool, with Neil Perry, one of the leading exponents and practitioners of Modern Australian cooking. He also worked at Mezza9 at the Grand Hyatt in Singapore; and then Aman Resorts, a group that owns 33 small luxury resorts around the world, with an emphasis on fine versions of local cuisine. Lusted was in charge of food and beverage for each of the hotels, supervising the food offer in culinary environments as diverse as Italy, Cambodia, China, Greece, India and America.

Such multiculinary training is not unusual in Australian chefs. And, as discussed by Anthony Corones, one consequence of multiculinarism is a raised culinary consciousness. In the review quoted above, Lethlean raises the issue of 'international cuisine' which, in one context, is used to describe the food served at large hotels around the world, usually what Revel calls 'false grand cuisine', debased versions of dishes from French haute cuisine. This is not the context here.

The food cooked by Lusted and other Australian 'bricolage' chefs is not from a body of recipes but, as

Revel writes, from 'a body of methods, of principles amenable to variations, depending on different local and financial possibilities'. And, as always, the imagination and abilities of the original chef. It does not always turn out as well as Lusted and Perry's food.

Freedom in the kitchen can be dangerous when it is not accompanied by wisdom and technical ability. But the judicious use of that freedom has resulted in the chefs of Australia being recognised as some of the finest in the world.

There are two main paths for Australian chefs wanting to be taken seriously for their cuisine. Firstly, they can choose a national/regional cuisine. Examples of the former include Damien Pignolet who, although Australian-born, chose to utilise his French ancestry and cook determinedly French food; and Kylie Kwong, also Australian-born, who chose to pursue her Chinese ancestry in the kitchen (and more recently incorporated Australian native ingredients). On the other hand, there is David Thompson, whose choice of Thai cuisine was based on his fascination with the culture and cuisine of Thailand; Tony Bilson, whose food, although contemporary Australian, is based upon French principles, especially those of the nouvelle cuisine; and Mark Jensen, Australian chef at the two Vietnamese Red Lanterns in Sydney. These are just a few of many chefs whose path is to 'choose' a cuisine not their own.

Then there is the more problematic – and perilous – path of Modern/Contemporary Australian, unrestricted by any particular national/regional culinary guidelines.

Such a course has been steered by Peter Gilmore at Quay (and now Bennelong) in Sydney who, although originally taught French technique – most institutions teach French technique – has utilised both French and Asian techniques and ingredients (and more recently native Australian ingredients), as did Phillip Searle at Oasis Seros in the late 1980s and early '90s. So too Ben Shewry of Attica in Melbourne, whose food was first influenced by his upbringing in rural New Zealand, where much of what his family ate was foraged or home-grown.

Apart from eating the food of these contemporary Australian chefs, the best way to get some idea of the breadth of their influences is to look at the dishes they serve and the ingredients and techniques used in them. Let's look at two dishes from two of these free-ranging chefs.

From Quay and chef Peter Gilmore, I've chosen 'Duck breast poached in fermented ume and oloroso master stock, forbidden rice, umeboshi, spring almonds' – for a quite 'outlandish' mixture of ingredients, even for contemporary Australian cuisine. Ume is a Japanese apricot often macerated in alcohol; oloroso a style of Spanish sherry; umeboshi the dried, pickled and salted version of ume; forbidden rice a black or purple Chinese rice; and 'spring almonds' are green, soft, uncured almonds, which I have never seen used before but which are well known to anyone who has tended almond trees. Which, I would surmise, is why they were on the menu at Quay: Gilmore is a keen gardener, growing a selection of fruit, vegetables and nuts.

By contrast, but equally apposite for the contemporary kitchen, from Attica and New Zealand-born Ben Shewry, 'A simple dish of potato cooked in the earth it was grown'. This seemingly satirical dish was the subject of an extended examination by Adam Sachs in the American magazine *Bon Appétit*:

> The dish is a hangi [A traditional New Zealand Māori method of cooking food, using heated rocks buried in a pit oven] in miniature and essential Shewry: a humble potato, buried in dirt and shrouded in personal narrative.
>
> The what is simple: a potato (variety: Virginia Rose, selected after Shewry tasted at least 39 varieties), peeled, lightly dressed in a touch of grape seed oil and salt, packed into layers of the very soil whence it had been dug two weeks before.

A list of a handful of the ingredients used by some of these contemporary Australian chefs includes organic Korean green rice, silken tofu, garam masala, Jerusalem artichoke, dates, aerated passionfruit, paperbark, foie gras, red cabbage granita, sangria jelly, Camargue organic red rice, mojama, kim chi, wallaby, Pedro Ximénez, prunes and forbidden rice.

This eclectic list, which includes some indigenous ingredients, is used by chefs in a country that, you will recall, until some fifty years ago was suspicious of the use of garlic. How did this happen? What was the impetus that drove young men and women to a career that, until thirty years ago, was seen mainly as a trade? In other words, when, in Australia, did the profession of chef become one of the arts rather than a relatively low status trade?

New kids in the kitchen

Between 1960 and 1970, an affluent, inquisitive and acquisitive middle class was emerging in Australia, with surplus income. Australians had been joined by large numbers of Europeans, and we began to use some of that surplus income to leave the country and return with a new-found respect for the way our new neighbours ate and drank. We were emerging from a long hibernation under the blanket of 'Britishness' and a people who had brought with them 'their culinary xenophobia [and] distrust of foreign food'. But it wasn't just in Australia that there were rumblings of revolution in the *Essengeist*.

As already noted, the year 1972 saw the codification of the principles of nouvelle cuisine by Gault & Millau, the French restaurant guide editors who were mounting a challenge to Michelin's never-before challenged position as the pre-eminent gastronomic guide. This coincided with a change in the economics of the restaurant business in France. Chefs emerged from the anonymity of the kitchen and opened their own restaurants. The nouvelle cuisine revolution meant that instead of merely churning out classic dishes according to the book (Escoffier, Carême), chefs began to create their own dishes. Now they were more than technicians, they were artists.

And media stars. In France, the late Paul Bocuse took up the position of spokesperson for the new breed of 'star' – not yet 'celebrity' – chefs. As Stephanie Alexander remarked, 'He rather revelled in being the strutting cocky Frenchman, and he got headlines everywhere'. He wasn't the only one. Books of the time, such as *Great Chefs of France*, eulogised star chefs of the day like Alain Chapel, Paul Bocuse and the brothers Jean and Pierre Troisgros.

It was during this time of expansiveness, curiosity, openness to new culinary experiences and the elevation of cooking from trade to craft (some would say art) that a handful of intelligent young Australian middle class men and women – who would normally have been expected to enter the more staid and 'respectable' professions – made what were then radical decisions to forge their careers in the kitchen. This was a time for Australians to make radical decisions. Let me explain with a personal story.

I knew Michael Manners (the subject of the first

story below) before he went to hotel school. Those of us from schools like Cranbrook (Michael's) and Scots (mine) didn't, in those days, become chefs or plumbers or carpenters. We were destined to be lawyers or doctors. That's not me being a snob, but just remembering back to the shock when Michael went off to hotel school. When he returned with a beautiful French wife, Monique, and we all queued to get into his first restaurant – Upstairs, in Darlinghurst – we understood. It was a revelation. There were other professions besides the law, medicine and stockbroking for the middle classes. And cooking was one of the arts.

A surge of nationalism was emboldening us in many fields aside from cuisine – advertising and a resurgent film industry being just two. Here are brief histories of four chefs who chose untraditional paths.

'Australians were realising that food can be an adventure whereas before it was a necessity.' Michael Manners left Cranbrook, one of Sydney's Greater Public Schools – public as in the English use of the word – to attend the Ecole Hôtelière in Lausanne, and returned after experience cooking in England to open the first of his many restaurants, Upstairs. Manners went on to take his food out of Sydney, spearheading the rise of good regional cooking and restaurants. The last of these was Selkirk's, in Orange.

'I went to the library and discovered Escoffier and it was as if the sun came down from the heavens and shone on me! The romance of it: "take 47 eggs". That was it!' Damien

Pignolet was born in Melbourne, and after leaving school went to the William Angliss Institute to study hotel management and catering. After graduating, he spent some time in Melbourne working as a hospital and institutional cook and running a cooking school. His career as a prominent chef–restaurateur began in Sydney, first at Pavilion in the Park in The Domain, next at Butler's and Claude's, and then Bistro Moncur at the Woollahra Hotel, which he owned with his business partner, the late Dr Ron White.

'I'd been brought up to think that if you couldn't use your brain you used your hands – and now when I look at many of the so-called chefs I can see that they have very good skills with their hands and they're bright too.' Anne Taylor began her life as a chef–restaurateur somewhat later than the others, but the restaurant she opened in Sydney's Taylor Square, Taylor's, was highly regarded by other chefs. Taylor was born on a dairy farm run by her parents in Cobargo on the New South Wales far South Coast, with Jewish and German grandmothers, both obsessed with food. After school she went to The University of New South Wales, where she started, but never finished, a PhD on the English seventeenth-century playwright Nathaniel Lee. She dropped out of university after a year-and-a-half and landed a job as censor with the Film Censorship Board. In 1976 Taylor took her first trip to Europe, spending six weeks travelling to the UK, France, Italy and Greece It was while on this trip that she first contemplated opening her own restaurant. She lost weight in London because 'the food was so bad', and regained it in France. But it was Italy that was the revelation. She realised that she could open an Italian restaurant in Sydney and serve the food she ate in Italy there.

'My contribution, I like to think, is one of good taste in the serious definition of that term, not its lesser and trivial definition.' Gay Bilson was born in Hawthorn, Victoria. Her mother worked when she was young and later gave up working outside the home. Her father was a foreman in a family-owned factory. Schooling was first at a suburban state school, then a girls-only public high school. Her parents had the usual aspirations for her, medicine being one because of the reverence for doctors in the middle class. She studied Arts at The University of Melbourne, but didn't finish her degree. She became a cataloguer in a library. Bilson cooked at Tony's Bon Goût, and later was (primarily) the pastry chef at Berowra Waters, but did not see herself as such. She regarded herself as and called herself a restaurateur.

It was the courage, curiosity and tenacity of chefs/restaurateurs such as these four – there were, of course, many more – that inspired another generation of chefs. They, like all these Australian chefs operating in a cultural vaccum, leapfrogged the usual path, as it was outlined by Revel: 'it is a striking fact that a truly great erudite [high] cuisine has arisen principally in places where a tasty and varied traditional cuisine already existed, serving it as a sort of basis'. Such a traditional cuisine never existed in Australia. Neither have we developed an identifiably Australian 'high' cuisine. Notwithstanding, we do have large numbers of chefs daily creating an 'erudite' cuisine in what we call 'fine dining' restaurants, and what I have called the high tables.

In *Goodbye Culinary Cringe*, Cherry Ripe quotes Alice Waters, who contends that 'it takes at least a hundred years for cuisine to develop'. Ripe goes on to suggest that 'it could be argued that the best Australia can hope to do is develop a "culinary identity"'. I would argue that since Ripe wrote those words in 1993 we have developed an identity which proclaims that our best chefs are remarkably resourceful and imaginative, taking advantage of the quality and variety of ingredients available to them.

It would no longer be possible for a visiting Frenchman such as Edmond Marin La Meslée to remark paradoxically, as he did in 1883, that '... no other country on earth offers more of everything needed to make a good meal or offers it more cheaply ... but there is no other country either where the cuisine is more elementary, not to say abominable'. How this happened, here, in this land of culinary contradictions, is a conundrum that I am examining.

But who can afford to eat at these high tables?

The bill

For another project (in 2013) I made an attempt to put a dollar figure on eating out at the high tables in Australia using data from 13 top Australian contemporary cuisine restaurants at the time. (If you are interested in my methodology, contact my publishers and I'll send you the entire project.)

Using that data, I have:

1   multiplied their average price by the number of seats by an average of 5 nights a week open (Tuesday to Saturday) by 50 weeks a year
2   taken 60 and 40 per cent of that figure (supposing 60 and 40 per cent seat-occupancy).

The resulting figures gave a very approximate expenditure on food only (the general industry practice is to add an extra 30 per cent for drink), and for dinner only: some are and some are not open for lunch and some are open 7 days. It's important to remember these were only 13 of the thousands of restaurants in Australia – there are over 600 in each of the Sydney and Melbourne *Good Food Guides*. The results of these calculations are:

Total expenditure: ($29 018 000 per annum)

Adjusted for estimated percentage occupancies
60 per cent: $17 410 800 p.a.
40 per cent: $11 607 200 p.a.

Number of patrons
Total: 296 500 p.a.
60 per cent: 177 900 p.a.
40 per cent: 118 600 p.a.

The average spend was $98 a head for both
60 per cent and 40 per cent occupancy rates.

Even with these 'back of the envelope' figures it is clear that, firstly, a lot of money is being spent in Australia on eating out at the top end. And secondly, there is a large audience. How large is hard to gauge. The lack of figures for the industry makes it very difficult to calculate the audience for our top restaurants, but I have attempted another rough calculation based upon the above figures.

Taking those earning above $100 000 per annum as the most likely regular users of the top restaurants, 17 per cent of 1.1 million diners is 187 000 – a figure somewhat lower than the 296 500 according to my first calculation.

But based upon those figures, I believe it is reasonable to suggest that the audience for the top

13 restaurants in Australia (principally Sydney and Melbourne) is somewhere between 200 000 and 300 000. If these calculations are anywhere near the (unverifiable) truth, then the audience for the top restaurants of Australia – again, mainly Sydney and Melbourne – represents just under three per cent of the population of Sydney and Melbourne aged between 25 and 64.

So, who are these people who eat in the best – or at least the most expensive – restaurants in the country? And how often do they do so? The figures I worked with were for those who dined out at least once a month. Again, without research, it is impossible to be definitive. But my 'field work' as a critic tells me this: the vast majority of that three per cent would come from the 'upper class'. For fear of disturbing the hornet's nest of class in Australia, let me quote Craig McGregor from his book *Class in Australia*:

> It is impossible to live in Australia without coming to realize that the different social classes have different sorts of jobs, live in different suburbs, go to different schools, get different incomes, speak in different ways, experience crucial differences in privilege and inequality, indeed live different lives.

Generally speaking, it is difficult to disagree with this, other than to add that the class divide is more porous in Australia than in older civilisations – we have no aristocracy – and so wealth plays a greater part in determining who lives 'different lives'. One aspect of the activity of those lives is regular dining at the more expensive restaurants. This has always been the case in the capital cities: Revel's 'appanage' again.

Before we had social media, we had the social pages. In the *Sydney Morning Herald* and *The Age*, from the 1950s until the 1980s, they featured the comings, goings, dining and lunching of 'society' – then a circumscribed group from the 'best families'. Typical of such notices was: 'Wednesday, June Hordern gave a dinner at Beppi's with Mari Livingston and David Vincent'. Today, the descendants of the social pages, for example 'Social Seen' in the *Sun-Herald*, record the comings and goings of the modern version of Sydney 'society': celebrities, actors and the recently wealthy. It only includes the scions of the older families if they're caught up in some scandal.

My observation (again as a restaurant critic) is that the three per cent also includes two other groups. Chefs and restaurateurs eating and drinking out to compare their offerings with those of their rivals. And those who could be described as 'hard-core foodies', not necessarily wealthy but whose obsession is eating out. Earning much lower wages than the three per cent, they will save to eat as regularly as they can afford to at the restaurants they read about in the food pages, magazines and blogs.

But with each new closure of an admired restaurant, it has to be admitted that 'fine dining' is giving way to fast and fashionable dining. And although I am no longer a regular habitué of the high tables, I admire the best chefs there, and hope there is always a place for them in our two capital cities. I am with Priscilla Parkhurst Ferguson when she writes, in *Accounting for Taste* (and accepting, as it is a book about French cuisine, her use of the word), that cuisine 'turns that act of nourishment into an object fit for intellectual consumption and aesthetic appreciation'. We may not have a haute cuisine, but if we lose our high tables and the chefs who furnish them, we have lost something important in our culture.

However, most of the furious interest in food exhibited in Australia and the world today is not concerned with the 'high' public tables.

The low tables

Since 1999, Scott Bolles has been the editor of the column 'Short Black', which appears every Tuesday in the *Good Food* supplement of the *Sydney Morning Herald*. This column is often referred to as the 'bible' of Sydney's restaurant business. Its main business is recording the openings and closings of restaurants, cafes and (lately) bars, and the comings and goings of the more prominent chefs and restaurateurs. In 2013, he wrote this:

> We're not entirely sure where Sydney is going
> to find the diners to fill them all, but you have
> to admire the pluck of the operators behind the
> tsunami of new venues headed on our way. The
> sheer number of new restaurant seats is staggering.

To illustrate his phrase 'tsunami of new venues' I first recorded the openings listed in his column between December 2012 and December 2013: this amounted to a total of 72 new restaurants, bars and cafes.

More recently, I recorded 107 openings from January 2016 to December 2016. Admittedly in that period two huge food precincts opened or began opening: the Tramsheds in Glebe, and Barangaroo on the harbour, with, respectively, an estimated 1400 and 1200 seats. A similar count done in the 'Espresso' column – the 'Short Black' equivalent in *The Age*, Melbourne – from February to December 2016, offers 124 openings.

Most of those openings are not restaurants, but bars with food, 'fast-casual' eateries and, especially in Melbourne, burger joints (note, burger, not hamburger).

As a story in *The Age Epicure* in February 2016 put it, 'Melbourne is living and eating in the Burger Age'. I tried counting them and realised it was futile – by the time you reached a number (I got to over 40, and that excludes the chains like McDonald's and Hungry Jacks) others will have opened. As *Epicure* puts it:

> You can get a $24 wagyu hamburger at Neil Perry's
> exclusive Rockpool restaurant at Crown, or a $5.50
> quarter pounder at any McDonald's outlet … 'Burgers
> fix everything,' it says on the window of Hello Sam,
> a gourmet burger bar on South Yarra's Chapel Street,
> and given how many we're consuming they may be
> right.

There will be – if there aren't already, academic papers on the explosion of the burger in Melbourne. Sydney, by comparison, is burger bereft. As is often said, with a shrug of the shoulders in Fitzroy and Newtown (Melbourne and Sydney's hipster centrals), 'Go figure'.

There is no doubt that food as a topic of conversation and eating out as a pastime has reached, at time of writing, a frenzy. As young food journalist Kate Gibbs writes: 'Foodism has, basically, taken on the sociological features of culture. Young people used to churn their scanty incomes on drugs and rock 'n' roll, but now food is their drug'.

Many such can now be found on food blogs. Technorati.com, the first global blog search engine (now defunct: they come, they go), listed over 21 000 food blogs. Typical is *Excuse Me Waiter*, whose creators describe themselves and their blog as 'a documented food adventure run by two hungry Gen Y food fanatics DK & Yvn. We can often be found roaming Sydney in search of interesting foods from food courts to high-end restaurants'.

Another from Melbourne is *My Town Melbourne*. Its creator, Daniel Machuca, describes himself as 'a 30 year old blogger living in central Melbourne. Lover of all things foodie, pop culture, science and history, and sharing all of this from in and around the heart of Melbourne'. (More than likely, by the time you read this, some of those blogs will have disappeared to be replaced by others.)

Our food is consuming us

The post-*MasterChef* world is undoubtedly food-obsessed. Particularly, in Australia, in the inner suburbs of the capital cities. 'I am not a foodophobe', writes historian Maria Tumarkin:

> But when I walk the streets of my city and sometimes not a single bookshop comes my way and instead I encounter – and this easily in the space of one walk – maybe 30 cafes and eateries, one after another, filled with people in what appears to be the perfect representation of the supply-and-demand model, and my eyes fall on tables that cannot possibly have any more stuff on them, and above those tables are jaws moving fast, waiters moving faster still, full plates in, empty plates out; what is my dizzy head meant to think?

The phenomenon is not confined to Australia. American journalist William Deresiewicz, writing in the *New York Times Sunday Review*, claims that food 'is a vehicle of status aspiration and competition, an ever-present occasion for snobbery, one-upmanship and social aggression. (My farmers' market has bigger, better, fresher tomatoes than yours.)'. This extreme 'foodism' is more widespread in the Anglosphere – Australia, Great Britain and North America. While our foodism is obsessive, it is also all-consuming. And, harking back to what Gibbs wrote – 'taking on the sociological features of culture' – Deresiewicz writes, 'food centers life in France and Italy, too, but not to the disadvantage of art, which still occupies the supreme place in both cultures'. As an Italian friend once said to me, 'it's like you [British/Anglo-Celtic Australians] think you invented food'.

This widespread foodism and its adherents, the foodists, represent the next level down from the 'high tables'. These affluent young food hobbyists swarm to the latest cheap restaurants, cafes and bars reviewed online or in the food supplements. And not just the latest new places. Many of the blogs – *Grab Your Fork*, and *Noodlies*, for example – specialise in discovering ethnic restaurants serving unusual and 'authentic' food in outer Sydney, and lately, around the world. On *Grab Your Fork*, for example, blogger Helen Yee in one of her posts writes about the food she discovered on a trip to Bulgaria.

It is not possible to even roughly calculate the size of this market as I did for the high tables. But like that upper end, it is obvious that the food hobbyist segment does not represent the majority of Australians who buy food outside the home. The really big market is fast food.

According to Intermedia's 'Eating Out in Australia' report for 2017 (as at 23 June 2016), the highest proportion of revenue belongs to fast food outlets, with a total revenue nationally of $6.6 billion. There were 81 991 eating-out establishments in Australia. The highest number (29 432) were fast food outlets, comprising 35.9 per cent of the national total. Below is the breakdown of their figures for annual spending per family:

New South Wales: Fast Food $2300; Cafes $816; Restaurants $1590

Victoria: Fast Food $2037; Cafes $773; Restaurants $1661

That works out to an average household spending approximately $100 per week eating out. Overall it equates to 50 million meals out each week, or 2.5 billion in a year.

Rebecca Huntley, writing of a visit to Munno Para shopping centre outside Adelaide, described the 'lurid ring of fast-food outlets that surrounds it: Red Dragon

Chinese, Hungry Jack's, McDonald's, Red Rooster, Pizza Hut and Barnacle Bill's'. This is the reality, a far cry from the smart eateries listed weekly in 'Short Black' and 'Espresso', or the obscure Vietnamese or Iraqi restaurants in the outer suburbs listed in the foodist blogs. An even wider gulf is discovered when we look at what Australians are cooking at home. But before heading home, let's stop off at the pub.

A piece by Josh Dabelstein in the online magazine *New Matilda*, 'The Great Australian Debate: Is It Chicken Parmi, Parmy or Parma?', alerted me to a whole subsection of the low tables that I have ignored. Mea culpa. I'm not much of a pub food eater, which is no excuse for a food historian. But Dabelstein's piece on the correct name for a pub staple, Chicken parmigiana, stopped me in my trackie daks.

> There is only one way of colloquially referring to your flattened and battered, fried and baked, sauced and cheesed and well seasoned dead bird atop hot chips and beside an untouched side salad. So please, leave your epistemological scepticism at the door … The correct abbreviation is pronounced 'Parmi/Parmy'.

Australian pub food requires a book on its own. There is a wealth of food lore to be discovered in the pub bistros of the nation, often reimagined as 'gastropubs', a term coined in 1991 when David Eyre and

Mike Belben took over The Eagle pub in Clerkenwell, London. But such a history would need to go way back into Australia's pub food to the days when the menu was limited to 'steak and eggs, ham and eggs, sausages and eggs and bacon and eggs' and God help any customer who wanted a substitution. When my father, then a commercial traveller, requested such, a roar came from the kitchen: 'What does 'e think it is, the fuckin' Ritz?'.

The home tables

In *A Cook's Life*, Stephanie Alexander writes: 'We have come a long way from chops on Monday, sausages on Tuesday, steak on Wednesday, cold cuts on Thursday, fish on Friday'. But have we? According to two pieces of research from Meat & Livestock Australia (MLA) – 'Last Night's Dinner', 2009, and 'Connected Cooking', 2011 – at home, most Australians are still eating much the same food as we were before the 'food revolution' and, in spite of the welter of television cooking shows, with no greater cooking ability. As the research states:

> In the qualitative stage of the research we found that consumers (both young and old) were being inspired to re-create the impressive masterpieces that they had seen in challenges on shows such as MasterChef or exotic molecular cooking by Heston Blumenthal, so they could impress their friends ...

when it came to cooking good meals for themselves or their family each night, they struggled to get beyond the basics.

Put another way, 'Australians are watching and reading more about cooking than ever before. Yet, they still have limited knowledge about how to cook a steak'. This lack of cooking knowledge – as opposed to lack of food knowledge – extends to all age groups.

> ... the twentysomethings right now are probably one of the most educated food generations ever. And by that I mean they can talk to you about foie gras or cooking sous vide. But what they can't do is truss a chicken or cook a pot roast.

Notwithstanding, the research found that:

> more than seven out of ten dinner meals [are] freshly prepared, cooked and eaten in the home. Typically, these home cooked meals are cooked from scratch with fresh ingredients. And these meals are not the exotic fare offered in cookbooks and on television: Interestingly, Australians seem to prefer familiar, traditional meals such as steak and vegetables, roast chicken and spaghetti bolognaise.

The research found that the typical meal on the domestic table would be a red meat dish with three or four fresh vegetable accompaniments: 'On average, Australian families sit down to steak and vegetables at least once a week'.

In her book *Does Cooking Matter?*, Huntley reminds us that 'everybody has their own definition of what "cooking from scratch" entails' and that spag bol could well be made with a bought pasta sauce: we no longer count the use of bought pasta.

The raw data from the MLA's 'Last Night's Dinner' research recorded 1007 meals. From those, I have chosen the following:

Most exotic meals
  (Usually only a single mention)
  Beef rogan josh
  Chicken provencale
  Kangaroo casserole
  Indian mutton curry
  Pork vindaloo
  Steak with curry pasta and veg
  Osso buco
  Beef Bourgion [sic]
  Moroccan stew
  Chicken princitessa [sic]
  Cray fish mornay and cold meat
  Steak Diane

Approximately 50 curries
> Chicken curry, chicken, curry powder, onions,
> mushrooms

Approximately 35 stir-fries

86 recorded meals of steak

Approximately 15 Mexican meals
> Including Tacos minestrone [sic]

176 Italian meals
> Including pizza; approximately 33 of these were
> Spaghetti bolognese

The MLA research correlates to a great extent with my own small study, TableWatch. As previously noted, this survey is limited in size – 50 respondents – and scope – five questions only. In addition, because it was conducted by telephone (by me), I could not survey non-English-speaking respondents. I think it is fair to say that they would be cooking the food of their own culture. As it was, I did speak to two Germans and one Italian, who did report cooking their own food. But even with all those provisos, the findings of Table-Watch are useful. Firstly, they show that those who eat out so adventurously, eat conservatively at home. Secondly, they echo the findings of the MLA research that many Australians do cook from scratch: only three of the 50 reported using pre-prepared food – others may have been hiding their sins.

Where it does differ from the MLA research is that the most mentioned ingredient was chicken (15), followed by vegetables (10), then rice, potatoes and steak (7). Casserole and barbecue were the most mentioned methods (4), followed by roasts (2). There were four mentions of Italian, two of Asian, one of Thai and one of English.

It is, with only a couple of exceptions (Scallops with chorizo; Filet mignon sous vide) an unremarkable list of dishes. People might be watching television cooking shows, but they are not taking the experience into their own kitchens. Of course, some are, but it is, I submit, very much like pre-1945 Australia: there were good cooks, interesting cooks but the vast majority of Australians were eating plain British/Anglo-Celtic food.

This preference for plain fare at home contrasts starkly with the food offered in the 2014 *AWW* book *Modern Australian Food*. There are no authors on the cover, but listed as food writers in the credits are Madeleine Jells and Abby Pfahl. The introduction – 'The Australian Table' – begins:

> Australian food is a celebration of the way we live: the generous abundance of country-style cooking, the simplicity of freshly-caught seafood and the vibrant café culture. It is our marriage of food and lifestyle that makes Australian cuisine truly unique.

It goes on to point out that what we eat has been 'heavily influenced by our multicultural society' and to name those influences. 'Over time', the authors opine, 'we have adopted the best ingredients, techniques and flavours from these foreign cultures. Ironically, it is this diversity for which Australian food is known and loved'. They end: 'Australian cuisine is not only a story of what we eat but where and how we enjoy food'. That baffling marriage of food and lifestyle. (At this stage, it might be worthwhile going back to chapter 11 and reviewing the *AWW* contribution now, and then.) A random flick through the 330-odd pages of recipes yields:

Chorizo and manchego rolls
Gyozas
Grilled mussels with jamón
Osso buco
Slow-cooked lamb with white beans
Porterhouse steaks with blue cheese mash
Tonkatsu don
Raspberry hotcakes with honeycomb butter
Beef shiraz pies
Moussaka
Roast chicken with tomato braised beans
Roast leg of pork with apple sauce
Raspberry almond crumble tart
Oyster shooters
Chicken and mango salad

Chilli and salt prawns
Cajun chicken burgers
Beef and reef with tarragon butter
Dukkah prawn skewers
Ice cream sundaes

If, as Gay Bilson suggested in a letter to *The Aus-tralian*, 'A cuisine is the collective aroma of everyday domestic food', then what is wafting out of Australian kitchens most often is the aroma of fried or grilled steak and roast or fried chicken. And the research demonstrates, fairly conclusively, that our own 'erudite cuisine', notwithstanding Revel, has arisen without the existence of 'a tasty and varied traditional cuisine ... serving it as a sort of basis'. That is the subject of my last chapter.

Recipes

LAURIE DEE

....

LAURIE DEE'S CHAMPION BURGER

Makes 4 single or 2 double burgers

Above I have discussed Melbourne's burger mania. So, when I discovered that one burger joint, Laurie Dee's in Epping, had won best burger in Melbourne twice, I had to get the recipe. When I did, I was curious that it had no beetroot. I asked Laurie why.

I believe Australians have used beetroot in hamburgers mainly to replace the formerly unavailable pickled gherkins to perform a similar function and that is, to add tanginess, sweetness and bite. Very similar to what pickled gherkins provide if you think about it. The only down side of the beetroot slice in my opinion, is that it tends to slide around inside the hamburger which detracts from its main function of being a portable, hand held meal. I am actually a big beetroot fan and in fact now and again, love to partake in the traditional Aussie Fish & Chip hamburger with the lot, including the obligatory fried egg.

This is the quintessential Aussie take on the hamburger – adding egg, bacon and sliced beetroot. Something you will never find in the US and we should be proud of it.

400 g freshly minced 85 per cent lean chuck

cheese – go for Kraft processed cheddar slices – not the
individually wrapped variety

soft burger buns from the bakery (if available), cut in half – the
supermarket variety is fine, but some bakeries offer perfect,
soft, hamburger buns

30 g butter

iceberg lettuce, middle leaves only

sliced tomatoes

onions, chopped, sliced, raw or grilled

bacon – cook it crispy!

pickles, sliced or chopped

tomato sauce

mustard, try French's or Masterfoods' American

mayo, pick the brand you like most

The patty

The secret behind Melbourne's best burger is fresh meat
minced the same day your burger is made. The meat should
be lean but not too lean, with a fat content of around 15 to
20 per cent. Some aficionados like to mince the meat
themselves but, for most, finding a butcher you can trust to
mince while you watch will suffice. Ask the butcher to mince
it twice, first through a coarse plate and then through a fine
one.

1. Form round 100 g balls of minced meat to create your
   patties. It is important not to overhandle the meat – the
   less moulding and shaping, the more flavourful and juicy
   the burger.

2. Heat a thick cast-iron skillet or pan (not non-stick) to a moderate–high temperature. A barbecue with a thick cast-iron plate is even better.

3. Press your patties down hard on the hotplate or pan using a steel spatula and a heavy object to create a wide, thin patty.

4. When the patty is almost cooked through, scrape it up with the spatula and turn it over. Salt the patty lightly. This is the perfect time to add your cheese. The patty should then sit until the cheese has melted.

5. During the last 2 minutes of cooking, place the cut hamburger buns face-down in another pan or on your barbecue hotplate. You may want to add a knob of butter to give the bun a golden crunch on the inside. Note: never toast the outside of your bun!

6. Build your ideal burger by adding your preferred garnishes and condiments. Some love to add grilled onions or bacon, others like to keep it simple with just a little tomato sauce – to each their own. Condiments should complement without overwhelming the meat.

DAMIEN PIGNOLET

....

DAUBE OF OYSTERBLADE WITH OLIVES
Serves 6–8

Damien introduced his recipe with this anecdote:

In 1976 I was travelling in France, and on visiting Arles dined in a small restaurant called Restaurant Van Gogh where an enormous older gentleman had command of the floor with his good femme dans la cuisine. A simple four-course menu of entrée (boudin noir for me) and Daube de boeuf aux olives.

While I had cooked a daube in Australia, the Van Gogh version was a revelation, to taste their humble offering redolent of the Provençal wine and served with fried heart-shaped croutons and a potato purée. I serve it the same way these days. Delicious food!

1.8 kg oysterblade, fat removed and cut in thick slices

The marinade
1–1.5 bottles red wine, such as Côtes du Rhône or even a quality
  cask merlot or pinot noir
A huge bouquet of herbs: thyme, parsley stalks, bay leaves and
  2 strips of orange rind (when you have a chance, dry some
  rind in a very low oven to intensify the flavour). Tie these in
  muslin.
30 cloves garlic, peeled

The daube

300 g pork back skin sufficient to line a casserole that will
accommodate the ingredients fairly tightly

250 g pork belly, skin on but boneless, cut in lardons,
5 mm sticks

1 pig's trotter, cut in 4 or 5 pieces

150 ml brandy

100 ml veal glace

salt and pepper

150 g black olives, rinsed well

plenty of chopped flatleaf parsley to garnish

a purée of potatoes or one with ¼ celeriac, boiled and blitzed.
Note that the potatoes have to be puréed through a mouli or
a sieve since they turn to glue in a food processor.

1. Use enough red wine to cover the meat, bouquet and
   garlic and leave for 24 hours.
2. Line the casserole with the pork skin, leaving aside
   enough to cover the contents. 3. Drain off and collect the
   marinade, then pack in the beef, pork belly and trotter,
   herbs and garlic.
4. Warm the brandy and pour it over the beef, then ignite,
   shaking the pan to allow the alcohol to burn off. Preheat
   the oven to 130°C.
5. Add the collected marinade, veal glace, salt and pepper,
   then press the remaining pork skin onto the ingredients.
6. Bring to the boil, cover the surface with a double thickness
   of baking paper that extends over the edges of the
   casserole, and press on the lid to seal as well as possible.

7. Check the tenderness after 1½ hours, cooking until really tender – it could take quite a bit longer.

8. Discard the top piece of pork skin. Allow the daube to sit on the bench for a while, then remove the bouquet of herbs and degrease with a spoon and lots of paper towel. Add the olives. Bring to a simmer for 5 minutes to allow the olives to add their flavour.

9. Transfer to a serving dish with or without the pieces of trotter. Traditionally some of the pork skin lining is cut in little squares and served with the daube, but the pork lardons are quite sufficient. Scatter with the parsley and serve with the potato purée.

15

MONGREL NATION, MONGREL CUISINE

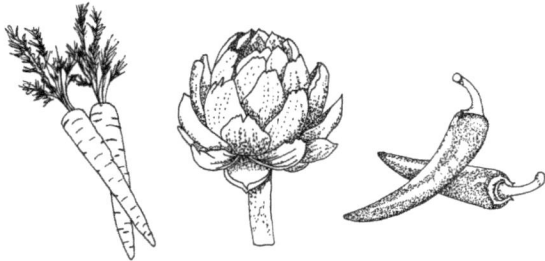

For let there be no mistake. Australia's future
culture will be plural. And there is no other way
forward but to think about how all of us can
learn to embrace its plurality.

Ghassan Hage, 'Roots will be with you always'

In 1988, Barbara Santich wrote: 'It seems to me that Australian cuisine ... is now in the proving stage and, depending on the power of the ferment, is ready to rise'. Thirty years on, if the ferment is still rising, it is the slowest proving ever recorded. So, what is needed for a cuisine – and here we are dealing with what I have called a high cuisine, prepared by professional chefs in the better restaurants – to develop?

In his essay on Sung cuisine, Freeman lays out the conditions.

Firstly: the appearance of a cuisine, a self-conscious tradition of cooking and eating, implies the confluence of the availability and abundance of ingredients – with a set of attitudes about food and its place in the life of man.

It also requires the use of many ingredients, and that (as previously discussed) 'sizeable corps of critical, adventurous eaters, not bound by the tastes of their native region and willing to try unfamiliar food'. And it needs to be 'the product of attitudes which give first place to the real pleasure of consuming food rather than to its purely ritualistic significance'. From my examination of Australian cooking at the high end, let me break down those requirements.

Firstly, there is the availability and abundance of ingredients. It would be fair to say no country on earth has more variety of ingredients from every country on the planet than Australia does. In 2002, in the *Sydney Morning Herald Good Food Shopping Guide*, it was recorded that according to figures supplied by the Sydney Markets Recording Service, 185 varieties of fruit, vegetables and herbs passed through the wholesale market at Flemington. In 2014, the same source reported 378, and in 2017, 382, which included, for the first time, an item of native Australian produce: finger limes.

What then of the requirement for a sizeable corps

of critical, adventurous eaters? By my calculations in chapter 13 there are between 200 000 and 300 000 out of 24 million Australians eating regularly at the high tables. This is a not-so-sizeable corps (say around 1.25 per cent), but large enough to be influential within the milieu of the high tables perhaps. As there are no 'native regions' as Freeman would define them in China, then that is not a consideration. They are more willing than most to try unfamiliar food, they are adventurous – but are they critical?

As mentioned in chapter 11, in 1977, Marion Halligan asked: 'Where is our Brillat-Savarin, our Carême, our Dumas – the philosopher, the cook, the man of letters to provide us with this food for thought?'. In 2018, the public discourse on gastronomy had not much improved. Outside the hermetic worlds of academia and the Symposium of Australian Gastronomy, there are only restaurant reviews and blogs. And when they do attempt analysis, as does the journalist quoted in a piece by Durack in the *Sydney Morning Herald* attempting to define Australian cuisine, it is usually banal: 'We live on the driest continent on Earth, most of us on the coastline, so we like to eat outside a lot and we eat a lot of seafood. And we don't mind doing that with a cold drink in hand'.

Finally, to the real pleasure of consuming food. Although it is not possible to contrast this, as Freeman does, with 'purely ritualistic significance', which is lacking in Australia – with the exception of Christmas (and religious observations, the Eucharist in the Catholic church for example) – then I would suggest that the 'not so sizeable corps' does give first place to the real pleasure of consuming food.

As to 'purely ritualistic significance': Japanese chef, educator and writer Hideo Dekura once contacted me for an article he was writing for a Japanese magazine, to ask what was the traditional food for the Melbourne Cup. He was mystified that we had none, so I suggested pie and beer if you were on the flat, and Champagne and chicken if you were in an enclosure.

Australia has the ingredients and an audience with a genuine liking for food. But there is one important component missing (apart from 'a set of attitudes about food and its place in the life of man'): 'People who have the same culture', Freeman writes, 'share the same food habits … the same assemblage of food variables'. For the first 200 years, we did have this 'same culture'. The problem was, it was fully imported from the other side of the world. Now that we are a multiculinary nation, this is at the same time our greatest problem and our greatest asset.

At the head of this section, I quote Ghassan Hage's statement that Australia's future culture will be plural, and that Australians must learn to embrace this plurality. He's right. That's why it's futile to search for an Australian cuisine, or a Modern Australian style. As our best chefs are showing us daily, we have a multiplicity of cuisines, just as we have a multiplicity of culinary cultures. To search for a defining Australian culture or a definition of Australian culture among the clamour of competing tongues, ways of life, ways of worshipping, eating, living and seeing in an increasingly globalised world, is regressive. To be Australian *is* to be multicultural, multiculinary – a mongrel.

To continue to attempt to slash through the thicket of difference and diversity in search of a single unifying idea that means Australia or Australian is pointless. This has long been understood. In 1985, Nicholas Jose wrote: 'In Australia, there is not the continuity and congruency of land, population, history, tradition and language that knit together a people's soul. The search for that elusive centre is the great Australian dream'. Does this mean we have no cultured food? No. As Malouf writes:

> The truth is that nations, like individuals, can live
> simultaneously in different places in the same place,
> and are no less complex and resourceful than minds
> are in using diverse paradoxical and sometimes
> contrary influences to make something that will be
> entirely their own.

This expresses the core tenets of a movement called Cosmopolitanism, which is discussed further in the epilogue. Australians must learn to swim in the polyglot pool, and the best we can hope for is to weave a rich and mutually supportive synthesis from all the strands of our population. A synthesis which, like the hand-woven rug alluded to in chapter 1, forms a whole from its many parts, a rich pattern rather than a separate and distinct national culture. In *Imaginary Homelands*, Salman Rushdie writes of his book *Satanic Verses* that it:

> celebrates hybridity, impurity, intermingling, the transformation that comes of new and unexpected combinations of human beings, cultures, ideas, politics, movies, songs. It rejoices in mongrelization and fears the absolutism of the Pure. It is a love-song to our mongrel selves ... Perhaps we are all, black, brown and white, leaking into one another ... *like flavours when you cook* [my emphasis].

This is a powerful definition of what the best Australian chefs are doing, 'using diverse paradoxical and sometimes contrary influences to make something that will be entirely their own'. Australian food is, as Rushdie writes of his book, 'a love-song to our mongrel selves', flavours, ingredients and origins leaking into one another.

It is this loosely linked network of Australia's multicultural population, each with its own ideas of what and how to eat, that at the same time denied us the chance of a traditional food culture and gave impetus to our most talented chefs at our high public tables to daily create a mongrel cuisine, a cuisine lauded globally. A perfect example is Stefano Manfredi's dish, Panna cotta with mango cheeks and prosecco (see above in chapter 13).

The same set of circumstances that prevented us from having a cuisine has resulted in our having something richer. The contradiction has enabled us to enjoy diverse, eclectic and original offerings from unconstrained chefs at our high tables, an unmatched multiculinarity on our low tables and, paradoxically (nostalgically?), mostly plain dishes on our home tables.

It makes sense. A mongrel nation has a mongrel cuisine.

I don't know about you, but my ancestry – as far as I'm aware – comprises Irish, German and Russian antecedents. I'd reckon most non-Indigenous Australians reading this book could claim the same or more. As I write this, 38 politicians have either been kicked out of the parliament, are on their way to the High Court, or are under a cloud for the crime of being undisclosed mongrels. Who knows how many by the time you read this? All of which sends me back to the Lévi-Strauss quote at the head of chapter 8: 'A society's cookery is a language into which it translates its structure, unless it reluctantly and no less unwittingly reveals there its contradictions'.

Again, let me paraphrase. Cookery is a code whose message is the structure of a whole society and its relation to the outside world – and (this is important) which exposes its contradictions. In what way can we decode Australia's cookery to reveal the structure of its society? I suggest we divide the answer into three epochs.

First, the 50 000 plus years before 1788, the epoch of the Dreaming when, as Gammage writes, for the original inhabitants 'theology is fused with ecology'. Their food (their cookery) was hunted, farmed, gathered and chosen always with an eye to balance and what the anthropologist WEH Stanner called the 'Everywhen', his word for the Dreaming, which posits an unchangeable universe. As you might imagine, one of the rules of the Dreaming is to leave the world as you found it. A clear structure is revealed.

The second epoch, the Displaced British, I would characterise as the time of clinging to a culture, a cuisine and a system of agriculture that had nothing to do with the land or its wellbeing, that indeed was in many ways antithetical to caring for country. If we measure this epoch from 1788 to the first signs of a move away from the total dominance of British cooking, it began in 1788 and ended, let us say, in the 1970s: around 180 years. A very long time to stick to a diet and culture that evolved in a very different climate. Why did we do it?

Firstly, we were a long way from our roots. We huddled in large part around the edges of the land, and viewed it – and its Indigenous inhabitants – with distrust, generally fearful of the interior which was often called 'the dead heart'. We looked back with longing at what we called the 'old country' when, ironically, we were living in the oldest country on earth. In his book *The Old Country*, George Seddon points out that the eroded rocks in the Pilbara have been dated to 3.515 billion years, the first record of rocks 'by over a half a billion years ... Now *that's* old'.

And it wasn't just a diet we brought with us. It was a set of social and cultural values, a way of life and a system of agriculture. There is a word for this set of values, a word used by the French intellectual and philosopher Pierre Bourdieu. And that word is 'habitus', meaning that 'culture is historically created and recreated under specific conditions'. In other words, when migrants move to a new land, they carry with them a set of behaviours and attitudes that are either anchored in the body (ways of walking, sitting) or daily practices (afternoon tea, time for eating dinner). The most obvious item of habitus is diet. We clung to our Sunday roast dinners, our Christmas puddings and our beer or tea with meals for almost 200 years. We were stuck in a cultural rut.

There are many reasons why this was so, including that the first settlers were dragged here against their will; that it was, in reality and in their time, as if they had changed planets. And then there was fear of the 'savages' of the land, the original inhabitants who had been beaten and shot into submission but who lived on in the popular imagination as a danger lurking in the bush. Below an excerpt from a poem. *The Creek of the Four Graves* tells the story of five settlers whose trip to the interior turns to tragedy when they are attacked and murdered by a group of Aborigines. The poet was Charles Harpur (1813–68), the son of convicts and described as the first native-born Australian poet.

His deadly foes went thronging on his track!
Fast! for in full pursuit behind him yelled
Men whose wild speech no word for *mercy* hath.

Aborigines are nothing more than (elsewhere in the poem) 'painted savages', whose right to the land is not at issue. Nor could he have known that their language contained 'no word for mercy'. Ignorance and fear were not one-sided, but on the other side, the fear, at least was justified.

During an interview, I asked Indigenous chef Clayton Donovan why there'd been so little communication, from both sides, about the food of the land. 'I don't know why', he said. 'Blatant ignorance on both sides? There was a period of time when I was growing up when knowledge would not be passed on – and it wouldn't be passed on to a white person.' Why was that? 'It would have been lack of trust. Knowledge is power. Would they give it to the new settlers to farm? In hindsight, it would have been great for our people … ignorance on one side, and mistrust on the other –

women were being raped, there were massacres, they would have been scared. It has to change.'

Alienation, isolation and fear prompted us British/ Anglo-Celtic Australians to cling to our diet and habitus for far longer than would normally have been the case. A destructive and shortsighted culture is revealed.

The third epoch, that of the Multicultural, the Multiculinary and the Mongrel, in which we now find ourselves, is reflected in the cuisines of the latest inhabitants and the creativity of its practitioners. And within that structure there does appear to be a growing awareness of the need to resurrect one of the rules of the Dreaming – not so much to leave the world as you found it (too late for that), but at least to farm and eat with an eye to the future.

What I find uncanny about aligning the Lévi-Strauss quotation with contemporary Australia generally, is how much it does unwittingly reveal our contradictions, and how our cooking runs parallel with them.

For instance, it was in 2010 that the Danish chef René Redzepi alerted Australian chefs to the Australian native foods around them that they had ignored for so long. It was also in 2010 that Social Justice Commissioner Mick Gooda introduced the question of constitutional recognition of the rights of Aboriginal and Torres Strait Islanders in his Social Justice Report. And as some of our best chefs add native Australian ingredients to their cooking, so too does the question

of constitutional recognition – and even more signifi-
cantly, an Indigenous voice in the parliament, a central
value in the Uluru Statement from the Heart (although
initially, and in my opinion arrogantly, rejected by our
politicians) – move closer to reality.

It was in 2017 that the absurdity of Section 44 of
the Australian Constitution was revealed, the bit that I
call the 'British to the bootstraps' or 'anti-mongrel' rule,
which insists that those seeking elected office must
be 100 per cent Australian and hold no allegiance to
any other nation. It's the constitutional equivalent of
legally binding us to a diet of roast beef and Yorkshire
pudding. Our multiculinary diet, our *Essengeist*, is a clue
to the real nature of the Australian people. How we eat
and who we are have changed dramatically since the
Constitution was written in 1901. Speaking of change,
it's time to get back to garlic.

Recipes

MARK BEST

....

CRISPY BEETROOT WITH TROUT ROE AND BEETROOT OIL

Serves 10 / Soak overnight

Many would say that Best, who began his working life as an electrician and came to cooking late (1990), exemplifies the first wave of restless, experimental, technically brilliant twenty-first century Australian chefs. He opened his Sydney restaurant Marque in 1999 and closed it, to the dismay of many, in 2016. When I asked Mark to define Australian cuisine, this is what he wrote:

> I think we struggle to define an Australian cuisine because there are so many answers to the one question. If you accept the fundamental premise that true creativity is not copying others, and you do not use imported produce, you are at least on the right path to achieving an Australian voice. It shouldn't only be defined by indigenous product but more by original cultural ideas. In terms of modern history, Australia is defined by its cultural mix, and that is the area I find most agreeable. My own patchwork heritage (British, Cornish, Scottish, German, Polish, etc.) has been a personal source of inspiration. An engagement with your own culture, your broader community and its produce.

Only the keenest among you will attempt this complex dish, which is from the last menu at Marque, his much-missed restaurant. It is here to illustrate the skills and creativity of a model modern mongrel chef.

Beetroot
10 medium beetroot, stalks trimmed to 10 cm, peeled
100 g hydrated lime powder
5 litres (20 cups) filtered water
1 litre (4 cups) vegetable oil for frying

200 g (preferably Petuna) ocean trout roe, for serving
sherry vinegar, for serving

1. To prepare the beetroots, using a wooden spoon combine the lime powder and filtered water in a plastic container. Carefully place the peeled beetroots in the water, ensuring they are completely covered. Leave to soak for 3 hours. Agitate the water every 10–15 minutes, as the lime powder will settle on the bottom of the container.
2. Preheat the oven to 140°C. Remove the beetroots from the lime water and rinse them thoroughly with cold water. Pat dry with paper towel. Bake on a wire rack on a baking tray for 2 hours – turn them every 10–15 minutes to ensure they dry evenly on all sides.
3. Once baked, cut off one side and scoop out all of flesh with a Parisian scoop [also known as a melon baller]. The lime will have created a thin leathery crust. Reserve the flesh.

4. Add the oil to a heavy-based pot or fryer. Bring up to 170°C and fry the beetroots until crisp. Place in a low oven on baking paper to fully crisp and drain any excess oil.

Beetroot 'oil'
10 kg beetroot
Texturas agar powder
xanthum gum

1. Peel and juice 10 kg of beetroot, then pass the juice through a fine chinois.
2. Add 0.18 per cent of Texturas agar according to the total weight of the beetroot juice. Whisk well.
3. Bring it up to boil over medium–high heat. Cool the liquid over a bucket of ice water straight away until it gels lightly.
4. Remove from the ice bucket and transfer to sous vide bags.
5. Compress each bag 5 times without sealing to break down the structure of the jelly.
6. Hang the liquid over a chinois with oil filter and let it drip in the fridge overnight.
7. Collect the juice and discard the solids on the next day. Reduce the juice over medium–low heat, checking the flavour from time to time. The reduction needs to be intense and full of beetroot flavour. Reduce to half the volume to intensify the flavour
8. Cold-smoke the liquid for 10 minutes.

9. Thicken with xanthum gum – allow 2 g per litre of liquid – using a wand blender.
10. Beware not to mix any air into the liquid.

To serve
Blend the cooked beetroot flesh in a food processor. Season with a little sherry vinegar, salt and freshly ground white pepper.

Half-fill each beetroot cup with the purée, top up with ocean trout roe. Spoon 2 tbsp of beetroot oil into large deep dish bowls and place a beetroot on each.

SOMER SIVRIOGLU

TARAMA WITH SALMON ROE AND FINGER LIMES
Serves 10 as an appetiser

From Somer Sivrioglu and David Dale, Anatolia: Adventures in Turkish cooking, *Murdoch Books, Sydney, 2015.*

Somer was born in Istanbul, Turkey, where his mother was a chef and restaurateur. He came to Australia when he was 25 years old, working in various hospitality businesses and restaurants before opening his first restaurant, Efendy, in Sydney in 2007. He has since opened Anason, in Barangaroo, in 2016.

White cod roe (also called tarama) is available from Greek, Turkish and Middle Eastern delicatessens. This recipe is difficult to make in smaller quantities – however, it keeps for a few days refrigerated and is delicious on sandwiches or served as a sauce with any fried seafood or vegetables. This is how Somer explained his Australian version of the classic dish:

> Taramasalata is a well-known Greek/Turkish dip made with
> salted cod roe, traditionally mixed with day-old bread
> soaked in water, then drained, or as in this recipe, mixed
> with boiled potatoes. Some add onions as well but I prefer
> this version. Adding Tasmanian hand-milked salmon roe
> and finger limes adds a unique native Australian touch to
> this century-old recipe from the Aegean Sea.

1 cup ice, or if your blender is not strong enough to crush ice,
    1 cup crushed ice
2 tbsp white cod roe
2 cloves garlic, crushed
2 chat potatoes, boiled and peeled
3 cups good-quality and clean-flavoured vegetable oil, such as
    rice bran or grapeseed
1 lemon, juiced
3 finger limes
1 tbsp hand-milked Tasmanian salmon roe
pide or salted bread sticks, for serving

1. Place ⅓ cup ice, and the cod roe, garlic and potato in a
   blender and pulse until smooth.
2. With the motor running, slowly drizzle in 1 cup of the oil.
   Be careful not to pour too quickly, it should be a thin and
   continuous stream.
3. Add ⅓ cup ice and blend until crushed.
4. Drizzle in another cup of vegetable oil slowly.

5. Add the last ⅓ cup ice and blend until crushed.
6. Pour in the remaining vegetable oil.
7. Add lemon juice slowly. Stop after 5 seconds or as soon as the lemon juice is blended in.
8. Remove the 'pearls' from the finger limes by cutting the finger limes in half, spooning out the pearls and removing any seeds, then mix with the salmon roe.
9. Put the tarama in a serving bowl, make a little well in the middle, and add the finger lime and salmon roe mixture.
10. Serve with pide or salted bread sticks.

CLAYTON WELLS

MORETON BAY BUG WITH GREEN PEPPER AND CITRUS BROTH

Serves 4 / Soak overnight

Here's what the Michelin Guide Newsletter says about Clayton Wells: 'He's known in Australia as one of the hottest chefs in the country. At his Sydney-based restaurant, Automata, crowds flock to the sleek, industrial space for a taste of his bold – and at times provocative – cuisine. His resume sparkles with fine-dining names such as Tetsuya's, Noma, and Quay'. This mid-thirties chef, who has also opened a restaurant in Singapore and a 'canteen' in Sydney near Automata, is calm, polite and fiercely focused: the very model of a modern mongrel chef.

(A romanesco, for those who have not come across it, is a form of broccoli, which has been described as part psychedelic broccoli, part alien life form. Seek it out.)

½ romanesco

2 large Moreton bay bugs

4 Cape gooseberries, peeled and sliced into 4 pieces

400 ml green pepper and citrus broth (recipe below)

20 g roasted kelp oil (recipe below)

Romanesco

Cut romanesco down to small same-size florets. Cook in salted boiling water for 1.5 minutes and then cool down in ice water. Reserve for later.

Moreton Bay bug

Cut each Moreton Bay bug in half lengthways and remove the meat. Steam in a Chinese steamer for 2 minutes and then place straight in the fridge. Once cold, cut each half into 3 pieces.

Roasted kelp oil

50 g kombu

100 g vegetable oil

Roast the kombu at 160°C for 45 minutes. Allow to cool down and then blend with vegetable oil. Strain though a coffee filter overnight. (The oil will last 1 month in the fridge.)

Green pepper and citrus broth

1 brown onion, diced

1 fennel, diced

2 sticks celery, diced

600 ml water
vegetable oil for sautéing
10 g white peppercorns
6 g cumquat koshu (see recipe below)
2 g yuzukoshu
20 g kombu extract
15 g yuzu juice
2 g kuzu (sweet potato starch)

Sauté onion, fennel and celery in vegetable oil in a saucepan.
    Add water and peppercorns and simmer for 45 minutes.
Allow to rest for 1 hour and then strain.
    Add the rest of the ingredients and bring to the simmer,
adjust seasoning with more yuzu juice if required, then strain
just before serving.

Cumquat kosho
50 g cumquat zest
50 g cumquat juice
7.5 g salt

Mix all ingredients together and then place in a sterilised jar
or vacuum pack. Place in the fridge and leave for 24 hours
before using. (The kosho will keep for 6 months in the
freezer.)

To serve

1. Bring the broth to the boil, heat up the romanesco and bug meat in the broth.
2. Scoop out romanesco and bug meat and place next to each other in a bowl.
3. Re-strain the broth.
4. Place gooseberry slices on top of the romanesco and then dress the dish with kelp oil.
5. Pour hot broth over the bug meat, table-side.

SHAUN QUADE

....

SANDALWOOD AND LEATHERWOOD NOUGAT

Serves approximately 8 portions

At Shaun Quade's Lûmé in Melbourne, you will not just eat his food but be immersed in the virtual reality of it. He once collaborated with a university in Melbourne to deliver an 'augmented reality dinner' called The Great Australian Road Trip – needless to say, he is one of our most fearless and creative mongrel chefs. Here is a recipe for the bravest (and best equipped in the kitchen) among you to try. Of himself and his recipe Shaun says:

I'm probably best known for my interdisciplinary and open-minded approach to modern cooking. For me, cooking is a constant, restless evolution. I draw inspiration from nature and the seasons but also from art, music, psychology and technology. I'm fascinated by the process and often look to other disciplines for inspiration and that very much influences how I cook.

This dish is one I would serve towards the end of the menu before moving into the dessert section. I like the fact that this dish is both savoury and sweet which helps bridge the tasting menu together. We use the nuts from the Australian sandalwood tree which is native to Western Australia. The 'nut' is actually the edible kernel of the tree's fruit.

Puffed fish skin
4 sides of ling skin
10 g N-Zorbit maltodextrin
sunflower oil for frying

Scrape the fish skin with a palette knife to remove any extra fat and flesh, then lay the skin out flat and dehydrate until completely dry.

Bring the oil to 190°C, then fry the dried fish skin until puffed and crispy. Drain well on absorbent towel. Break the skin up and place into a Thermomix with the maltodextrin and lightly pulse the skin until it is uniformly chopped.

Nougat base
87 g caramelised cream
3 g gold leaf gelatine
75 g white chocolate
137 g full cream milk

20 g leatherwood honey

18 g bottarga

Heat the milk to 70°C in the bowl of a Thermomix. Turn off the heat setting, then add the gelatine and white chocolate and process until homogenised. Add the remaining ingredients and process on speed 9 for 30 seconds.

Strain the mix through a fine sieve and allow to mature in the fridge for 12 hours. Pour the mix into an iSi gun and charge with 2 nitrous oxide bulbs.

Sandalwood nuts

50 g Western Australian sandalwood nuts

Roast the nuts in the oven at 175°C for 12 minutes. Place into a container and allow to cool.

To assemble the nougat

Using rectangular silicone moulds, place enough fish skin in the base of each mould to cover to a depth of 2 mm. Using the iSi gun dispense the nougat base into the mould, filling it halfway. Place 4–5 sandalwood nuts into each mould, then fill the remainder of the mould with more nougat base. Cover the top of each mould with more fish skin, then place into a blast freezer at -40°C until frozen solid.

Place the moulds into the chamber of a freeze dryer, then proceed with the freeze-drying cycle, which will normally take 12 hours.

Once completed, remove the nougat from the moulds and using a serrated knife cut in half lengthways to serve.

EPILOGUE:
GARLIC. WE GET IT.

There are five elements:
earth, air, fire, water and garlic.

Louis Diat, French chef (the inventor of Vichyssoise),
1885–1957

When taking an oath, the Egyptians swear by
garlic and onions as though they were gods.

Pliny the Elder, 23–79 CE

Once we had decided to gather up, and cuddle up to,
the cuisines of our new neighbours, the whiffy lily
sprouted in kitchens everywhere. Australian farmers,
recognising an opportunity, began to plant garlic.
About thirty years ago, to represent the emerging band
of garlic farmers, the Australian Garlic Industry Association (AGIA) was formed. At its peak, there were
700 members. And then disaster.

In the mid-1990s, tariffs on imported garlic were removed and Chinese garlic began pouring in. Garlic farming is a labour-intensive business, and China has an abundance of cheap labour. Membership of the AGIA plunged to about eight.

By 2011, according to the then chair of the AGIA, Leon Trembath, membership had climbed back up to double figures. But the problem was still there: the little Aussie garlic farmer couldn't compete with the massive Chinese garlic industry. How massive? Well, in 2014 (latest figures) China was easily the largest producer in the world, producing around 1.752 million metric tonnes annually. In 2010, about 1.8 million hectares were devoted to growing garlic worldwide, producing about 18 million tonnes (Food and Agriculture Organization of the United Nations figures). The overall production area within AGIA membership is 70 hectares.

According to the AGIA Strategic Plan (2015–19), Australians consume approximately 12 000 tonnes of garlic a year, and about 80 per cent of that is imported. In 2010–11 Australia imported just over 10 000 tonnes of garlic, with 8000 of these from China, 1307 from Mexico, 540 from Argentina, 299 from the USA, 285 from Spain and 218 from Chile. We eat around 12 000 tonnes a year, and the AGIA estimates we produce around 3000 tonnes a year. China isn't the only problem, just the biggest one.

Our farmers fought back, and the dedicated garlic munchers soon learnt a few things about Chinese garlic.

One, it's whitened using things like sulphur and wood ash, and two, the Chinese use growth inhibitors (hormones or chemicals) to stop it from sprouting. Three, although gamma radiation to sterilise is not accepted for food in Australia, it sneaks in. And, like all imported garlic, it's fumigated with methyl bromide on the way in. As if that isn't bad enough, it has very little flavour: not surprising after all that chemical interference.

That's Chinese garlic. But if your greengrocer or supermarket is honest, and labels country of origin, you will have noticed garlic sneaking in from many other countries (such as those mentioned above). That's because at the end of their seasons, the Central American and European countries dump their garlic on the Australian market for prices as low as $2 a kilogram. Again, hard for the Australian farmer to compete on price. But do we really want to eat this garlic?

You may have noticed, as I have, that a lot of the imported garlic has unpleasant, hessian baggy or rancid flavours, like corked wine or stale onions. That's because this dumped garlic is on the way out before it gets here.

So, if you are not eating local garlic, you are exposing yourself to some unpleasant – even dangerous – chemicals and processes. And not even getting good flavour. We garlic munchers are beginning to take notice of this.

Since that low of 19 or so members in 2011, membership of the AGIA has shot up to 78 in 2013, and today stands at 160. They're growing well over 300 varieties. Why? Because different varieties thrive in different climatic conditions and will ripen at different times, which will mean a longer garlic season. Those of you who have lived in garlic countries (Italy, France, Spain ...) will have noticed that garlic is available all year round. One of the keys to a longer Australian garlic season lies with the varieties planted.

Our garlic farmers are getting better and better, learning more every season. Garlic is a tricky crop to grow and store, but the AGIA is encouraging farmers to grow more diverse varieties. There are over 1000 garlic cultivars (a plant variety that has been produced in cultivation by selective breeding) grown around the world, and they can be divided into around 11 groups. Depending on their climatic conditions, farmers will choose varieties from those groups.

For instance, the five varieties from the Créole group do well in South Australia and areas that have mild and dry springs. The heads are a little smaller, with white skins and purple or red cloves. They'll store for a year or longer, and maintain their flavour. Some will even improve over time.

And there is much to learn: not just the right varieties for the soils, but how to store, cure and when to pick for maximum flavour. As grower Jan Goroncy of Barrington River Organic Farm told me: 'When spring garlic is freshly pulled it's milder and fresher, it doesn't keep, but it's celebrated in Europe'.

The good news is that there is now a group of dedicated if not fanatical Australian garlic farmers, and as we know from past experience, when Australian farmers take on a new challenge – wine, olives, truffles – they soar. In Victoria, fresh garlic is judged at their agricultural show, and there are garlic festivals or celebrations in Melbourne and Tasmania. Penny Woodward is a member of the AGIA, and one of the garlic judges at The Royal Agricultural Society of Victoria (RASV) garlic competition at the Australian Food Awards. How do you judge garlic? 'You pull apart a head, smell them, taste them raw and then roast them.' (And as I was writing this book, garlic was added to the schedule of the Fine Foods Show at the Royal Agricultural Society in New South Wales.)

Hunter Valley grower Jocelyn Colleran organises seminars on marketing, facilitates garlic dinners and can be found at farmers' markets around New South Wales offering garlic tastings. Garlic tastings? 'Different varieties of garlic have different flavour characteristics. And as with olive oil, there are a whole range of flavours', she told me.

I took part in one of these tastings at the Northside Produce Market in North Sydney. Three samples were offered, raw and grated. My favourite was the small red variety, Rojo del Pais Baza from the Créole group. It had a sweet and savoury flavour. I was intrigued by the variety of flavours, but relieved that we only tasted three. 'Garlic', said Jocelyn, 'really does capture people's imagination. I've even got garlic groupies who come to all my dinners'.

According to Penny Woodward of the AGIA, 'the answer to beating the cheap imports lies in educating consumers and retailers'. To enrich your knowledge of garlic, visit Australian Garlic, a website run by Penny and other garlic lovers: you'll find the address in the bibliography.

Before closing, I'd like to examine the broader ramifications of our post-garlic society: where our mongrel cuisine intersects with our broader culture.

Defining or dividing

I once met a man whose mother was Indigenous, his father Spanish. Where do you feel most at home? I asked him. In Spain, he said sheepishly. It shouldn't have worried him. He was being cosmopolitan, practising what is called today 'cosmopolitanism'. I knew the word, cosmopolitan, but didn't know it was an -ism.

The strict definition goes like this: cosmopolitanism is the ideology that all human beings belong to a single community, based on a shared morality. A person who adheres to the idea of cosmopolitanism in any of its forms is called a cosmopolitan or cosmopolite. Well, that's the theory, but it's a little rigid.

I learnt the word for the first time reading an article by Stan Grant, 'My Grandfather's Equality', in

Griffith Review 60. In it, he quoted the cosmopolitan thinker Kwame Anthony Appiah: 'Difference matters, but it need not define or divide us'. I got this immediately and it took me back to mongrel cuisine.

Multiculturalism works when we can live together in respect and enjoy our differences. In a culinary sense, this is the antithesis of One Nation – it is Many Nations, in culinary harmony. As in a dish that combines indigenous, Ethiopian, Italian and Greek ingredients to make a harmonious whole. Our best and brightest chefs are doing that every day.

Cosmopolitanism stands opposite the politics of One Nation and some extreme Australian conservatives which divide us and grade us according to skin colour and religion. Unfortunately for them, Australia is one of the most successful multicultural (and multiculinary) nations on earth. Of course, nothing is perfect. There are pockets of resistance, and one notable exception: Indigenous/non-Indigenous relations. This stain on our conscience still remains.

Then there is the opposing view of some right wing conservatives who (like Jordan Peterson) assert issues such as racism don't exist – or at least shouldn't exist – and that we should drop our identifying labels (Indigenous/Arab Australian/feminist/transgender) and just identify as human beings. That is not going to happen, and as a successful multicultural and cosmopolitan state we should resist attempts to obliterate our identities. They enrich our lives and our palates.

But there was one event in recent history that in a strange way reinforces both the importance of multi-culinarism to harmony between different groups, and the rarity of serious conflict. The Cronulla riots of December 2005.

It is fair to say that the size, intensity and physicality of the Cronulla riots were unique in recent Australian history. I'd like to propose not the usual two causes, but three. First, territory. In a suburb with a very low level of non-British/Anglo-Celtic penetration, the gradual increase in the numbers of Middle Eastern males on Cronulla beach was seen as a threat. Second was the enabling 'inflammatory broadcasts' of Alan Jones and other right wing 'shock jocks'. Jones was later fined $10000 for racial vilification. And thirdly, the lack of understanding of 'the other' (in this instance Middle Eastern culture) through culinary contact.

Cronulla is (or was then) what is known as a 'white bread suburb'; that is, in the Australian context, one with a largely British/Anglo-Celtic population: 77.8 per cent Australian born, with only 8.5 per cent who speak a language other than English at home. Only 46 per cent of the population of the City of Sydney, by contrast, is Australian born, with 29.9 per cent speaking a language other than English at home. An Eatability search in 2014 for Lebanese restaurants in Cronulla yielded this response: 'Sorry, no listings for Lebanese restaurants in Cronulla, Sydney'.

A similar search in the City of Sydney yielded 116 Lebanese restaurants.

A study carried out in Malaysia offers a comparative analysis on the extent to which acculturation – through education, social interaction and media – influences the foodways between three Malaysian major ethnic groups (Malay, Chinese and Indian). It concludes by noting that 'When two or more ethnic groups share foodways, they become closer'. More specifically it concludes: 'food could also act in strengthening the integrative force, solidarity and social bonding and alliances among the communities and ethnic groups'. In other words, if we eat each other's food, we are more likely to understand each other's culture.

Nothing is perfect. But I do believe we are moving slowly towards making the choice that Grant writes about: 'We can choose to be united by values or divided by race and culture'. With a little help from our multi-culinary tables.

A search in 2018 turned up at least three Lebanese restaurants in Cronulla, all serving the delicious whipped garlic sauce, toum, with fried chicken. It may be coincidence, and perhaps Australian society has moved on, but there have been no more riots.

To close, wisdom from a remarkable Frenchman, Marcel Boulestin, living in England, the land of the alliophobes. Boulestin was a journalist, novelist, restaurateur and prolific writer on food and gastronomy in the 1930s and 1940s. He was also the host of the first-ever cooking show on television, which ran on the BBC between 1937 and 1939, in television's experimental days.

Elizabeth David was influenced by him and adopted many of his teachings. In her book *An Omelette and a Glass of Wine* she wrote a long and affectionate essay on Boulestin. There we learn one more reason why it is fitting that he should be mentioned here.

He was not a chef – he employed one in his restaurant – but a wonderful cook and, as David wrote, 'he was nothing if not open-minded, adapting English ingredients to his own purposes and forever exercising his gift for fantasy'. A fantasy that involved inventions such as Maltese curry, and a dessert, Peaches Barbara, which comprised tomato jam, cream, kirschwasser and pistachios. Monsieur Boulestin, we suspect, would have been at home with Australia's mongrel cuisine.

There is a Boulestin quote in the Introduction to David's *A Book of Mediterranean Food*. And as we have now embraced garlic in our lives and food, let us hope he is correct when he writes: 'It is not really an exaggeration to say that peace and happiness begin, geographically, where garlic is used in cooking'. Amen to that.

Recipes

MARGARET FULTON

....

SHOULDER OF LAMB WITH
TWO HEADS OF GARLIC

Serves 4

From Margaret Fulton, A Passionate Cook, *Lansdowne, Sydney, 1998.*

Of this dish, the doyenne of Australian cooking wrote:

I like this long, slow way of cooking a shoulder of lamb on the bone. Carving can be difficult, but the meat is so tender I pull it away in large pieces. The drippings from the lamb give a delicious flavour to the potatoes baked at the bottom of the dish. The anchovies, garlic and vinegar do wonders, as does the long, slow cooking.

My copy of A Passionate Cook *falls open on the page. It illustrates like no other recipe I know how far we have come PG. A fitting end to this book, a tribute to a wonderful cook, the godmother of Modern Australian cooking.*

1.75–2 kg shoulder of lamb on the bone

salt and freshly ground black pepper

1.5 tbsp light olive oil [I use extra virgin olive oil: since 1998 we
    have learnt that 'light' is meaningless]

30 g unsalted butter

1 kg potatoes, peeled and sliced

2 medium onions, halved and sliced
4 anchovy fillets
2 heads garlic
fresh rosemary sprig, broken into small twigs
1.5 tbsp white wine vinegar
2 cups (500 ml) water [I use stock and much less – 1 cup]

1. Preheat the oven to 180°C. Trim any excess fat from the lamb. Rub the lamb with salt and pepper and some of the olive oil. Heat a heavy flameproof baking dish over a moderately high heat and add the rest of the olive oil and the butter.

2. Add the lamb and brown all over, turning frequently, until well browned. Lift out of the pan onto a plate.

3. Spread the potatoes and onions in layers on the bottom of the baking dish. Dot with anchovy fillets, sprinkling each one with a layer of salt and a small amount of pepper.

4. Remove any excess layers of papery skin from the garlic, cut the garlic heads in half across and place in the potatoes.

5. Lay the lamb on top of the potato mixture. Sprinkle the rosemary and vinegar over the whole dish. Cover with foil and bake in the oven for 3 hours, taking off the foil off after 1½ hours and reducing the heat to 160°C.

6. To serve, transfer the lamb to a hot platter and the vegetables to a separate warmed platter. Cut the meat off in chunky pieces – it will almost fall apart. Serve with the potatoes. Good with a green salad.

BIBLIOGRAPHY

Books

30th Anniversary Cookery Book & Household Guide, Croft's Stores Pty Ltd, 1935.

Albala, Ken (ed.), Food Cultures of the World Encyclopedia, Volume 3: Asia and Oceania, Greenwood, Santa Barbara, 2011.

Alexander, Stephanie, A Cook's Life, Penguin, Camberwell, 2012.

—— The Cook's Companion: the complete book of ingredients and recipes for the Australian kitchen, Viking, Ringwood, 1996.

Baker, James W, Thanksgiving: the biography of an American holiday, University of New Hampshire Press, Durham, 2009.

Bannerman, Colin, A Friend in the Kitchen, Kangaroo Press, Kenthurst, 1996.

—— Acquired Tastes: celebrating Australia's culinary history, National Library of Australia, Canberra, 1998.

Beckett, Barbara (compiler), Australian Food, Lansdowne, Sydney, 1999.

Beckett, Gordon, A Brief Economic History of Colonial NSW: the golden years of the colonial era re-examined, Trafford, Bloomington, 2012.

Beckett, Richard, Convicted Tastes: food in Australia, George Allen & Unwin, North Sydney, 1984.

Beeton, Isabella, Mrs Beeton's Book of Household Management, first published by SO Beeton Publishing, London, 1861. Online edition published by Project Gutenberg, 2003.

Bell, David & Hollows, Joanne (eds), Ordinary Lifestyles: popular media, consumption and taste, Open University Press, UK, 2005.

Bienvenu, Marcelle, Brasseaux, Carl A & Brasseaux, Ryan A, Stir the Pot: the history of Cajun cuisine, Hippocrene Books, New York, 2005.

Bilson, Gay, Plenty: digressions on food, Lantern, Camberwell, 2004.

Bilson, Tony, Fine Family Cooking, HarperCollins, Sydney, 1994.

—— Insatiable: my life in the kitchen, Pier 9, Millers Point, 2011.

Blake, Anthony & Crewe, Quentin, Great Chefs of France: the masters of haute cuisine and their secrets, HN Abrams, New York, 1978

Bober, Phyllis Pray, Art, Culture and Cuisine: ancient and medieval gastronomy, The University of Chicago Press, Chicago & London, 1999.

Bibliography

Bromby, Robin, *The Farming of Australia*, Doubleday, Lane Cove, 1986.

Burgmann, Verity & Lee, Jenny (eds), *A Most Valuable Acquisition: a people's history of Australia since 1788*, McPhee Gribble, Fitzroy, 1990.

Cameron-Smith, Barbara, *Starting from Scratch: Australia's first farm*, Royal Botanic Gardens, Sydney, 1987.

Campbell, Joan, *Bloody Delicious: a life with food*, Allen & Unwin, St Leonards, 1997.

Castles, Stephen, Cope, Bill, Kalantzis, Mary & Morrissey, Michael, *Mistaken Identity: multiculturalism and the demise of nationalism in Australia*, Pluto Press, Sydney, 1988.

Cherikoff, Vic, *The Bushfood Handbook: how to gather, grow, process & cook Australian wild foods*, Bush Tucker Supply Australia, Boronia Park, 1993.

Clark, Pamela (editorial and food director), *Australian Women's Weekly Modern Australian Food*, Bauer Media, Sydney, 2014.

Cookery the Australian Way: by a committee of Australian home economists and teachers of home economics in Melbourne, Macmillan, South Melbourne, 1966.

Covarrubias, Miguel, *Bali*, Oxford University Press, Kuala Lumpur, Singapore & Djakarta, 1972.

David, Elizabeth, *A Book of Mediterranean Food*, John Lehmann, London, 1950.

—— *An Omelette and a Glass of Wine*, Dorling Kindersley, London, 1985.

Downes, Stephen, *Advanced Australian Fare: how Australian cooking became the world's best*, Allen & Unwin, Crows Nest, 2002.

Drake, Lucy, *100 Tested Recipes and Cookery Hints*, Fitchett Brothers Pty Ltd, West Melbourne, 192-?.

Drummond, JC & Wilbraham, Anne, *The Englishman's Food: a history of five centuries of English diet*, Readers Union Jonathan Cape, London, 1959.

Dupleix, Jill, *New Food: from the new basics to the new classics*, William Heinemann, Port Melbourne, 1994.

Duruz, Jean: 'Food as Nostalgia: Eating the fifties and sixties', Australian Historical Studies, 29: 113, 231–250, 1999, <http://dx.doi.org/10.1080/10314619908596100>

Edwards, Ron, *Traditional Torres Strait Island Cooking*, The Rams Skull Press, Kuranda, 1988.

Egan, Jack, *Buried Alive: Sydney 1788–92*, Allen & Unwin, St Leonards, 1999.

Faas, Patrick, *Around the Roman Table: food and feasting in ancient Rome*, The University of Chicago Press, Chicago, 2003.

Falk, Pasi, *The Consuming Body*, Sage Publications, London, 1997.

Ferguson, Priscilla Parkhurst, *Accounting for Taste: the triumph of French cuisine*,

The University of Chicago Press, Chicago, 2004.

Flannery, Tim, *Watkin Tench 1788*, Text Publishing, Melbourne, 2009.

Freeman, Michael, 'Sung', in KC Chang (ed.), *Food in Chinese Culture*, Yale University Press, New Haven, 1977, pp. 141–76.

French, Maurice, *The Lamington Enigma: a survey of the evidence*, Tabletop Publishing, Toowoomba, 2013.

Frost, Alan, *The First Fleet: the real story*, Black Inc., Collingwood, 2011.

Fulton, Margaret, *A Passionate Cook*, Lansdowne, Sydney, 1998.

—— *I Sang for My Supper: memories of a food writer*, Lansdowne, Sydney, 1991.

—— *Superb Restaurant Dishes: over 200 delicious recipes to cook at home*, Octopus Books, Sydney, 1982.

Futter, Emily, *Australian Home Cookery*, George R Phillip & Sons, Sydney, possibly 1924.

Gallegos, Danielle, 'Cookbooks as Manuals of Taste', in David Bell & Joanne Hollows (eds), *Ordinary Lifestyles: popular media, consumption and taste*, Open University Press, New York, 2005.

Gammage, Bill, *The Biggest Estate on Earth: how Aborigines made Australia*, Allen & Unwin, Crows Nest, 2011.

George, M Dorothy, *London Life in the Eighteenth Century*, Routledge/Thames Press, London, 1996.

Glasse, Hannah, *The Art of Cookery Made Plain and Easy*, first published by the author, 1796. Reprint published by United States Historical Research Service, Schenectady, 1994.

Goody, Jack, *Cooking, Cuisine and Class*, Cambridge University Press, Cambridge, 1982.

Grant, Bruce, *The Australian Dilemma: a new kind of Western society*, Macdonald Futura Australia, Rushcutters Bay, 1983.

Graves, Tomás, *Bread & Oil*, Prospect, Totnes, 2000.

Halligan, Marion, *Eat My Words*, Angus & Robertson, Sydney, 1990.

Haskell, Arnold L, *Waltzing Matilda: a background to Australia*, Adam and Charles Black, London, 1940.

Heldke, Lisa M, *Exotic Appetites: ruminations of a food adventurer*, Routledge, New York & London, 2003.

Heuzenroeder, Angela, *Barossa Food*, Wakefield Press, Kent Town, 1999.

Higman BW, *How Food Made History*, Wiley-Blackwell, Chichester, 2012.

Hitchcock, Tim, *Down and Out in Eighteenth Century London*, Hambledon Continuum, London, 2004.

Hughes, Robert, *The Fatal Shore*, Collins Harvill, London, 1987.

Huntley, Rebecca, *Does Cooking Matter?*, Penguin, Melbourne, 2014.

Isaacs, Jennifer, *Bush Food: Aboriginal food and herbal medicine*, New Holland Publishers, Sydney, 2002

Bibliography

Jose, Nicholas, 'Cultural Identity: "I think I'm Something Else"', in
Stephen R Graubard (ed.), *Australia, The Dædalus Symposium*, Angus &
Robertson, North Ryde, 1985.

Karskens, Grace, *The Colony: a history of early Sydney*, Allen & Unwin,
Crows Nest, 2009.

Keesing, Nancy, *Lily on the Dustbin: slang of Australian women and families*,
Penguin, Ringwood, 1982.

Kraig, Bruce, *Hot Dog: a global history*, Reaktion Books, London, 2009.

Lang, Tim & Heasman, Michael, *Food Wars: the global battle for mouths, minds
and markets*, Earthscan, London, 2004.

Lawson, Jane, *Grub: favourite food memories*, Murdoch Books, Sydney, 2007.

—— (commissioning editor), *The Country Women's Association Cookbook:
seventy years in the kitchen*, Murdoch Books, Sydney, 2009.

Leitner, Gerhard, *Australian English; The national language*, De Gruyter
Mouton, Berlin, 2004

Lenoir, Philippe & de Ravel, Raymond, *Exotic Cuisine of Mauritius*, Editions
de l'Océan Indien, Mauritius, 1988.

Levenstein, Harvey, *Paradox of Plenty: a social history of eating in modern
America*, University of California Press, Berkeley & Los Angeles,
2003.

Lévi-Strauss, Claude, *The Origin of Table Manners*, Jonathan Cape, London,
1978.

Liew, Cheong with Ho, Elizabeth, *My Food*, Allen & Unwin, St
Leonards, 1995.

McGregor, Craig, *Class in Australia*, Penguin, Ringwood, 1997.

McMichael, Philip, *Settlers and the Agrarian Question: foundations of capitalism
in colonial Australia*, Cambridge University Press, Cambridge, 1984.

Malouf, David, *A First Place*, Random House Australia, North Sydney,
2014.

Manfredi, Stefano & Newton, John, *Fresh from Italy*, Hodder Headline,
Rydalmere, 1993.

Marcellys, *French Cooking for Everywoman*, Charles Scribner's Sons, New
York, 1930.

Marinato, Vince, *The Shop on the Wharf*, published by V Marinato,
Watsons Bay, 1996.

Markham, Gervase, *The English Huswife, Containing the Inward and Outward
Virtues Which Ought to Be in a Complete Woman*, first published by
R Jackson, London, 1623.

Meudell, George, *The Pleasant Career of a Spendthrift*, George Routledge &
Sons, London, 1929.

Mintz, Sidney, *Tasting Food, Tasting Freedom: excursions into eating, culture, and
the past*, Beacon Press, Boston, 1996.

Moloney, Ted & Coleman, Deke, *Oh for a French Wife*, Shepherd Press, Sydney, 1952.

Montanari, Massimo, *Food Is Culture*, Columbia University Press, New York, 2006.

Moorhouse, Frank (ed.), *The Drover's Wife*, Penguin Random House, North Sydney, 2017.

Mundy, GC, *Our Antipodes, or, Residence and Rambles in the Australasian Colonies*, Richard Bentley, London, 1852.

Muskett, Phillip E, *The Art of Living in Australia (together with three hundred Australian cookery recipes by Mrs H Wicken, lecturer on Cookery to the Technical College, Sydney)*, first published by Eyre & Spottiswoode, London, Edinburgh, Glasgow, Melbourne, Sydney & New York, 1892. Republished by Sydney University Press, Sydney, 2004.

Naccarato, Peter & LeBesco, Kathleen, *Culinary Capital*, Berg Publishers, Oxford, 2012.

Newling, Jacqui, *Eat Your History: stories and recipes from Australian kitchens*, Sydney Living Museums/NewSouth Publishing, Kensington, 2015.

Newton, John, *The Oldest Foods on Earth: a history of Australian native foods*, NewSouth Publishing, Sydney, 2016.

—— *Wogfood: an oral history with recipes*, Random House, Milson's Point, 1996.

O'Brien, Charmaine, *The Colonial Kitchen: Australia 1788–1901*, Rowman & Littlefield, Maryland, 2016.

O'Connell, Jan, *A Timeline of Australian Food: from mutton to Masterchef*, NewSouth Publishing, Sydney, 2017.

O'Donnell, Mietta & Knox, Tony, *Great Australian Chefs*, Bookman Press, Melbourne, 1999.

Olsen, Kirstin, *Daily Life in 18th-Century England*, Greenwood, London, 2017.

Park, Ruth, *The Companion Guide to Sydney*, Collins, Sydney & London, 1973.

Pascoe, Bruce, *Dark Emu Black Seeds: agriculture or accident?*, Magabala Books, Western Australia, 2014.

Pascoe, Elise (recipes) & Ripe, Cherry, *Australia the Beautiful Cookbook*, Cumulus/AR Bookworld, Melbourne, 1995.

Patten, Marguerite, *500 Recipes from Australia*, Paul Hamlyn (in association with *Australian Women's Weekly*), London, 1965.

Pearson, Margaret J, *Cookery Recipes for the People*, ML Hutchinson, Melbourne, 1888.

Perry, Neil, *Rockpool*, William Heinemann, Melbourne, 1996.

Polese, Beppi with Newton, John, *Beppi: a life in three courses*, Murdoch Books, Sydney, 2007.

Pollan, Michael, *The Omnivore's Dilemma: the search for a perfect meal in a fast-food world*, Bloomsbury, London, 2006.

Rawson, Mrs Lance, *The Antipodean Cookery Book and Kitchen Companion*, George Robertson & Co., Melbourne, Sydney, Adelaide & Brisbane, 1907.

Revel, Jean-François, *Culture and Cuisine: a journey through the history of food*, Da Capo Press, New York, 1982.

Reynolds, Allison, *Anzac Biscuits: the power and spirit of an everyday national icon*, Wakefield Press, Mile End, 2018.

Rickard, John, *Australia: a cultural history*, Addison Wesley Longman, United Kingdom, 1996.

Ripe, Cherry, *Goodbye Culinary Cringe*, Allen & Unwin, Crows Nest, 1993.

Robson, LL, *The Convict Settlers of Australia*, Cambridge University Press, Melbourne, 1965.

Roden, Claudia, *A Book of Middle Eastern Food*, Penguin, London, 1970.

Rolls, Eric, *A Million Wild Acres*, Hale & Iremonger, McMahons Point, 2011.

Root, Waverley, *The Food of France*, Vintage Books, New York, 1977.

Rushdie, Salman, *Imaginary Homelands*, Granta Books, London, in association with Penguin Books, 1991.

Rutledge, Jean (Mrs Forster Rutledge), *The Goulburn Cookery Book*, first published 1895. The 28th edition published by WC Penfold & Co., Sydney, 1928.

Salatin, Joel, *The Sheer Ecstasy of Being a Lunatic Farmer*, Chelsea Green, Vermont, 2010.

Santich, Barbara, *Bold Palates: Australia's gastronomic heritage*, Wakefield Press, Kent Town, 2012.

—— *Looking for Flavour*, Wakefield Press, Kent Town, 1996.

Sawyer, Jesse & Moore-Sims, Sara (compilers), *The Coronation Cookery Book*, compiled for The Countrywomen's Association of New South Wales, Australia, Publicity Press, Sydney, 1937.

Schauer, Amy, *The Schauer Australian Cookery Book*, Edwards, Dunlop & Co., Brisbane, 1909.

Schofield, Leo, *Eating Out in Sydney*, Angus & Robertson, Sydney, 1976.

Shun Wah, Annette & Aitkin, Greg, *Banquet: ten courses to harmony*, Doubleday, Sydney, 1999.

Sinclair, Ellen (food editor), *Australian Women's Weekly Chinese Cooking Class Cookbook*, 1978.

Smith, Andrew F, *Eating History: 30 turning points in the making of American cuisine*, Columbia University Press, New York, 2009.

Solomon, Charmaine, *The Complete Asian Cookbook*, Paul Hamlyn, 1976.

Southwell, Daniel, *Journal and Letters of Daniel Southwell*, published in *Historical Records of New South Wales*, 1893. Online edition published by Project Gutenberg, 2012.

Spang, Rebecca L, *The Invention of the Restaurant: Paris and modern gastronomic culture*, Harvard University Press, Cambridge, 2000.

Spencer, Colin, *British Food*, Grub Street, London, 2011.

Symons, Michael, *A History of Cooks and Cooking*, University of Illinois Press, Urbana, 2000.

—— *One Continuous Picnic*, Melbourne University Press, Melbourne, 2007.

—— *The Pudding That Took a Thousand Cooks*, Viking, Ringwood, 1998.

Turner, Graeme, *Making it National: nationalism and Australian popular culture*, Allen & Unwin, St Leonards, 1994.

Twopeny, REN, *Town Life in Australia*, first published by Elliot Stock, London, 1883. Reprint published by Sydney University Press, Sydney, 1973.

Walker, Kylie (publisher), *The Country Women's Association Cookbook 2: more treasured recipes*, Murdoch Books, Sydney, 2011.

Walsh, Richard, *Ferretabilia*, University of Queensland Press, St Lucia, 1993.

White, Patrick, *The Twyborn Affair*, Jonathan Cape, London, 1979.

—— *Voss*, Viking, New York, 1957.

Wilkinson, Alfred J, *The Australian Cook: a complete manual of cookery suitable for the Australian colonies*, George Robertson, Melbourne, Sydney & Adelaide, 1876.

Wilson, Gavin, *Cuisine & Country: a gastronomic venture in Australian art*, catalogue, Orange Regional Gallery, Orange, 2007–08.

Wrangham, Richard, *Catching Fire: how cooking made us human*, Basic Books, New York, 2009.

Journal articles and online sources

Abel, Ernest L, 'The Gin Epidemic: much ado about what?', *Alcohol and Alcoholism*, 9 November 2012, pp. 401–05, <alcalc.oxfordjournals.org/content/36/5/401.full>

Appadurai, Arjun, 'How to Make a National Cuisine: cookbooks in contemporary India', *Comparative Studies in Society and History*, vol. 30, no. 1, 1988, pp. 3–24.

Black, Sarah Jane Shepherd, '"Tried and Tested": community cookbooks in Australia, 1890–1980', PhD thesis, School of History and Politics, University of Adelaide, 2010, <hdl.handle.net/244064979>

Burns, Crayton, 'The Army in Australia Before Waterloo', *Digger History*, <diggerhistory.info/pages-conflicts-periods/other/before-waterloo.htm>

Collins, David, *An Account of the English Colony in NSW Vol. 1 With Remarks On The Dispositions, Customs, Manners, Etc. Of The Native Inhabitants Of That Country. To Which Are Added, Some Particulars Of New Zealand, Compiled, By Permission, From The Mss. Of Lieutenant-Governor King*, first published 1798. Online edition published by Project Gutenberg, 2004, <gutenberg.org/files/12565/12565-h/12565-h.htm>

Corones, Anthony, 'Multiculinarism and the Emergence of Gastronomy', *Proceedings of the Third Symposium of Gastronomy: A Multiculinary Society*, 1987, pp. 17–27.

Dabelstein, Josh, 'The Great Australian Debate: is it Chicken Parmi, Parmy or Parma?', *New Matilda*, 8 February 2018, <newmatilda. com/2018/02/08/great-australian-debate-chicken-parmi-parmy>

'Food at Sea in the Age of Fighting Sail', *British Food in America*, no. 57, summer 2018, <britishfoodinamerica.com/Our-First-Nautical-Number/the-lyrical/Food-at-sea-in-the-age-of-fighting-sail/#.WXp1q9OGOV5>

Hage, Ghassan, 'Roots will be with you always', *Higher Education, The Australian*, 23 April 2008.

Harper, Melissa, 'Feeding the Public Stomach: dining out in the 1970s with restaurant critic Leo Schofield', *History Australia*, vol. 9, December 2012, pp. 43–66.

Karskens, Grace, 'The Rocks', *Dictionary of Sydney*, 2008, <dictionaryofsydney.org/entry/the_rocks>

Malouf, David, 'Made in England: Australia's British Inheritance', *Quarterly Essay*, no. 12, 2003.

Martin, Megan & Crockett, Gary, 'Oiling the Wheels of Patronage', Sydney Living Museums, first published in *Insites*, winter 2009, <sydneylivingmuseums.com.au/stories/oiling-wheels-patronage>

Maxwell-Stewart, Hamish, University of Tasmania & Kippen, Rebecca, University of Melbourne, 'Sickness and Death on Male and Female Convict Voyages to Australia' (A much extended version of the arguments in this paper is available in Baskerville, Peter & Inwood, Kris (eds), *Lives in Transition: longitudinal research from historical sources*, McGill-Queen's University Press, Montreal & Kingston, 2014), <femaleconvicts.org.au/docs/seminars/Voyages_HamishMaxwellStewart.pdf>

Newling, Jacqui, 'Dining with Strangeness: european foodways on the Eora frontier', *Journal of Australian Colonial History*, vol. 13, 2011, pp. 27–48.

Newling, Jacqui & Hill, Scott, 'First Fleet fare', Sydney Living Museums, *The Cook and the Curator*, 7 February 2013,

Newton, John, 'Pick & Nick', *Slow: the magazine of the slow food movement*, no. 17, April–June 2000, pp. 76–83.

Phillip, Arthur, and various others, *The Voyage of Governor Phillip to Botany Bay. With an Account of the Establishment of the Colonies of Port Jackson and Norfolk Island, compiled from Authentic Papers, which have been obtained from the several Departments to which are added the Journals of Lieuts. Shortland, Watts, Ball and Capt. Marshall with an Account of their New Discoveries*, first published by John Stockdale, 1789. Online edition published by University of Sydney Library, 2003, <adc.library.usyd.edu.au/data-2/phivoya.pdf>

Reynolds, Anne, 'A Short History of Italian Cafés and Restaurants in Sydney', *Modern Greek Studies Australia and New Zealand*, vol. 10, 2002, <openjournals.library.sydney.edu.au/index.php/MGST/article/view/6696>

Rozin, Paul & Segal, Michael, 'Vegemite as a Marker of National Identity', *Gastronomica: the journal of food and culture*, vol. 3, no. 4, 2003, pp. 63–67.

Schultz, Julianne & Phillips, Sandra (eds), *Griffith Review 60: First Things First*, South Bank Campus Griffith University, 2018.

Symons, Michael, '"The Cleverness of the Whole Number": social invention in the golden age of Antipodean baking, 1890–1940', *Petit Propos Culinaire*, issue 85, 2008.

Sheridan, Susan, 'Eating the Other: food and cultural difference in the Australian Women's Weekly in the 1960s', *Journal of Intercultural Studies*, vol. 21, issue 3, 2000, pp. 319–29, <dx.doi.org/10.1080/713678985>

Timbury, Cheryl, 'Marines', *First Fleet Fellowship Victoria Inc.*, 8 June 2012, <firstfleetfellowship.org.au/marines/marines/>

Woodward, Penny, Australian Garlic,

ACKNOWLEDGMENTS

Firstly, Luisa Deacon, the membership manager of the New South Wales CWA for not only allowing me access to the archives, but also seeking out elusive documents.

Pamela Clark, long-term editorial and food director of the *Australian Women's Weekly Cookbooks*, for astute memories of her time there and for allowing me access to the invaluable *Australian Women's Weekly* archives.

Once again, Michael Symons, Anthony Corones, Barbara Santich and Colin Bannerman for their pioneering works on Australian food. They lit the path.

To Penny Woodward of the Australian Garlic Industry Association for guidance through the maze of garlic cultivars, groups and history.

Jacqui Newling and Scott Hill, whose online series *The Cook and Curator* (Sydney Living Museums) has led me up the right garden paths and into corners of colonial kitchens I would never have found without them.

The members of the Food Group I belong to, voraciously well-read and trenchantly critical. They are, in addition, supportive and generous. They know who they are.

My publisher Phillipa McGuinness saw the value in the book, and who chose two critically focused pairs of eyes to look over it: firstly, inquisitor Mathilde de Hauteclocque, and then editor Diana Hill – an exhausting but exhaustive process that has resulted in a better book.

To all who provided me with recipes and permission to publish them. For those recipes alone, I'd buy this book if I hadn't written it.

And as always, my in-house critic, editor and stronghold of sanity, De Brierley Newton.

INDEX

Page numbers in italics indicate a recipe. Apart from those beginning with a proper noun, only the names of dishes for which a recipe is supplied have an initial capital letter in this index.

Index

Index

Index

Index

Index

Index